PRAISE FOR *REDI*

'This book has the potential to transform the future of HR. Lars Schmidt is a beacon of light, and his bold vision may well elevate a long-marginalized field into the force for good that it deserves to be.'
Adam Grant, *New York Times* bestselling author of *Think Again* and *Originals*, and host of TED podcast *WorkLife*

'The uniquely uncertain circumstances during 2020 reinforced the importance of HR as present, communicative, empathetic, innovative, courageous and creative. This book is a window into that world. Lars Schmidt is a gifted storyteller and harnesses his own unique voice and those of many other people leaders to paint a picture of what great HR can be. This book is essential reading for anyone looking to build people teams for today and tomorrow.'
Katarina Berg, Chief Human Resources Officer, Spotify

'The events of 2020 reinforced the need for progressive and agile capabilities. We must be continually willing to disrupt ourselves and our talent practices in a disruptive world. As such, Lars Schmidt lays the groundwork for transformative people teams and approaches in this book. This is a bold window into modern people practices including real-world examples and essays from leaders building the future of the field.'
Pat Wadors, Chief People Officer, Procure Technologies

'Lars Schmidt has a unique vantage point on all things people. What makes him so special is his ability to distill so many sources and inputs through his unique lens to paint a picture of what we can be at our best. *Redefining HR* is a blueprint for modern HR and people operations. It blends relatable stories, struggles and practices in a way that only he can bring to life.'
Claude Silver, Chief Heart Officer, VaynerMedia

'You want a window into the future of our profession/industry? Then I suggest you start flipping through these pages. It chronicles fantastic thought leaders and insights about people and culture, respecting the history of our

industry while pushing forward and challenging the status quo in HR. If you're serious about driving behaviour and mindset change in your organizations, you don't want to miss out on the collective wisdom he's curated in this book. Lars Schmidt is the compassionate people and culture crusader of our time and what he's captured in these "next" practices is truly a gift to people leaders in our industry.'
A J Thomas, Head of People Products, Strategy and Operations, X, the Moonshot Factory

'A book project born out of curiosity, acknowledgement of transformation and need to do better. I appreciate how the author touches on the varied aspects of serving the people function within the organization without coming across as the authority. He thoughtfully weaves in the experiences and thoughts of others to deliver a read that is sure to add value as we journey to build companies and teams over the next decade.'
Torin Ellis, Diversity Strategist, the torin ellis brand

'Lars Schmidt has absolutely nailed the future of HR. This book is a must-read for business and HR leaders alike. This book is a fantastic, delightful read, full of insight and innovation. I couldn't put it down and now find myself forever changed on how I think about where we are headed. This is a homerun.'
David Hanrahan, Chief Human Resources Officer, Eventbrite

'The field of HR is evolving dramatically and it's never been more important to be on the front end of the curve. Lars Schmidt has pulled together some of the leading minds in the industry to pose the questions we should all be asking ourselves of what it means to great at people.'
Maia Josebachvili, Former Head of People, Stripe

'Lars Schmidt has been at the forefront of redefining what the HR function should be for many years. His ability to collaborate and seek out the input of leaders in this field is unparalleled. I highly recommend reading this book – it will open up and challenge your thinking on getting the best out of people in the workplace'.
Beth Ann Steinberg, VP People & Talent, Chime and Founder, Mensch Ventures

'I've worked with Lars Schmidt as a peer, customer, and co-founder for the past 10 years, and he is one of the most progressive practitioners in the field today. He not only spearheads modern HR practices but also elevates the field of his peer practitioners on a global scale. This book cuts through the corporate jargon and helps HR leaders understand the elusive "why" and "how" to implement results-aligned strategies. A rare blend of emotional intelligence and exceptional execution, Lars balances building from both the employer and employee perspective. He is a holistic thinker, a fearless advocate and a heck of a community builder.'
Ambrosia Vertesi, Operating Partner, Operator Collective

'Lars Schmidt has long been a forward-thinking expert in the people space, so it's phenomenal to see all of that greatness come together in a book that's both informative and practical. It is packed with thought-provoking ideas that provide exactly the kind of inspiration that the people space so woefully needs.'
Ruth Penfold, People Practice Lead, bp Launchpad

Redefining HR

Transforming people teams to drive business performance

Lars Schmidt

KoganPage

First published in Great Britain and the United States in 2021 by Kogan Page Limited

2nd Floor, 45 Gee Street
London
EC1V 3RS
United Kingdom

122 W 27th St, 10th Floor
New York, NY 10001
USA

4737/23 Ansari Road
Daryaganj
New Delhi 110002
India

www.koganpage.com

Kogan Page books are printed on paper from sustainable forests.

© Lars Schmidt, 2021

The right of Lars Schmidt to be identified as the author of this work has been asserted by him in accordance with the Copyright, Designs and Patents Act 1988.

ISBNs

Hardback   978 1 78966 706 6
Paperback 978 1 78966 704 2
Ebook   978 1 78966 705 9

British Library Cataloguing-in-Publication Data

A CIP record for this book is available from the British Library.

Library of Congress Cataloging-in-Publication Data

Names: Schmidt, Lars (Employer Brand Strategist), author.
Title: Redefining HR : transforming people teams to drive business
   performance / Lars Schmidt.
Description: Great Britain ; United States : Kogan Page Limited, 2021. |
   Includes bibliographical references and index.
Identifiers: LCCN 2020047888 (print) | LCCN 2020047889 (ebook) | ISBN
   9781789667042 (paperback) | ISBN 9781789667066 (hardback) | ISBN
   9781789667059 (ebook)
Subjects: LCSH: Personnel management.
Classification: LCC HF5549 .S2448 2021 (print) | LCC HF5549 (ebook) | DDC
   658.3–dc23
LC record available at https://lccn.loc.gov/2020047888
LC ebook record available at https://lccn.loc.gov/2020047889

Typeset by Integra Software Services, Pondicherry
Print production managed by Jellyfish
Printed and bound by CPI Group (UK) Ltd, Croydon CR0 4YY

This book is dedicated to the next generation of HR and people leaders who will continue transforming the field and push us all to be better.

CONTENTS

ABOUT THE AUTHOR

My name is Lars Schmidt and I'm thrilled to share this book with you. It's the culmination of hundreds of hours of work: writing, interviews, reading, podcasts and more. Before you dig in, it might be helpful to know a bit more about me, what I value and how I operate.

I'm the Founder of Amplify (AmplifyTalent.com), a boutique HR executive search and consulting firm based outside of Washington DC that helps companies build progressive people teams and capabilities.

Before founding Amplify, I was fortunate to lead digital talent transformation at NPR and do some groundbreaking work recognized by Mashable, the *Wall Street Journal*, the *Washington Post* and others. In prior roles, I was responsible for creating scalable high-growth global talent strategies at Ticketmaster, Magento and several startups in Los Angeles.

I'm an advocate for modern HR and work to accelerate the evolution of people team capabilities and impact through efforts like the HR Open Source initiative I co-founded, regular columns in *Fast Company* and *Forbes*, co-authoring *Employer Branding for Dummies* (Wiley, 2017), the Redefining HR (formerly 21st-century HR) podcast and media series, and talks around the world.

I love to build. I'm drawn to projects that combine transformation and impact – even better when combined at scale. I'm at my best when I'm faced with a new problem set where I can get creative.

I'm passionate about open-source projects and helping amplify and democratize access to templates, tools, resources and practices to help practitioners innovate and make an impact.

When I'm not doing things related to the above, I can be found at my Northern Virginia home where I'm dad to two wonderful daughters and husband to an amazing wife.

FOREWORD

It was 2015 and Lars Schmidt was on a crusade: he wanted to end the war on talent. His solution was to open-source the work of HR practitioners. He had an earnest belief that employers shouldn't battle each other for candidates, but instead join forces to build a better workplace for all. In a different silo, I had been fighting this battle myself in a far less organized and far more hair-on-fire-frantic kind of way. His vision for a collaborative HR ecosystem was inspiring. The HR Open Source community he and his co-founder Ambrosia Vertesi created around that mission was vibrant. Without hesitation, I enrolled in the movement to better the world of work.

But this wasn't the start of the Human Resources revolution, no; it was simply the beginning of my relationship with Lars. The kindest rebel you'll ever meet, his punk-rock people philosophies have had a significant impact on the HR industry. Our community knows him to be a servant thought leader, one who cares deeply about giving platforms to the people who are changing the way the world goes to work. For over 20 years, Lars has been addressing and challenging the traditional institution of HR, imploring a dynamic shift in approach.

The reality is that the field of Human Resources had been woefully out of date for decades. Only in recent history has HR made the dramatic shift from the backroom to the boardroom, bringing people strategy to the forefront of business strategy. No longer are we relegated to compliance and benefits administration alone. We are detailed operators, yes, but also strategists, coaches and sherpas to this brave, new world – a world that doesn't view humans as resources, but rather as people who have unique perspectives, experiences and feelings. This book is a roadmap to that world.

Redefining HR gives us an opportunity to better understand the evolution of this field and how each of us can play a role in shaping its future. From leveraging policy to operationalizing culture to having fun with data, Lars focuses on practical, actionable approaches to catalyse change – within your organization, your career and the workplace at large. He includes case studies from forward-thinking people leaders, offers his own operational expertise and shares snippets from his podcast.

For those who didn't recognize the shift before, the events of early 2020 made it known that businesses that refused to lead people-first would suffer the greatest tolls. Public health concerns, civic unrest and economic uncertainty plagued our communities; HR teams had never been more needed or more recognized as critical business partners. The urgency to create sustainable, equitable, diverse cultures of inclusion became non-negotiable. The HR community came together quickly to right the ship, sharing critical information openly to ensure all had access to supporting their teams. Pandemic playbooks, reductions in force toolkits and new workplace safety policies swept inboxes like wildfire. There was no competitive advantage to keeping things to ourselves. The battle wasn't between us but in front of us, and we were stronger together.

Lars' suggestion to simply *share more* has now become a flat-out imperative. *The world of work will never be the same again.* It is our responsibility to ensure we're building this next chapter with intention and care. Take from our past the good, but leave behind the things that weren't serving our mission to create a better workplace for everyone. Starting here, book in hand, I challenge each of you to rethink HR.

Katelin Holloway
Founding Partner, 776

PREFACE

It's time to redefine HR.

I'm not talking about whether we call the function 'Human Resources', 'People Operations', 'Talent and Culture' or any of the other terms we use to define ourselves. I'm talking about our capabilities. Our impact. How we develop and support each other to evolve our field. This is about shaking free of the legacy perceptions and dogma of our past and building something new.

Redefining HR means setting a new expectation of what HR can be. Higher expectations. For our companies, our employees and ourselves. Redefining HR is about building a new narrative of what it means to practise HR today, and tomorrow.

This book is a bridge to that world.

Redefining HR is an exploration of modern HR and people practices. It's an overview of how the field has evolved, with an emphasis on modern approaches that are redefining the field.

When I set out to write this book, I wanted to marry the theory and elements of modern HR with their practical application – interviews with progressive people leaders, case studies, examples. I didn't want to write another theoretical HR book. I wanted to create something tangible, real and relatable for practitioners out there doing the work. A blend of inspiration and education. Real stories. Real impact.

This book is the culmination of over 20 years in the field of HR. I've worn many hats during that time: individual contributor, executive, consultant, writer, author, speaker, podcaster, student, writer of overly complex bios. It's based on hundreds (thousands?) of interviews, consulting engagements, jobs, conversations, mistakes, and a drive to explore the boundaries of modern HR.

I've been fortunate throughout my career to work for and with progressive people leaders – mentors and muses who saw HR as a vital function to maximize the employee experience, but more importantly, a fundamental driver for a business's success. This book is a tribute to them – for lighting a spark in me that became a quest to spotlight all the good work that's happening in the field.

Before we dig into the meat of the book, I wanted to provide a brief introduction to give you some context on where I'm coming from when you read this.

I'm often asked what I do. The answer always feels embarrassingly complex and self-important. The truth is, I've managed to create a unique role for myself that allows me to tap into a range of 'day jobs' – HR executive search, consultant, speaker, podcaster and writer. If you had told me five years ago that this is what I'd be doing, I would have laughed in disbelief. If you had asked me 20 years ago, it certainly wouldn't be spending my career in HR. So how did I get here?

Where it all began

In 1998, I entered the workforce as a fresh-eyed graduate ready to tackle the world. Following my five-year Marketing and International Business degree (I justify the fifth year with my double major, at least to my dad), I envisioned I'd be getting into advertising or marketing, or even PR. HR was never on my radar: I didn't even have any misconceptions about HR at that point.

The one thing I was certain of was that I wanted to move to Los Angeles, so I applied to the one company with an office in LA that came to my university career fair: Pencom Systems, a technical recruiting firm based in New York with offices across the United States. and Canada. Though I had no idea what recruiting was, after a series of interviews I accepted an offer and moved to New York for a six-month training programme on all things technology and recruiting. In December 1998, I arrived in Los Angeles ready to see what the 'dot-com craze' was all about.

The bubble was real. It was the Wild West in technology recruiting in those days. Every noun.com was falling into venture capital money. Few had revenue.

I worked with a lot of the Idealabs companies and others, including Goto.com, eToys and Netzero. Companies were hiring and relocating candidates and their families based on phone screens. It was crazy. It didn't last. The dot-com bubble burst a year after I arrived.

At an early stage of my career, I was at a crossroads: I enjoyed building connections and relationships in recruiting, but I struggled with the lack of control and influence on the client side that came with agency recruiting. I knew I needed to go in-house to see if staying in the field was right for me.

After a year in-house as a recruiting consultant building a software company, I moved into my first full-time in-house recruiting role at

Ticketmaster, where I spent the next seven years in seven jobs. This was my first deep dive into modern HR. I spent most of that time reporting to someone who became a mentor and shaped my career and views on the field more than anyone – Beverly Carmichael. Beverly was the former Chief Human Resources Officer (CHRO) of Southwest Airlines. Her leadership – informed by intelligence, competence, empathy and confidence – stretched me into roles outside my comfort zone. I loved that team. I loved what we built. I'm incredibly proud of the work we did at Ticketmaster. To this day, some of my fondest work memories reside in that experience.

When I moved on to Magento, an open-source e-commerce company that was later acquired by eBay, I met another mentor in their President, Bob Schwartz. Bob was a visionary leader who taught (and still teaches) me the power of communities, ecosystems and connection.

In 2010, I was recruited to National Public Radio (NPR) to run talent and innovation for a newly hired CHRO tasked with leading their transformation from radio/broadcast to digital – Jeff Perkins. Jeff gave me the keys to drive their talent strategy. It was my first time working in a non-profit. We were competing for talent on two fronts (digital/tech and journalism), mostly against for-profit companies. I knew traditional recruiting playbooks wouldn't work, so I built our strategy around the newly developing field of employer brand. We launched one of the first culture hashtags with #NPRlife in 2010 and developed brand ambassadors, aligned with marketing to leverage our consumer brand. It was an experimental lab and I loved it.

Jeff encouraged me to write and speak about what we were working on. In hindsight, that shaped much of my lean towards open-source and 'working out loud'. Looking back, it's easy to connect the through lines between all of those roles to extrapolate what I'm doing now, but at the time I was just living and working in each moment.

At the end of 2013, I decided to go out on my own. I was inspired by friends and young entrepreneurs I worked with through an NPR initiative I supported called Generation Listen. I wanted to see what I could build.

You know those stories about natural-born entrepreneurs destined to build great things? That was never me. I always wanted to be a 9–5'er working for the man and getting a steady pay check. Then I found a Blackberry strapped to my waist (my Blackberry came with a heavy holster and light shame). I got involved in social media and realized I'd never have a 9–5 job. So, I did what all sensible middle-aged, soon-to-be first-time fathers would do – I quit. Perhaps I need to rethink 'sensible' in that sentence?

In December 2013, Amplify Talent was born. My initial focus was employer branding and recruiting optimization consulting. I broadened to HR executive search in 2019 as I wanted to find a way to add more value to a growing global people executive network I was building.

Along the way I co-authored a book on employer branding, and began writing for *Fast Company*, *Forbes* and LinkedIn. I launched a podcast. I launched and shuttered a podcast about different careers (highlight: interviewing 'Chunk' from The Goonies). I travelled the world speaking at dozens of conferences and events. I cofounded a not-for-profit (HR Open Source) with my good friend Ambrosia Vertesi. Most importantly, I became a dad to two amazing girls. It's been a wild ride.

I've seen a lot over those 20 years. I've notched a few wins and plenty of losses. I fell in love with the word 'pilot'. I've done big things with small budgets and small things with big budgets. I've iterated – a lot. I've battled imposter syndrome when given tasks that I clearly had no business doing.

Through all of that, what I was really doing was realize that I had somehow managed to fall into a career I loved. A field that I felt made a difference in people's lives. A job that could swing between maddeningly frustrating and the kind of complete elation that made me want to chase that high again and again.

The past five years in particular have really galvanized my views on the evolution of HR. As a cofounder of HR Open Source, I travelled the world meeting with practitioners and learning about their wins, struggles and barriers. As a writer and podcast host I've had many conversations with leaders who are transforming the field. I could distil them all into one clear takeaway: there's never been a better time to work in the field of HR.

I wrote this book because I truly believe that, and I want you to see it for yourself. This book is written to educate, hopefully to inspire some ideas, and to challenge legacy perspectives around HR.

Let's do this.

ACKNOWLEDGEMENTS

This is actually one of the more difficult sections of the book to write, as hundreds of people have inspired and supported me over my career and deserve credit for this book. I can't possibly capture them all below, and I'm sure I'll miss people who *should* be here. Know that any omissions reflect my current quarantine-impaired memory, and not your impact on me.

One of the things that make this book special is the range of contributors adding deep subject-matter expertise, perspectives and stories.

When I set out to write this book, I knew it would need those tangible and relatable perspectives to frame the content with context. I didn't want to write an analyst or academic take on modern HR. I wanted to write a book for practitioners, by practitioners. The following people made that possible and I'm deeply grateful for their contributions to this book.

Massive thanks to Adam Ward, AJ Thomas, Al Adamson, Ambrosia Vertesi, Amy Thompson, Andrew Saidy, Anna Binder, Aubrey Blanche, Becky Cantieri, Beverly Carmichael, Bryan Power, Carmen Hudson, Caro Widenka, Ciara Lakhani, Claire Kennedy, Claude Silver, Colleen McCreary, Daniel Harris, Darren Murph, David Green, David Hanrahan, David Lee, Deb Gran, Dipti Salopek, Dominique Taylor, Garrison Gibbons, Guissu Baier, Jaison Williams, Jason Fried, Jeri Doris, Jessica Yuen, Jevan Soo, John Bersin, John Vlastelica, Johnny Sanchez, Josh Bersin, Joy Sybesma, Karen Eber, Katelin Holloway, Katie Burke, Kelly Jackson, Kelly Rew-Porter, Kristen Lisanti, Dr Laura Morgan Roberts, Leah Knobler, Madison Butler, Mai Ton, Maia Josebachvili, Matt Buckland, Matt Hoffman, Melissa Thompson, Michael DeAngelo, Michael Fraccaro, Mitasha Singh, Pat Caldwell, Perry Timms, Richard Mosley, Sarah Morgan, Sehr Charania, Stacy Zapar, Tara Turk and Zoe Harte. Your expertise, stories and perspectives helped bring life to this book.

There are so many people who've inspired and influenced me along the way. Too many to mention all of them by name, but some I want to call out below.

To my friend Katrina Collier. Thank you for introducing me to Kogan Page and making this book possible.

My deep gratitude to Anne-Marie Heeney, Lucy Carter and the entire Kogan Page team. Thanks for your editorial guidance and patience with my many inquiries. I'm sure I lived up to my warnings on my wannabe designer preferences.

Behind every writer are editors who make their words come to life. I'm grateful to have had the opportunity to work with a trio of editors at Fast Company who've helped me become a better writer – Rich Bellis, Jay Woodruff and Julia Herbst.

Beverly Carmichael, my former boss and mentor who showed me what great HR can be. Bob Schwartz, my entrepreneurial and ecosystem mentor and friend who always answers the call when I need his guidance. My former boss and friend Jeff Perkins who set me on this path by giving me the freedom to experiment, write and share at NPR.

To my many industry friends and modern work muses who inspire me and push the field to be better: Craig Fisher, Bill Boorman, Hung Lee, Matt Charney, Torin Ellis, Stacy Zapar, Maren Hogan, Marc Coleman, Amy Thompson, George Anders, Jamie Leonard, Ciara Lakhani, Marta Riggins, Johnny Sanchez, Gerry Crispin, Dr Erin L Thomas, Kelly Rew-Porter, Chris Hoyt, Alexis Ohanian, David Green, Leela Srinivasan, Al Adamson, Sree Srinivasan and too many more to list. Big thanks to my editorial friends, including for contributing some of the visuals and charts to the book: Kristin Altorfer, Liana Pistell, Maria Ignatova, Dinah Alobeid and Kim Maynard.

Every author needs someone who's been there and willing to answer all the random texts and questions, and I'm grateful that my friend Laurie Ruettimann is that person for me (#CHO!). I also want to recognize the entire People Tech Partners community. I'm inspired by the openness and support across this entire community to make us all better.

Editing the chapter on diversity and inclusion in the early days of the heightened consciousness around the Black Lives Matter movement and social injustice reinforced how important it was to get that chapter right. I'm deeply grateful for the editorial guidance and suggestions from Beverly Carmichael, Torin Ellis, Sarah Morgan and Victorio Milian to help broaden the perspective of the chapter and drive home the importance of embedding diversity-focused practices throughout the book.

This book is infused with inspiration from some of the titans of modern people thinking about approaches, who inspire and inform my work, including Laszlo Bock, Patty McCord, Adam Grant, Katarina Berg, Nellie Peshkov, Reid Hoffman, Katie Burke, Josh Bersin, Claude Silver, Katelin Holloway, Beth Steinberg, Ambrosia Vertesi, Dan Price, and others.

To my parents, Lillian and Kai Sr, and my brother, Kai Jr. I miss you every day and wish you were still alive to share this with me. Know that I carry the love, wisdom and kindness you invested in me every day and that desire to give back is embedded in this book. To my nephew Kyle, your dad would be so proud of the man you've become – and so am I.

To my daughters, Eve and Maya. It's been so much fun sharing this writing experience with you and answering your countless 'How many more words do you have left to write, daddy?' I'll never be able to convey how much joy you bring me. Thank you for reminding me what's most important in life every day.

Lastly, and most importantly, I want to thank my amazing wife Janet Ciciarelli. This book wouldn't have been possible without you and all you do for me and our family. Thank you for supporting my career, being a sounding board for this book (and my other work and projects), and saving me from my over-excited self sometimes (though I haven't given up on mandarin collars... yet).

Introduction

A framework for modern HR and people operations

Human Resources

People Operations

Talent and Culture

People and Places

Human Capital

Talent Operations

Personnel

Do any of those terms describe your team? Perhaps something different altogether? I'm not surprised.

The field has been going through a bit of an identity crisis for several years. Much as the evolution from 'personnel' to 'human resources' was marked by an increase in capability, the current evolution is driven by the increased capabilities and impact of next-generation people teams.

This evolution in nomenclature is not unique to HR. Software engineers used to be programmers. Account representatives used to be sales reps. Even within the field of HR, we've seen the gradual shift from 'recruiting' to 'talent acquisition'.

Let's be honest, the term 'Human Resources' has an image problem. We have ourselves to blame for some of these self-inflicted perception wounds. I'll get into this more later in the book, but in short, our thirst for power and control as a path to the cherished *seat at the table* created resentment and frustration in our teams.

While we have to own our role in some of those legacy perception issues, the reality is that as a function we were rarely given the respect equal to our importance in building a successful organization.

The field of Human Resources today is a spectrum. On one side you have a relic from the days of personnel, defined by words like administrative, reactive, transactional, or less flattering terms. Swing the pendulum in the other direction and you have a very different function defined by words including strategic, transformative, proactive, inclusive, embedded, essential. Your views on the field will largely be informed by where you sit on that spectrum.

This book explores the leading edge of HR. It breaks down some of the ways in which the field has evolved, highlighting shifts in mindset, approaches, technology and more. It blends research, interviews with modern people executives, personal experience and case studies from practitioners around the world who are embracing next-generation people practices to transform their companies.

Human resources or resources for humans?

I love the question above. I wish I could claim it, but it came from Basecamp co-founder and CEO Jason Fried. We were discussing the role of modern HR on my 21st Century HR podcast when he made this comment (Schmidt, 2019). The simplicity was profound. Too often when we think of legacy HR we conjure visions of impersonal policies and procedures that strip humanity and leave our employees feeling as if they have to have a master's in bureaucracy navigation to thrive. Jason's comment was a great level-setting reminder of whom we serve. His views were echoed by Rainmaking Venture Studio Head of Talent Matt Buckland, in the *Fast Company* story referenced above: 'The Truth is HR did themselves a disservice in the pursuit of a "seat at the table". They became police for the organization and lost the respect/ trust of workforces. Any name change that implies some employee advocacy or treats "people" as people should be welcomed.'

Whatever your preferred nomenclature for the function, the reality should be your focus on supporting and enabling your employees to do their best work. 'How' to do that is obviously the art. This book will really be focused on the 'what' and the 'how' of modern HR. You're already reading this, so I trust we can skip the 'why'.

The capability and value to the business of modern people teams go well beyond compliance. Modern people operators bring a much broader skill set to their role, often infused with experiences, perspectives and capabilities from outside the function. People leading these functions possess business acumen on par with their peers across the C-suite. They're embedded in the business and embraced as part of the teams they support. Their teams leverage data that inform their strategy and allow them to address people challenges before they become a crisis. Rather than striving for ownership with centralized command and control structures, their decentralized business partner models focus on empowering and enabling employees to thrive.

How to read this book – what it is and what it isn't

Throughout the book I'll be presenting a view of modern HR that will shape your perspectives on the field. My views are formed by my own experiences, of course. They're far from comprehensive. When thinking about this book, it was important to me to add a range of voices, perspectives and views beyond my own.

That old cliché about surrounding yourself with people smarter than you is a good metaphor for this book. I've been incredibly fortunate in my career to build a network of relationships with subject-matter experts throughout different HR, talent, recruiting and technology disciplines. Many of them have weighed in throughout this book to lend their expertise and insights. I lean on them to ensure that deep domain expertise is infused into each chapter.

Each chapter includes stories and case studies from practitioners who are practising modern HR. I want to balance my own views with their stories and real-world experience to present a more multidimensional view on each topic.

Practitioner spotlights and case studies are highlighted to help them stand out throughout the book. It was important to me to include a range of voices and real-world experience, practices and stories to bring the ideas in each chapter to life.

This book is not about best practices. I personally don't believe in 'best' practices as they're too subjective. For a practice to be 'best', it requires the perfect mix of ingredients – culture, budget, resources, workforce, locations, facilities and so on. That's a lot of variables. I think the idea that you can take a specific practice that is aligned with all of those elements, transplant it to another company and yield the same results is naïve.

I prefer 'proven practices'. They've worked well for an organization with all their unique variables. That doesn't mean replicating it will work for you, but it can inspire you to build something similar that's localized to your own unique circumstances.

What I hope to do in this book is to expose you to a range of varied practices, approaches, views and more. I won't be suggesting any of them as 'best' or suggest your people practices are inferior if they're not built the same way. What I do want to do is expose you to a range of novel ways to think about solving non-novel (and some novel) challenges – an assortment of views and ideas. Maybe they'll inspire you to build something similar? Maybe they'll inspire you to build something better? Maybe you'll reject that approach altogether? You'll have to make your own call.

This book is also not comprehensive. HR is a broad field, made even broader when you look at its applications across companies, industries, sizes, geographies and a range of other variables. We won't dig deeply into fields like academia, union environments, non-profits and so on. The case studies and executive spotlights lean a bit tech as that's where I spend a lot of my time and where much of my network resides, but I worked to get perspectives and experience beyond technology as I know that innovation and great people practices can happen anywhere.

You'll be surprised where you might find inspiration. My goal in writing this book is to introduce you to a range of inspiring practices and practitioners to feed that inspiration and light a spark about what's possible.

Before we get into the main chapters, it's important to add some context to what redefining HR means. We'll do that in Chapter 1.

Reference

Schmidt, L (2019) Why It's Time to Include Compensation Range in Job Descriptions, *Fast Company*. Available from: www.fastcompany.com/90394268/why-its-time-to-include-compensation-ranges-in-job-postings (archived at https://perma.cc/3GNC-BNFD)

01

What is redefining HR?

As the book title and introduction might indicate, this book is about progressive HR and people practices. It lays out foundational elements of modern people practices and how they've evolved from HR's past.

What's different about HR today? Quite a lot, it turns out. While not comprehensive, this chapter will spotlight some of the key shifts from legacy HR to modern HR to set the tone for the book. We'll go deeper in future chapters to contextualize and bring these to life even more.

I also wanted to use this chapter to define modern HR. Not in my words, but in the words of leading people executives who are driving this shift.

Defining modern HR and people operations

This book is a deep dive into modern HR. As we get started, I feel it's important to define that from multiple perspectives. I'm privileged to speak with a range of modern people executives on my podcast – each with their own take on the direction of HR.

As we get into the core of the book, I wanted to share some of their perspectives on the direction of the field in their own words. I also wanted to provide a glimpse into some of the topics we'll explore in the following chapters.

The quotes throughout this chapter come from my 21st Century HR podcast and illuminate modern people executives' views on how they define modern HR.

DAVID HANRAHAN, CHRO, EVENTBRITE

I think of 21st-century HR as re-engineering people programmes towards humanity. We've entered and exited a period, at least in the US industry and workplace, that was largely grounded in compliance in the workplace. We've lost touch with our humanity in HR as part of that.

We've engineered people functions towards risk aversion and creating rules in the workplace. We need to shift our focus to understanding the potential of humans: what makes us human; how to get the most from the human experience at work; empathy; kindness.

As a society we're seeing mental health rates, anxiety, incidents of depression and so on skyrocketing. People are having fewer children. Society is changing. In many ways it feels as though we've lost connection. We've lost connection with what it means to be a human, particularly at work. If we can't find that again, we're going to lose people. We're going to lose their productivity, their potential, their passion.

Decentralize and empower (Chapter 4)

Old-school HR teams obsessed over getting that coveted seat at the table. They designed elaborate programmes that put them as the gatekeeper of many corporate decisions – bonuses, promotions, budgets, headcount. This usually came from a place of insecurity. Employee resentment grew as these needlessly complex machinations slowed things down.

Next-generation HR leaders (and teams) are much more secure in their impact on the business. They are focused on success enablement and designing programmes that allow leaders to lead and employees to thrive.

MATT HOFFMAN, PARTNER AND HEAD OF TALENT, M13

Instead of simply managing performance from the top down, 21st-century HR is about developing and elevating performance from every aspect. 21st-century HR is an appreciation of the power of diversity. It's an appreciation of the benefits of inclusion, compelling companies to respect and appreciate people for their whole selves – as human beings, with everything they bring to the table.

I think so much of HR in the past has been about fitting people into specific boxes and then just building better practices to find the right people for the right box. But the advancement and the value of HR in the future is that you no longer have to worry about fitting people into specific boxes all the time. You can let them create their own experiences, let them create their own structure. Let them build their own containers and really unleash their full potential rather than just help people live up to predetermined 'boxes'. The more you can create an environment for employees to do their best work and break through those predefined expectations of what their job should be, the better they will do and the better your organization will do.

Rather than focus on personnel and processes, 21st-century HR is focused on building a culture based on creating healthy foundations where you can trust employees as you scale, get manager and leadership behaviours to drive high growth and high performance in the future, and then find ways to unleash people's potential across that entire foundation.

Policy for the many (not against the few) (Chapter 4)

How many HR policies have you read that were written to cover the absolute edge case of the worst possible scenario, and then assume that all of your employees will do exactly that? It's stifling to feel that your employer has zero trust in your ability to make correct decisions.

Modern HR leaders are able to balance their need to mitigate risks while implementing common-sense programmes aimed at reducing friction and enabling employees to do their best work.

COLLEEN MCCREARY, CHIEF PEOPLE OFFICER, CREDIT KARMA

I always say that our teams are really designed around saying yes and we've really moved into this space where there is an appreciation for the idea that there are a lot of business problems that are almost always rooted in our number one cost, which is labour. Our job is helping our business leaders get to a position where we're able to actually give them solutions that will help them solve those business problems.

The fact that we have that trust right now to do that, and that platform, means that we are in this great consultant position to be this expert on talent.

We don't necessarily have to put that burden back on the business leader. We have to give them choices. My operating philosophy is 'we say yes unless it's illegal or stupid'. The reason I say that is because when a business leader comes to you with an idea and your response is actually, 'Oh my god, this is so dumb', it's because they have a problem and they don't understand. We have all these tools now, so we can be great at saying: 'Here's all this data. Let me help you understand. This is your problem. Here is some data around your talent and your employees, or the outside market, or labour costs, or all of these kinds of things. Then here's my experience and here's who you have. Let's go forward and find a better solution.'

We have that opportunity now. We don't have to be, nor is there an expectation that we will be, hiding behind our employee handbook and that this is the rule. As soon as we continue to be those partners where our leaders say, 'I don't know what I'm going to do if I don't have that HR business partner', or 'That recruiter was so right when they said, "Hey, this job is going to take probably this amount of time to fill because there's nobody who works in those roles in this geography and you're probably going to have to go and import somebody"', they now know we can have this data. We have this knowledge set. We can solve their problems. That is 21st-century HR.

Building a company for everyone (Chapter 3)

The language we use matters – as does the intent. The traditional framing of 'diversity' is actually limiting. Modern HR teams are expanding their focus to building inclusive organizations based on representation. Too often, legacy HR teams viewed diversity as a check-the-box initiative entirely focused on hiring. We're now going deeper with a more nuanced lens, shedding notions of 'culture fit' and weaving inclusive thinking and practices throughout our people programmes – recruiting, pay equity, promotions, training, development.

ANNA BINDER, HEAD OF PEOPLE, ASANA

Your investment in the culture that drives your business results and enables you to achieve your mission is what defines 21st-century HR. That's my North Star. That is everything. I've come to believe, that there are two things that drive engagement over and above everything else. The first is: Does my work matter? Am I working on stuff that matters? Those questions use some of the same words but they mean different things. How can I connect the work that I'm doing up to the bigger project or up to the bigger objective? How does that objective connect to the company's strategy and ultimately allow us to achieve our mission?

When I'm trying to figure out how to prioritize between two tasks that seem equally important, but I only have time for one of them, how do I connect it to the higher purpose and does it really matter? The second thing that is a fundamental driver of engagement is belonging. I might not look and feel like everyone else around me, but am I in an environment where my voice is heard? Where I can mostly be my full self? Where it's okay to show vulnerability?

We've invested tremendously at Asana in trying to create that sense of belonging. Belonging means different things to different people, so it's very hard to impact it. Part of it is ensuring that expressing vulnerability is a core leadership trait that is not only allowed but actively encouraged, celebrated and held to account. Those two things. I think that's the modern workplace. 21st-century HR is enabling those two things and making them alive. Not just because they're the right things to do, but because they will help your organization achieve its mission.

Performance reviews get agile (Chapter 10)

Does anyone still think the tired annual review cycles provide value? In a world of real-time feedback, the idea of waiting 364 days to hear how you're performing is as valuable as an eight-track cassette.

Employees want ongoing feedback on how they're doing and what's expected of them. If we hope to retain them, we'd better be prepared to have those conversations more than once a year.

MICHAEL FRACCARO, CHIEF PEOPLE OFFICER, MASTERCARD

There's a need for HR to continually reinvent itself and transform beyond its traditional day-to-day activities. The same fundamentals apply, but I think HR functions now have the opportunity to influence and shape the future of the organization. That opportunity has never been more pronounced than it is today. When we think about the trends driving the future of work, we read a lot about the threat of automation and artificial intelligence; that is, the robot's taking jobs. There's a huge role for HR to play in terms of the tone and the messaging of these developments within organizations – and the realization that there's probably more opportunity as a result of these new technologies coming into the workplace. I think it's fertile ground for interesting work and meaningful contributions. It's a great time to be in Human Resources.

The house that data built (Chapter 11)

There are few components more fundamental to modern HR than analytics. We've never had more data at our fingertips. How we interpret, measure and act on those data is often the difference between good and world-class people teams. There's a reason why people analytics skill (and demand) is on the rise. Companies are building their own internal data teams or moving others from outside HR into the function to elevate their ability to synthesize and act on the massive stores of employee data they've accumulated.

JEVAN SOO, CHIEF PEOPLE AND CULTURE OFFICER, STITCH FIX

We're just starting to see the beginning of technology becoming embedded in everyday work life as it pertains to HR and people operations. Things like Laszlo Bock's Humu with their behavioural nudges are just the tip of the iceberg. I draw a ton of inspiration from other innovations in other business functions. I think about things like 'always on' sensors in the Internet of Things, devices that send you tons of insight throughout the day – what's the work version of that?

There's so much there for us to unpack because of the continued challenges of improving people data – both quality and quantity. Too much of what we currently collect essentially requires someone to fill out a survey. I have to believe there's more we can do there. There is so much technology advancement and opportunity ahead of us.

I think about tools that can help coach employees in real time, perhaps intervening in the moment where someone is unconsciously being less inclusive or decision bias is happening. The world of possibilities is really pretty expansive. When I think about 21st-century HR, I think about the continued collision of technology with humanity and the ability and responsibility of the HR function to really harness that in a way that's proactive and used for good. Hopefully it's more *Star Trek: The Next Generation* than *Black Mirror*.

HR goes open source (Chapter 5)

It used to be really hard to learn how to design and execute HR initiatives. Not anymore.

One of the single biggest shifts that's fuelling next-generation HR practices is the shift to open-source practices. Legacy HR viewed their processes as secret ingredients under lock and key. This proprietary approach stifled innovation.

Progressive people teams embrace open-source approaches. It's common to find modern people leaders contributing case studies, writing blog posts, sharing their learnings (and failures). You rarely saw that a decade ago – now it's common.

KATELIN HOLLOWAY, FOUNDING PARTNER, 776

I owe every single ounce of where I am today to the people who helped me get here and the sharing communities that exist.

In my first role as a people executive, the CEO asked me to start organizing things around talent acquisition and policies and come up with a handbook. I'd had a few handbooks as an employee in the past, but if it had not been for the HR and people community, it would have taken me a lot longer to produce something. The shared thinking was: *We should be spending our time with people, not recreating and reinventing wheels. We have to help each other.* I know every single people professional out there wishes they could spend more time with people. They do not want to be stuck behind a computer hacking away at things that someone else can do better or has already done anyway.

I wish I could contribute more to those communities. I'm a huge fan of open source.

Bringing business acumen to HR (Chapter 2)

Employment law? Required.

Succession planning? A given.

Talent mapping? Fundamental.

HR has always had HR acumen. In today's complex business world, though, that's not enough. Look across HR leadership in sector-leading companies and you'll find HR leaders from a range of non-traditional career paths. Why? The complexity of business today requires an HR leader to possess an intimate grasp of the business, industry, market and more.

Chief people officer is one of the toughest jobs in the C-suite. They're expected to understand the financials like a chief financial officer, grasp product–market fit like a chief marketing officer, gauge the revenue pipeline like a chief revenue officer and be the right hand to the chief executive officer, all while synthesizing that understanding to develop programmes and systems that optimize your most volatile resource: your people. It's a difficult job even with business acumen – and I'd argue it's impossible without it.

MICHAEL DEANGELO, EXECUTIVE COACH, DEANGELO DEVELOPMENT

The future of HR is much more business minded. There are two core parts of our role. There is a focus on how you create a culture that is supportive, an environment that allows the work to be done really effectively while allowing people to feel that they're not an 'only'. They feel included and they understand that their work has a meaning and a purpose.

There's that culture side of every role, but then there is a business capability side that is critical. Most of us under-index on that, and that's a key need for modern HR. You have to learn the business. What drives user growth? What drives engagement for users? How do you make money? Only after understanding those questions can you know what levers you need to pull in order to make those things better. That allows you to look two to three years out with the business and say, 'This is the business we're in now, but what's the business we're going to go to in two years and how do we have the capability so that when that starts we can do that work?'

It's all about understanding and adjusting capabilities, because, especially in tech, the industry will just continue to evolve and disrupt, and you will not be supporting the business if you are just working on what they're doing currently. You have to be thinking about where it's going to go, and largely those capabilities are probably going to be different. Maybe you'll take on a new business model. Maybe you'll shift into subscription, or content, or enterprise model. All of those things have very different needs from a leadership, from a board dynamic, from how you structure the organization and the decisions you make.

You constantly have to be thinking of that. Maybe your CEO is very progressive and she thinks about that, but she would at the very least need a partner who's helping her think two years out, which means we have to start now.

'Why isn't HR here?' over 'Why is HR here?' (Chapter 4)

Remember the 'Why is HR here?' comments that were often delivered with an eye roll in meetings? You don't hear many of those with next-generation people teams. Quite the opposite, actually.

Modern HR practitioners are vital partners to the business. They combine data, research and experience to help teams think through their most complex talent challenges. They're respected, requested and needed.

The key takeaway from these discussions was that HR is a spectrum. While the majority of the field is somewhere in the middle, the leading edge of HR is having a transformational impact on business and redefining the field itself. These new teams are coveted by the C-suite. They make a lasting impact on the business, employees and organizational capability.

CLAUDE SILVER, CHIEF HEART OFFICER, VAYNERMEDIA

I define 21st-century HR as practitioners becoming coaches. We are in the service of human beings and looking at the whole human being in a holistic way. In today's day and age, that means people are coming into the office after dropping their kid off at school, after going to the gym, after paying their electricity bill. They have a life before they come into work and they have a life after.

I'm interested in knowing how they're managing their energy. I want to make sure that they know they have access to meditation, a wellness room, a 1:1 with their manager, an impromptu chat with me or others in leadership... whatever it is they need. They need financial advice? They can have that too.

We look at the whole person. We have a wellness wheel here that helps us look at the different needs of a human, whether or not that is environmental wellness, financial wellness, exercise and so on. We don't have all the answers, but we're going to do our very best to provide you with what you are looking for.

The role of HR has never been more important. That importance was brought into the spotlight in 2020. Covid-19 underscored the impact of competent and agile people teams. The events of 2020 allowed companies who saw the importance of investing in their people function to navigate the turbulent times much more successfully than those who viewed and resourced the function as an administrative entity.

Josh Bersin has been at the forefront of the field of HR for years. He's seen a range of cycles for the function, and shares his comments on the current state of HR in the practitioner spotlight here.

PRACTITIONER SPOTLIGHT
The heroic role of HR today

Josh Bersin, Founder and Dean, Josh Bersin Academy

The HR profession has been thrust into a heroic role in business. Why? Because virtually every economic, political, business and financial issue that companies face is now all about people. In fact, I like to say 'every business challenge is a people challenge', leading to the ever-increasing importance of HR.

The challenge we face in HR is often our identity. Are we a compliance and payroll function? Are we responsible for culture, leadership and change? Are we leading the push for diversity and inclusion? And how well can we digitize all that we do to make it easy, transparent and productive? We have to do all of this.

In this new era of the pandemic, these truths are being proved. Today, as companies worry about safety and health in every geography, HR is playing a lead role in redefining the work experience, creating well-being and support programmes for employees and families, and helping to redesign all the protocols that make work productive, healthy and financially rewarding. And what the pandemic also shows is that HR teams must be agile (not 'do agile'), collaborative, and learn all the time.

Among the many things HR professionals must do, we must be closely aligned with the business, highly empathetic to workforce needs, acutely aware of social and political issues, and well versed in technology, economics and all the practices of our trade. And more than ever we have to think about ourselves as craftspeople – not just copying what other companies do, but inventing and crafting solutions that are unique and well fitted to our companies.

I believe the HR profession is one of the most valuable roles in business today, and while most of us come into the profession from many different places, we have to come together to learn, share and advance our thinking. Business plays an enormous role in society: when companies treat people well, give them the development they need and pay them fairly, the company succeeds, the people succeed and society is better as a result.

This is modern HR: relevant, savvy, inventive, bold, well trained, connected, and empathetic most of all.

This is our mission – and I feel proud and honoured to support HR in every way I can.

As you can see, the differences in approach and thinking on modern HR are vast. The aim of this book is to go deeper in most of these areas to help you better understand the shift, spark ideas and thinking, and share real stories and tangible examples from practitioners doing this work.

In the next chapter, we'll explore how the role of the chief human resource officer (CHRO) has evolved to support these new practices.

02

The evolution of the CHRO

Take a moment and think back on all the chief human resource officers (CHROs) you've worked with in your career. What traits stand out to you? What was their communication style? Did they enable change or stand in the way of it? Chances are, if you've worked long enough, your answers are all over the place.

The profile of a modern CHRO has been evolving over the past decade. Historically this role followed a linear career path from within the field. HR leaders worked their way through functional career progression as they climbed their way to the top job. Their experience and perspectives often went deep in HR, but often lacked cross-functional exposure and experience. The times are changing.

A few months ago, I was doing a radio show interview and the host was asking me about 21st-century HR. It was clear he had a perception of HR based largely on legacy views. At one point he asked if HR is still 'where careers go to die'. Yep – live on the radio. I redirected him with the comment that: 'HR is now where careers come to thrive.'

PRACTITIONER SPOTLIGHT
Journey to HR

Anna Binder, Head of People, Asana

After college I travelled around the world for a couple of years and explored different cultures. I ended up in San Francisco and started my job search. When you've never had a job and you don't know what you want to do, your ability to make criteria-based decisions in your job search is really limited. You don't even know how to assess. I remember pretty clearly, I had three job opportunities given to me in one week.

It was the late 1990s and it was the heyday of the internet in San Francisco, so that was kind of the norm. I ended up joining a company based solely on the fact that I thought I wanted to follow the CEO. He seemed really impressive. He was a rigorous interviewer. I believed in his vision. I believed in his leadership as much as I could. I started out doing everything. I was part HR, part recruiting, part legal. I coordinated the board meetings. I was his assistant. Sometimes I sat at the front desk. I definitely paid all the bills and reviewed the contracts. I did everything and we were a ten-person start-up.

We eventually grew that company to 300 people. Bit by bit, parts of my job got 'taken away'. I still remember at one point he said to me, 'You've really added a lot of value here. You're early in your career. You get to do whatever you want. Tell me what you want to do?' I said, 'I want to do corporate development.' He laughed. 'Why do you want to do corporate development?' I said, 'Well, it just seems that there's smart people over there doing smart stuff. I just want to go be with them.' He laughed, not with me, but at me. He truly laughed at me. He said, 'Don't be an idiot. You're really good at this HR stuff. It comes naturally to you. You're having a tremendous impact. Do the things in life that bring you joy and that you're good at. All of the success will happen after that. It will naturally follow.'

I said, 'But John, whenever I go to a party and I tell people that I work in HR, they roll their eyes. I don't want to work in a function that people roll their eyes at. That just doesn't feel good.' We had a set of conversations, but I said, 'Okay, well, you know what? I'll try it. I'll see how it goes.'

Eventually, I built the capability. I got better at it. I moved to another company. I got mentorship from other people who were not in HR but believed in the function. Bit by bit, I built my capability and my strength in the discipline. Eventually, I just shifted and I realized I didn't see a lot of people I looked up to in the function at that time and who I felt would really teach me something. It felt a little bit lonely. It hurt my ego to have people roll their eyes. Eventually I shifted and I just said, 'I actually really love this work. I believe in its impact. I actually think it's what I'm good at, so maybe I can just do it. Then eventually I can be one of those people that other people who are starting their careers can look to and say I want to be like that.'

I can't tell you how gratifying it is to be able to do work that you feel you were meant to be doing, and to have impact on human beings and on businesses. I feel like I've had an ocean of good fortune in my career and very, very blessed.

Anna's comment about people 'rolling their eyes' when she shared that she worked in HR earlier in her career really resonated with me, and particularly with those of us with some tenure in the field. It illustrates that legacy perception of HR and what we've moved from to get to the concepts and capabilities in this book.

I still see it on occasion when I introduce myself, but I now know it's a reflection of how they've worked – not what I do.

Non-traditional career paths

Human Resources evolved out of a personnel-based function rooted in administrative and compliance-driven tasks. The value-add to the business was rarely viewed in the same way as sales, marketing or engineering. When you break down old-school HR teams, you'll find many practitioners who've spent most of their careers in the field.

As I outlined previously, those career paths tended to be linear, rising from coordinator to manager, ultimately all the way up to top CHRO. This path meant the function was rarely infused with perspectives and practices from outside the field, leading to insular ideas on what it means for an HR professional to support the business.

Today's modern HR executives are finding their way to this role through a range of disparate fields, even skydiving. Maia Josebachvili leads the people team at Stripe. She's one of my favourite people leaders in the space – and certainly has one of the more interesting paths that led her there.

PRACTITIONER SPOTLIGHT
My unlikely path to HR

Maia Josebachvili, Former Head of People, Stripe

When people ask me how I got into HR, I often joke and say I'll list out my previous jobs to see if they can come up with a good hypothesis because I don't really know. :)

Of course, that's not really true (okay fine, maybe a little), but I certainly have not had the obvious career path to get to where I am. I studied mechanical engineering in college, was a derivatives trader on the floor of the stock exchange, and a founder and CEO of an early e-commerce and outdoor adventure company. We sold that company to daily deals site LivingSocial, where I became GM (General Manager) of New Initiatives, incubating and running several business units. That's where I had my first encounter with hypergrowth – LivingSocial went from 300 employees when they bought my company to 5,000 in the two short years I was there.

That experience really piqued my interest in HR, as I saw first-hand the criticality of having an exceptional people function. It led me to explore early-stage HR tech companies and I took an advisor/consultant role with Greenhouse as they were just starting out. As is often the case in start-ups, I wore many hats there, including VP of Strategy and New Initiatives, CMO, and my first stint as VP of People. All of that led me to where I am now – leading the people team at Stripe, a global company with over 3,000 employees.

There was also a small stint as a pro-skydiver sprinkled in there, but that one didn't last too long.

While my career path has not exactly been linear, I can point to almost every experience I've had and explain how it's played a pivotal role in my ability to do my job. Some examples of skills I developed outside the function that have proved most helpful are:

- Organization leader, manager and previous 'user' of HR. During my time at LivingSocial, we spun up an entire new division of 75 full-time and 700 part-time people within my first six months. While my primary job was to build the business and be responsible for the P&L, ultimately I described my job as a crash course in all things HR: hiring and onboarding at scale, career pathing, internal communications and so on. It's really helpful to have had that experience on the business side as we develop products and interfaces for our managers and leaders.

- Entrepreneurial, product mindset. As Lars is articulating here, the future of work is evolving. This means that while we can draw on past experiences, we must simultaneously throw out the old playbooks and chart a new course. I'm writing this in the middle of the Covid-19 pandemic. In the past six months we've meaningfully shifted our talent and geo-location strategy, rolled out our approach to increasing opportunities to work remotely permanently, and are in the process of re-imaging the role of the office in our culture. I lean on what I've learned when developing products for users. We start every new project with user research: what challenges are our managers facing, or what matters most to employees? We use a combination of user surveys and focus groups, and then each programme we develop has a go-to-market launch plan to maximize adoption, followed by frequent feedback and iteration cycles.

- Analytical skills. People are often surprised when I share how much of my time I spend in Excel (or Google Sheets these days). Just to run the business we need sophisticated recruiter capacity models that can flex to accommodate shifts in our geographical or level mix. To truly build a high-performing organization over the long term, it's also important to be able to dive into data to answer big picture, strategic questions. For example, our team recently did a study of interview notes and performance reviews of high-impact employees, as well as people who left for performance reasons. The goal was to better understand what attributes are most predictive of long-term success, so that we could use that information to inform interview questions going forward. The analytical skills I've developed over the years have been really helpful to be able to work with our analytics team on these studies and more.

My path to HR was not linear, and I imagine it will continue to bounce again in the future. I wouldn't be surprised if I go back to the business at some point, and I'd be less surprised if I end up in people again after that. I think that's the beauty of how our function is evolving – non-HR experience is very helpful in the role, and people experience is increasingly becoming valuable, and almost necessary, in non-people roles.

If you're considering a jump into, or a dip outside of, people, my two cents is to give it a shot. The odds that it's net-positive to your career are quite high.

When you look across the field of HR today, you'll find employees from a range of different backgrounds and experience. As our people operations continue to scale in their sophistication and capabilities, we're seeing an influx of talent from across the organization – marketing, analytics, project management, data science, creative. The list goes on.

At times, HR leaders may take a detour into other areas of the business and become 'customers' of the HR team. That perspective can help uncover blind spots and develop a more empathetic view towards the teams that HR supports. Consider this experience from Stitch Fix Chief People and Culture Officer Jevan Soo when he left HR earlier in his career to join the Sales Operations team at Square:

> I learned so much about being a great people operations leader from the multiple opportunities I had to be in the business very close to revenue, close to customers. I remember after one role change from the people team to

leading sales operations, all of a sudden I was the recipient of all of the emails, programmes and initiatives that the people team I just came from would send forth. I would have a moment here and there where I'd think, 'This process is so hard, they don't understand, they're not being thoughtful about what I have to deliver for the business.' Then I'd remember I was in that same seat three months ago, shipping those same people programmes! It instilled in me a lot of empathy for both sides and the challenge of balancing competing priorities.

That time was really instructive for me in showing me how lucky we are on the people side of the house – people stuff is all we think about. Unfortunately, other leaders in the business can't dedicate 100 per cent of their mindshare and capacity to those people initiatives – and it's not simply because they don't care or aren't trying. And so now I really try to have my teams design their initiatives with that perspective and empathy in mind.

In a global survey from HR Open Source (HR Open Source, 2018), 70 per cent of respondents worked in areas outside Human Resources at some point in their careers. This cross-pollination of skills and experience is having a profound impact on the field – increasing capabilities, accelerating agile practices and making the field both more data-driven and creative.

Stitch Fix Chief People Officer Jevan Soo agrees, as he shared on the 21st Century HR Podcast (21st Century HR, 2019):

One of the exciting things I see in the HR function is the influx of people coming over with non-HR functional experience working alongside people who have grown up in HR who are really disruptive and innovative and excited to see things change. You're seeing people bring in all these great insights and innovations from other business functions. Think about operations and supply chain and agile product development thinking and approaches entering our field, or everything that's happened in marketing over the last couple of decades: brand affinity, authentic connections with consumers, CRM and top-of-the-funnel nurture campaigns, lead generation approaches for sales being adapted to recruiting. There are so many lessons to apply from other areas of the business.

As Jevan notes, these new skills sets, perspectives and capabilities are having a huge impact on the field. This is one of the biggest catalysts of the up-levelling of HR and people teams and capabilities.

PRACTITIONER SPOTLIGHT
Traverse the jungle gym

Guissu Baier, Co-founder, The People Collective

'Hi, my name is Guissu Baier and I'm a recovering employment attorney.' That's how I typically introduce myself. While, to many, my career path from lawyer to VP of HR at a Silicon Valley Unicorn may seem non-linear, for me it was a natural progression from playing defence as a lawyer, to playing offense and leveraging an organization's greatest asset – its people – to drive the business forward.

In law school, I was drawn to employment law because it was a fascinating intersection between business and people, economics and psychology. After years as a litigator, I joined the payment technology company, Visa, as one of the only two employment attorneys globally. When the opportunity arose to join a high-growth on-demand grocery delivery start-up as its first employment attorney, I pounced.

The company's speed of execution, ability to hit aggressive goals, and culture were infectious. In the true spirit of joining a high-growth start-up, I soon ended up wearing multiple hats. In addition to a full workload as the company's only employment counsel, at the request of the CEO I took on leading the company's first diversity, equity and inclusion initiative. Immediately I was hooked. The chance to have a direct impact on the organization in a way that was meaningful for its people and tangible for the company was incredibly rewarding.

Several months later, the CEO asked me to step in and lead all of HR on an interim basis. I agreed, but made it clear that I wasn't planning to just babysit the function. I had ideas on how to propel it from an operational function to a strategic, competitive advantage. At first, the CEO was sceptical. After a quarter of 70+-hour weeks, gathering data, and leaning on a network of mentors, like Jo Dennis, I delivered an end-to-end people strategy proposal.

It was ambitious. The CEO loved it. He promoted me to VP of HR and I quickly got to work with the team on executing the vision I presented. We began measuring engagement and belonging in a data-driven way, launched a bespoke manager and leadership training programme, and challenged convention on how to approach performance and compensation. It wasn't perfect but we had the latitude to innovate and make a lasting impact.

When my husband and I decided to leave the Bay Area, I made the hard choice to leave the company. Many people asked if I would return to the law. 'No way!' I exclaimed. I am and will forever be grateful for my legal training but, for me, the ability to have an impact on people's lives, on the direction of a business and on its heart and culture is energizing and addictive.

After venturing into venture capital as an operating partner, I saw an opportunity to partner with the venture capital community to deliver strategic services to early-stage companies and co-founded The People Collective, a boutique talent, people and culture firm.

My advice to those who are considering a 'non-linear career path'? Life isn't linear and opportunities are everywhere if you are brave enough to peek beyond the blinders. So dream big, and not just in one direction. Traverse the jungle gym. Don't wait for someone to draw you a ladder.

Guissu's non-linear path from law to Human Resources to venture capital is no longer an anomaly. More and more business operators are moving in and out of the HR department.

The influx of skills is also being seen in the executive seat. Look across the chief HR executive role today and you'll find a range of leaders from other areas of the business: Google's Eileen Naughton (Sales), Facebook's Lori Goler (Marketing), Microsoft's Kathleen Hogan (Services), Apple's Deirdre O'Brien (Retail), Amazon's Beth Galetti (Operations), HubSpot's Katie Burke (Media Relations), VaynerMedia's Claude Silver (Advertising), SpaceX's Brian Bjelde (Engineering) and New Relic's Kristy Friedrichs (Consulting), just to name a few.

These shifts are often triggered by the desire to infuse more business acumen into the function. Many of the transitions are internal moves, situations where leaders already had a grasp of the business and the trust of their C-suite peers. I've spoken to many of them and they often have a refreshing humility towards the role. They admit what they lack in HR operational depth and savvy, and they ensure they have a team around them that is able to complement their experience and unique skill set. Consider Claude Silver's transition to the Chief Heart Officer role at VaynerMedia:

> Ten years ago I was working in London and I was the head strategist on many large global brands. I got a feeling, that voice in my head was loud, which was saying to me, 'You really only want to work with people. You really want to be a coach or a therapist and somewhere where you could more directly impact humans.' I shoved that voice away because I had a great career and advertising was allowing me to be creative.

Then I met Gary Vaynerchuk. I had always wanted to work with him. He was like that one missing piece in my advertising arsenal, which was social strategy. He and I connected through my best friend. We met and we kind of fell for one another. We instantly had an incredible bond. The next thing I knew, he hired me. He brought me from London to New York City. I was his first senior vice president (SVP). I ran our large Unilever account and I had a team of 45 people, so in reality I was operating a little mini agency. I just loved the people part, growing and developing them, enjoying the camaraderie we were building, the trust and all of that stuff. Then that voice came up loud again: 'You really don't care about advertising, you only care about these people.' I went to Gary on my year anniversary. I said to the greatest salesman in the world, 'Thank you so much for this opportunity. I think you are amazing and I love this place; however, I'm no longer interested in advertising or selling a product.' He said in his incredible, generous fashion, 'Cool. What is it that you want to do?' I responded, 'I only care about people. I only care about the heartbeat of this place.'

Within a few months I had sourced my replacement and left the agency. Four months later, Gary asked me to breakfast. We sat down and he literally said, 'Hi, how are you? You're coming back. You're going to be chief heart officer.' I said, 'Okay, cool', because I already knew what that was. If you're a people person, you've always been a people person. I was always that person, whether or not it was to the team of 45 or to the whole agency. So, I just said to him, 'Awesome. How do we know if I'm successful? Because that's pretty damn lofty.' He said, 'You'll touch every single human being and infuse the agency with empathy.' I was like, 'Okay, let's rock and roll.' So, four years later we're here.

Claude represents a new mould of HR leader. Anyone who knows her knows that her title goes deeper than terminology. Heart and empathy are hard-wired into how she operates as a leader. Gary brought her into that role for that very reason. 'Chief Heart Officer' is a non-traditional title for a non-traditional leader hand-picked by a non-traditional CEO to lead VaynerMedia. It's a perfect, non-traditional, fit.

Sometimes these non-traditional profiles are exactly what founders are targeting – and become their secret formula to success.

PRACTITIONER SPOTLIGHT
My journey to HR

Sehr Charania, Venture Partner, NextGen Venture Partners

I took a non-traditional path to become a people leader, but hypergrowth has always been a constant in my career journey. After spending a few years in the consulting world, I co-founded an energy company which became the fastest-growing company in Houston at the time. After a whirlwind few years, we exited to a now-public company, and I took my first real break since college and travelled.

My travels took me to the Bay Area, and a few days later a recruiter at IPSY reached out. IPSY's founders were looking for an untraditional Head of People that brought a more commercial mindset than the more traditional candidates they had met. At the time, I knew very little about the people space and, quite frankly, was not convinced that it would be a great fit for me. However, I thought IPSY's founders were brilliant, so I took the leap.

As an outsider in the people space, my first few months on the job were challenging. I inherited a small people team and was working 15-hour days to shore up organizational debt while simultaneously scaling the company at a fast clip. I also experienced imposter syndrome for the first time. I was working with experienced founders and felt I had to constantly prove myself. I was nearing burnout during my first few months, but I was fortunate to have mentors that I could lean on.

Over the next few years, IPSY became the world's largest beauty subscription company, valued at over a billion dollars. On the heels of IPSY's massive growth, my family decided to move to Austin, where I joined the team at RigUp as their VP of People & Talent. Over the next two years, RigUp tripled headcount, built a category-defining product and became a tech unicorn. Looking back, here's what I've learned:

- Experience isn't a prerequisite for the Head of People role, but it does help. We grew faster and navigated through much more change at RigUp than at IPSY. However, having the ability to recognize patterns and know the fundamentals of the people function helped me move faster and better.

- Functional experience outside the people space can give you an advantage. Having led other functions, I was able to partner very effectively with leaders, managers and teams since I could deeply empathize with and relate to them. As a former founder, I could more easily perspective-share with other founders and discuss business and strategy in a way that resonated with them.

- Networks are essential. As an untraditional people leader, leaning on others with HR experience was critical. Without the support of other people leaders, I would not have been able to get up to speed as quickly as I did and I probably would have made more mistakes along the way.

- Work for great founders. Founders can make for a great experience or a suboptimal one in the Head of People role. Their view on culture, their vision for the people function and their willingness to allocate resources to build out the people function deeply influence the type of impact a people leader can have.

When you consider your career options in the field of HR and people operations, you have so many options to pursue today. Want to be a generalist? There are a range of generalists and HR business partners to explore in most companies. Want to be a specialist? In most teams today, you'll have expanded opportunities beyond the traditional choices such as recruiting, benefits, compensation, HR information systems (HRIS) and so on. The world is your oyster.

While that assessment is admittedly sunny, there's another side to consider – especially if you aspire to the top job.

Navigating the pressures of a modern CHRO

The modern CHRO holds one of the most difficult positions in the C-suite. You have to possess a deep understanding of the business that's on par with your executive peers. You need to be able to influence and guide the CEO as a trusted advisor on all things people. You must grasp the nuance of your business and strategic plan so that you can align your people strategy for where you are today and where you're going over the next several years. All while overseeing the company's most volatile asset – its people.

Add to this external factors like #MeToo, Black Lives Matter and social justice, political and geopolitical change, generational shifts, technological change and more, and it's a wonder the people in these roles find time for sleep. The expectations on modern people executives are massive. That's one of the reasons the tenures are declining and the number of vacancies seems to climb each year. It's a hard job. It's a lonely job. You often deal with some of the most traumatic experiences humans face – death, divorce, disease, loss, dishonesty and more. You also rarely have internal support networks where you can talk about all of the above. That pressure can be incredibly isolating. It takes a special skill set and ability to navigate these waters.

You're also under tremendous pressure from the business and your C-suite peers to make an impact – quickly. Michael DeAngelo is the former Chief People Officer at Mozilla. He's an experienced people leader, with past HR executive roles with Pinterest, Google, Pepsico, Microsoft and others. He weighed in on the importance of developing your onboarding plan during our 21st Century HR podcast:

> Be very clear about your plan and take the time to understand the organization before acting. You're going to get pressure to make key decisions. Your team's going to be asking you to do things that have been holding for 6–12 months. As a new CPO, the best thing you can do and explain to your team is to convey that it's really important you learn here first.
>
> You need to understand before being understood. You want to get the culture. You want to understand the history and you need to understand what the background is for problems and the things we need to go fix, because that's what's going to help us make the most progress. You have to have a mindset of 'what is the client's first need?' You may think that this flashy thing would give you the fastest start, but if that is not what the clients think is broken, it's going to actually impede your progress.
>
> Start with what they're asking you to do, and then, once you get credibility there, they're going to give you permission to do things that are more progressive.

HR executives arrive with an immediate slate of problems to fix. You're expected to quickly get up to speed on a range of variables, including culture (strengths and risks), talent, marketing positioning, business model, growth plans, what's working well, what must be fixed, and a lot more.

If you jump into fix mode before you have a firm grasp of these variables, you can create even more problems. According to a study by the *Harvard Business Review* (Byford, Watkins and Triantogiannis, 2017), 70 per cent of new executives cited a poor grasp of how their organization works as a stumbling block for effective onboarding. Getting aligned with your executive peers is essential to setting yourself up for success. Part of this is managing the expectations of the CEO, as Credit Karma Chief People Officer Colleen McCreary explains:

> There are a lot of start-up CEOs who think the talent part is easy. I laugh at the number of start-up CEOs I've met where they will say to me, 'Wow, all of my problems are around people and leaders and I feel like I have to do their jobs and I don't know what I'm going to do.' Then literally the next sentence will be,

'But I don't really need to hire any super senior HR person. I just need somebody that can help a little bit.' Do they even understand what came out of their mouth? It's hard not to laugh. I think it's that investment in the entire employee experience. It's understanding that the investment in cultivating the culture, processes and tools that align with the vision that the company's espousing is hard and expensive. It does take a lot of people to do that really well.

The rapport and connection between the CEO and the CPO are key – particularly when it comes to building healthy and scalable cultures. If you're ever interviewing for a people executive job and are told you'll be owning the culture, you should thank them for the clue and run away. Fast. You can't win there.

If, however, you find a leader who truly values, prioritizes and resources what it takes to build a healthy culture – that's a different story. Leaders who can balance and co-prioritize building a healthy business and building a healthy culture are the ones who tend to have the best cultures and most impactful people teams. Asana Head of People Anna Binder explains:

> There are three different ways to think about the people-related or culture-related work. For CEOs, there's a range of focus areas pulling their attention – trying to get products market fit, trying to get a product to market, or trying to get from 5 to 20 million in revenue. Some feel they can't really focus on culture and values and people. They have to focus on these things and fundraising. They view that people stuff as a distraction. They're going to outsource that, either to a Head of People or to somebody else.

> Then there's the other type of CEO who says, 'You know what, it's not a distraction. We can actually balance the two. We can spend time building the business, and we can spend some time building the culture.' This balance is truer today than ever. It is 100 per cent true at Asana. One of the reasons I'm thriving here is that Asana rejects the concept that there needs to be a tradeoff between building business and building culture. It is actually your investment in culture, and your commitment to defining and making the values real, that will drive your business success and ultimately enable you to achieve your mission. It's not either/or, it's not balancing the two. It is actually that investing in your culture ultimately drives your business success.

> One of the big evolutions for me in the role is that shift in perception on the work of culture building and the culture evolving that has driven that change. It's not the sole role of the CPO. It's an all-team sport. At Asana, I experience it at the board level where they want to know what we're doing to evolve our culture. If you look at our weekly leadership team meeting, I would say 50 per cent of

the topics are either people or culture related. Every employee here feels they are participating in evolving the culture. My job is as an orchestrator of that. I never feel that I'm in a room by myself thinking about culture.

When culture building is viewed as a shared responsibility across the organization, magic happens. The co-ownership of culture is a core ingredient in high-performing companies and cultures. It permeates through the leadership team into the employees and is reinforced through daily behaviours. Culture can't be pushed by individual(s) – it must be a collective set of shared values, expectations and behaviours.

The business complexity that modern HR leaders must navigate in today's world is much more robust. Michael DeAngelo considers this here:

> The field is much more complicated now. The business environment is much more complicated. It's constantly moving. The pace of change is super-fast. Much faster than I remember ten years ago. There's a lot of consolidation in particular companies. The difficulty of companies trying to compete and stand out is changing very quickly and you have to continue to differentiate. In technology companies you're constantly being disrupted. There's a lot more stress in the system for people and everyone from top to bottom in the organization, and that's a big challenge.
>
> As a CPO, we worry about capabilities a lot more now. Do you have the capabilities to compete? Not just in the current business model you have, but the next one you're planning on, because you're going to get disrupted.

As Michael explains, the ability for modern people executives to navigate this complexity is essential to their success. You have to have an eye on what's now and what's next to successfully lead your company and your teams through today's complex world.

When HR leaders get vulnerable

Let's go back to that exercise at the beginning of the chapter. Is one of the words that came to mind when you thought about your past CHROs 'vulnerable'? Probably not.

As our conversation in HR broadens to terms such as empathy, inclusivity and belonging, we're seeing a change in the behaviour of leaders being willing to open up about their struggles, challenges and circumstances. This openness allows them to connect to employees in ways their predecessors couldn't. Claude Silver describes her views on the field of HR when she moved into it:

When we think about the HR of the earlier days, I remember always thinking that the people in HR must be perfect at their job. That's what I really thought. Pristine and perfect. No flaws. I think that was my perception because they were walled off. What did you go to HR for? When you got into trouble? When you needed to sign your contract? I had this really strange perception that they were just perfect people and all of us on the floor were flawed.

The fact is, we're all just figuring it out. We're now letting those HR practitioners, who are so great and dedicated, out of that cage to open up and share with us. Becoming more human is a real gift. That's what we're seeing more and more of with modern HR teams. I'm human just like every single one of our employees. For them to be able to relate to me and for me to be able to relate to them is really where the alchemy occurs.

I'm extremely fortunate that I have found a home at Vayner and with Gary in which I can do my life's work. I can use the tools in the toolbox that I have, and build something special.

Standing in front of your employees and baring your soul isn't easy. It's not for everyone – but it's honest and real. That realness is what allows employees to relate. No one is perfect – nor do they need to be. When leaders work hard to present a veneer of perfection, employees see through that. It chips away at your trust and credibility as a leader.

When I recorded a podcast with (then) Niantic VP People & Places David Hanrahan in 2019, something special happened. Halfway through our conversation he opened up with a story about his sharing his struggles with mental health at a company all-hands meeting. I was moved by the vulnerability, honesty and realness of the moment. His refreshing candour, which you can read below, reinforced that importance of authenticity and vulnerability in leadership.

PRACTITIONER SPOTLIGHT
Discussing mental health

David Hanrahan, CHRO, Eventbrite

When I was VP People & Places at Niantic (creators of Pokémon GO), I was in a fireside chat that one of our leaders had decided to set up in partnership with a YouTube influencer, who has a huge following on Pokémon GO. The two of them had just talked about mental health. Each of them was very open about mental health and the struggles they've had or their families have had. The leader knew that I was passionate about this topic. I don't think he knew why I was passionate about it; he just knew that I was interested in introducing our tech solution called Spring Health, which is a kind of on-demand therapy. When planning the fireside chat, he said, 'Hey, why don't you tag along and at the end you can talk about how to use Spring Health.'

During the fireside chat they had this very passionate and vulnerable conversation about mental health and depression. Without even really thinking about it, he handed me the microphone, saying, 'Hey, why don't you talk about Spring?' I started talking about the reason I was personally passionate about this, which was because months prior to this, I struggled with my mental health. I had a lot of negative repeating thought patterns where I thought I was going to lose it. I have two kids at home. I have a wife. I also had this personal struggle with depression that I was unprepared for. It was in that moment that I realized what these two were talking about.

I felt this was my opportunity as a leader to also similarly share my struggle with this. I was sharing exactly what I was thinking about in my mind, about losing my passion in life, and thinking there's going to be an end coming up soon for me. Just sharing that, sentence after sentence, it was like my mind went numb. I don't even remember exactly what I shared, but I just knew immediately that my relationship with all the employees in the room suddenly changed. They saw there was a different reason for why I was talking about this and unveiling this new Spring Health tool, beyond just 'it's a good thing to do'. It was my opportunity to share personally what it meant to me.

I'm often asked what HR leaders can do about creating space for conversations around mental health. One very simple thing we can do is find the opportunity for the discussion, whether it's a fireside chat or you as an HR leader having coffee with a VP who says they've had this struggle. Let's create a forum. Let's create space to talk about the struggle. One of our leaders talks about it. He calls it the Black Dog, which is a euphemism that Churchill used to talk about depression. Just talking about it in a way that says, 'I struggle with this. Do you struggle with it, too? What do you do?' It's seemingly simple, but I think sometimes HR leaders would lean against that because: 'Oh, that's private. That's a HIPAA (Health Insurance Portability and Accountability Act) compliance violation. We're going to enter into private health territory. Let's just refer people to the EAP (employee assistance programme). That's your solution.'

Look at what companies like EY and Starbucks are doing. Some of the things they're doing are simple. They're not huge monetary solutions. They are just creating a discussion, a forum for leader-led discussions. EY calls it the 'Are You Okay?' series. A leader will just talk about how they have changed over the years. Things they've struggled with personally. Then field questions. Maybe some of those questions would be, 'Hey, here's something I do to actually help.' That's what we did at Niantic. From that, a Slack channel emerged. These are not major things. The HR leader just needs to lean into the discussion and find the opportunity for it. It could be about masculinity. It could be about empathy. It could be about something that is only tangentially related to mental health. Creating the opportunity to discuss these things, and doing it on a semi-recurring basis, gets it out in the open. It starts to get things de-stigmatized.

When you're able to open up about your own connection to different initiatives, you're able to set a different tone with your employees. In 2019, SurveyMonkey revamped their benefits programmes to include fertility benefits to all employees through a partnership with Carrot Fertility. This could have been rolled out with a standard internal communications programme like most new benefits are, but their CPO Becky Cantieri took a more personal approach and shared her own struggles with infertility. The struggles her employees faced starting a family mirrored her own. She understands the fear, frustration and anxiety that brought. Rather than stand behind a boilerplate communication strategy, she opened up about her own struggles and journey with infertility:

> Sharing my own experience and being vulnerable allows people to not be embarrassed or hide behind the challenges they face. By opening up the conversation, this is brought to life in a way that resonates with people. They can then embrace the issue, and ask and seek support. I was open to the idea of sharing in the spirit of helping people. I understand that many of us struggle with infertility, and I know that there are tools and resources out there to help. Success for our employees and for the business starts with being willing to support employees in their journey.

Vulnerability is strength, not weakness. It sets an example for your leadership team and employees that it's okay to bring their whole self to work. It unlocks some of the anxiety your employees carry when they feel they have to leave a part of themselves at home.

Let's be honest, the role of today's HR executive is extremely challenging – physically (hours, stress) and emotionally (anxiety, stress, traumatic life events, bad behaviour, isolation). Never has it been more important to practise self-care. Every single CPO I know has battled burnout at some point in their career. The next section will explore this in more detail.

Navigating burnout

As you reflect on the dynamic nature of today's people executives, you have to consider the toll that a job like this can take: the stress, the isolation, the emotional burden, dealing with bad behaviour, fighting for budget and resources, the loneliness. It all adds up.

Burnout is becoming a real issue as people executives move from one company and its unique challenges to the next, particularly in the start-up world where the pressures are unique and acute. If you're lucky enough to experience an exit or liquidity event, you might not need to put yourself through that stress again. It's common to find seasoned operators moving on to consulting roles after a few turns in the CHRO seat. Their skill set is still in demand, but approaching the role from a detached third-party view allows them to make an impact without the emotional and psychological burden that in-house roles create. This point is illustrated by Credit Karma Chief People Officer Colleen McCreary:

> I'd had a couple of board members who are venture capitalists and who seemed surprised at the number of CPO job postings. Multiple people had come to me and said, 'What is it? The number one opening in all my portfolio companies is the Chief People Officer. Why is that?' I often get asked by CEOs about hiring their first CPO or Head of HR. What should they look for? What is that role? Where do they go to find one? I was having to explain over and over that this is a hard job.
>
> At least for me, and for a number of my peers, it is hard to feel you are on the line for all of the employees' experience that you can't actually control. I always say, I still worry at night about the rogue manager who just won't listen and just does something stupid. I could end up on the front page of whatever because this person did something stupid, despite trying to do all of the right things.
>
> It's like any CEO of a business. The things that you are making decisions about – people's careers, their jobs, their promotions, their development, their compensation, their benefits – all of these are things that people really deeply care about and want to have conversations about. It's hard. It's hard to be that person always on the line. And doing that multiple times, having to come in and prove your credibility. Prove your worth. Prove who you are or how you're making those decisions, and then having to sometimes be the bad guy. That's just hard.

What I told all these CEOs and VCs is: who does that for a long time? If you've done well and maybe you've had a couple of IPOs, and you've had some experiences so that maybe you're in a position where you can make some different choices – why would you do that again? It can be exhausting for people. I don't think there is a general appreciation, and this sounds like whining a little bit maybe, for how hard that job can be and how lonely it can be because you really don't have a peer set in the building that you can just open up to all the time. Unless you have a support network of people between your home and personal life and professionally outside, these are really sensitive issues. It's not as if you can just run and talk to everybody about them.

Ensuring you have a robust 'phone a friend' network can help HR executives navigate the loneliness, stress and isolation of the role. These peer networks may not prevent burnout, but they'll help you keep that at bay and know you're not the only one experiencing these feelings and stress.

As a modern HR leader, your network equity is as valuable as your skill and expertise. As you can see from the examples above, the value in building a robust network to support your continual learning, lean on when you need answers to difficult situations, or help you during difficult times is key to your success – and longevity in the field.

Onboarding: setting yourself up for success

There are few jobs more demanding in the C-suite than the CHRO. Despite the immense responsibility and expectations, most HR executives get very little onboarding support.

HR leaders often arrive with an immediate set of problems to address. To do this effectively, they need to understand and interpret a range of variables: business models/growth plans/risks, market positioning, financials, budgets, culture (strengths and risks), talent, what's working well, what must be fixed, and more.

This illustrates why the profile of a CHRO is changing. Many of today's HR executives are business operators focusing on people strategies and alignment. They view their role as aligning the people strategy to support the business needs and objectives, not just compliance and oversight of core HR functions like benefits and recruiting.

Getting onboarding right is essential to an HR leader's success. Deb Gran shares some valuable tips on how to approach your onboarding.

PRACTITIONER SPOTLIGHT
Successful onboarding

Deb Gran, Chief HR and People Leader, DiaSorin

When you are hired as the new HR leader at a company, you can be sure that it is because you have all the right qualities that your new company needs in the HR leader role. But, unfortunately, being hired does not immediately endow you with credibility, respect and trustworthiness in the eyes of the head of the organization or anyone else. That must be earned.

Becoming established happens with time in the job – showing who you are, what you stand for and how you lead. Over the years, I have learned some simple methods that may help to accelerate your transformation from 'new HR leader' to 'trusted advisor' at your new organization.

First, avoid the temptation to get sequestered in the HR bubble. In fact, try to spend as little time as possible with the HR team during your first few weeks on board. Briefly introduce yourself to the HR team members and tell them that you are giving them space to work while you navigate your way through the first few weeks on the job. They've lasted this long without you, so a few more weeks should be just fine. You are demonstrating that you trust your team, which will be as positive a first impression as any other.

In the meantime, immerse yourself in understanding the people and culture outside the walls of HR. Concentrate your time and energy on meeting as many people as possible, at all levels in the organization, especially the 'ground zero' of whatever product or service your company provides.

In one of my first assignments, a rather brave employee told me that if I wanted the true picture of the organization, I wasn't talking to the right people. I took the bait and asked her to make a list of suggested connections and to spread the word that I had time on my hands and wanted to talk. What followed was nearly four weeks of the best onboarding experiences I could have hoped for. Each meeting started with, 'What should I know?' and ended with, 'Who else should I speak with?'

In the end, I gained valuable insight into the structure of the organization, general opinions, unwritten rules, how the company communicated, and views on HR's role and reputation. It was an invaluable lesson. Importantly, I was able to demonstrate who I was as a leader with an audience that may not have otherwise been so available to me.

The next step is to take all of these nuggets of information and to do something with them. Prepare presentations for the leadership team and for the HR department that fill the gaps between perception and reality as you see it at this organization. Are there any strengths of the HR department that go unrecognized? What gems can you grab onto and quickly educate others on the competencies that HR brings?

Just as importantly, what are the current inadequacies of the HR department? In the future, your colleagues will not take your advice to heart if they believe you do not keep your own house in order before doling out criticism. Taking a circumspect and honest view of the work that is on your plate early on in your tenure will allow you to speak with increased authority and credibility later on.

Michael DeAngelo's career has spanned people leadership roles across a veritable who's who of corporate leaders: Merck, Microsoft, PepsiCo, Google, Pinterest, Mozilla. He shares his thoughts on successfully setting your onboarding priorities and approach.

PRACTITIONER SPOTLIGHT
Executive onboarding

Michael DeAngelo, Former Executive Coach, DeAngelo Development

The more senior you get, the more your role becomes about the decisions you make on where you prioritize. You're not always going to get it right. I do the same thing for every new role and I do a listening tour. My target was 100 one-on-ones across the organization. I talked with every level of employee from all different functions and asked really basic questions like, 'What's going well with the people function?', 'What's not going well?', 'What would you change?', 'Who is and isn't stellar in the people team?' and 'If you were in my role, what do you think you would focus on first?'

I did that initially just to get a groundswell of the sentiment out there and where the top priorities were. It's easy to get those data; the trick is to have enough volume that you start to see where the preponderance of the issues is. I had a cohort that was just the leadership team: the CEO and direct reports. I knew what their key issues were. Then I looked at individual contributors, what their key issues were. I looked at people who were remote and at those who were outside the United States. I combined all that feedback to look for themes. I saw some things, like the top five themes I thought were showing up the most.

When I was 25 per cent through the listening tour, I checked in with the leadership team. I checked in with my direct reports. Here's what I'm hearing. Does it resonate? Does it not resonate? These are the people I'm planning to meet with. Who else should I meet with? Throughout, I did maybe one more check-in and then a final review. Most of that comes down to: what does the leadership expect and what are you hearing from individual contributors on what we should prioritize? Then you make a bet and you look at what's most important. The thing I've learned in the last couple of roles is: get the foundation in place first. Oftentimes, the things that are the most important to people are not the cool shiny projects. They typically need you focused on getting your people operations in order.

The first step of elevating the field of HR is often with leadership, like the profiles described in this chapter. While you'll struggle building progressive people teams without the right leadership profile, the actual work of up-levelling your HR and people team capabilities is often rooted in HR transformation. We'll go deeper on that topic in Chapter 4.

Before we do, we have to spend some time on a topic that is essential for modern HR – diversity, equity and inclusion. Modern people teams understand that this has to be woven into all aspects of their people programmes and initiatives. In Chapter 3, 'Building a company for everyone', we'll show you how.

References

21st Century HR (2019) Jevan Soo. Available from: https://21stcenturyhr.fireside.fm/ep46-stitch-fix-chief-people-and-culture-officer-jevan-soo-building-an-hr-operating-system (archived at https://perma.cc/NWH9-LK4N)

Byford, M, Watkins, M D and Triantogiannis, Lena (2017) Onboarding Isn't Enough, *Harvard Business Review*. Available from: https://hbr.org/2017/05/onboarding-isnt-enough (archived at https://perma.cc/HP2S-54J5)

HR Open Source (2018) Future of Work Report – 2018. Available from: https://hros.co/future-of-work-2018 (archived at https://perma.cc/4E3C-UKFE)

03

Building a company for everyone

di·ver·si·ty

Definition of *diversity*.

1: the condition of having or being composed of differing elements

especially: the inclusion of different types of people (such as people of different races or cultures) in a group or organization

2: an instance of being composed of differing elements or qualities: an instance of being diverse

The Merriam-Webster (2020) dictionary defines *diversity* as above. In the context of Human Resources, it's often applied broadly in the context of race, gender, sexual orientation, disabled, military veterans, and different religions. For the purposes of this chapter, I'll largely be focusing on this term in relation to race and sexual orientation.

Throughout the chapter I use a range of terms that are branches on the diversity tree. Equity, belonging, inclusion, representation, LGBTQ+, diversity, equity and inclusion (DEI), diversity inclusion and belonging (DIB), and others. In some instances, I'll use the terms above to specifically highlight and define them. In other instances where appropriate, I'll use them interchangeably with the intent of getting readers accustomed to the different idioms of the field.

It was important for me to cover this topic early in the book before getting into some of the other core elements of HR, such as recruiting, learning and development, analytics and so on. The reason? To build modern HR and people capabilities, we must embed inclusive approaches, and mindset, throughout our people programmes and initiatives.

We can't continue to expect we'll make a difference in our organizations by approaching diversity as a separate effort bolted on to our recruiting efforts. It must be integrated into how we think and plan, as well as into programmes we design across the employee lifecycle. I'll get into specific examples in later chapters for each of those areas, but I want to start by establishing the foundation for modern approaches and thinking on diversity.

The business value of diverse teams has been well established, not to mention the moral imperative. This chapter isn't designed to make the case for why diversity is important. That's a baseline assumption, so I won't waste words on justifying the importance so we can focus on how HR/people teams can support better outcomes.

To be a progressive HR leader, you must hold that belief in diversity as true. If you don't, I'm afraid the other suggestions in this book won't be enough to overcome that shortcoming.

The topic of diversity is not new to HR, but how we think and act on the topic has evolved quite a bit over recent years, as has our language.

As we'll be using terminology in this chapter that may be new to some readers, I want to define them before contextualizing them as the chapter unfolds:

Discrimination: The unequal treatment of members of various groups based on race, gender, social class, sexual orientation, physical ability, religion and other categories (Racial Equity Tools, 2020).

Microaggression: The everyday verbal, non-verbal and environmental slights, snubs, or insults, whether intentional or unintentional, which communicate hostile, derogatory or negative messages to target persons based solely upon their marginalized group membership (Racial Equity Tools, 2020).

Equity: Equity refers to social justice or fairness, and is one of the central pillars of many health, education and livelihood programmes (Equity Tool, 2020).

Systemic inequity: A condition where one category of people is attributed an unequal status in relation to other categories of people. This relationship is perpetuated and reinforced by a confluence of unequal relations in roles, functions, decisions, rights and opportunities.

LGBTQ+: An acronym for lesbian, gay, bisexual, transgender and queer/questioning (one's gender identity or sexuality). The plus was added to expand the definition to encompass a range of other identities that fall under the broader LGBTQ umbrella.

White privilege: Inherent advantages possessed by a white person on the basis of their race in a society characterized by racial inequality and injustice.

This last term may be controversial for some readers. It shouldn't be if you're aligned on the definition. In short, it doesn't mean white people didn't have personal difficulties and obstacles in life, or even necessarily gain specific advantages by their skin colour. White privilege means your skin colour won't create disadvantages based solely on the pigment of your skin.

White privilege is often directly connected to systemic inequity. Both are terms the field of HR must name and understand to be able to make meaningful change. I'll explain more as the chapter unfolds.

Before we can see the future we have to understand our past

Our workplaces are littered with examples of companies struggling very publicly with issues related to their lack of diversity, from systemic issues including inequity, microaggressions and pay gaps all the way to blatant discrimination. Discrimination has long been a part of the workplace, well before laws were enacted in the United States to provide protections from discrimination – and unfortunately long after.

I wanted to open with US history on laws (US Equal Employment Opportunity Commission, 2020), and then transition to where we've still fallen short and what can be done about it as this chapter unfolds.

Let me also own that I am not an expert in this field. In order to get this story and chapter right, I've enlisted a range of DEI experts and practitioners to help me tell this story as it must be told.

In the United States in 1963, Congress passed the Equal Pay Act (EPA). This Act protected men and women from sex-based wage discrimination for performing the same job. That same year, 250,000 Americans marched on Washington, DC to protest for racial equality – an event etched in history, including Dr Martin Luther King Jr's famous 'I have a dream' speech.

In 1964, the Civil Rights Act was signed into law by President Lyndon B Johnson. It included a section, referred to as Title VII, which prohibited employment discrimination. The Equal Employment Opportunity Commission (EEOC) was created to enforce that Act.

In 1967, Congress passed the Age Discrimination Employment Act, which expanded employment protections to employees between 40 and 65 years of age from employment discrimination.

Nine years later, Congress amended Title VII with the passing of the Pregnancy Discrimination Act of 1978, which decreed that discrimination against pregnant women would be included under the category of sex-based employment discrimination.

In 1990, the Americans with Disabilities Act was signed into law. This expanded employment discrimination protections to Americans with disabilities.

In 1993, The Family Leave Act (FMLA) was passed, guaranteeing employees unpaid time off for family or medical reasons (in the United States, pregnancy leave falls under this category).

In 2019, I sat down with Dr Laura Morgan Roberts to record a podcast on her *Harvard Business Review* series, *Advancing Black Leaders*. She shared this perspective on the evolution of diversity in HR.

PRACTITIONER SPOTLIGHT
The intersection of diversity and HR

Dr Laura Morgan Roberts, University of Virginia Darden School of Business and CEO and Co-founder, RPAQ Solutions

It's a wonderful evolution when we think about when organizations began devoting focused attention and resources to questions of diversity and inclusion. It began in response to legislative and social pressure, when people who had been legally oppressed and marginalized for centuries began to mobilize on behalf of their right to work and have the same opportunities for growth and development as other members of society had had up to that point.

Following the Civil Rights Movement of the mid-20th century, DEI efforts focused on a number of Equal Employment Opportunity (EEO) protected categories, including race, gender and religion. We now include age and ability status, and of course sexual orientation, as important dimensions of difference that need to be welcomed, honoured and recognized in the context of our work.

Over time, we've shifted from a purely legalistic response to one that tries to help organizations to be more proactive and take the initiative because they recognize that the individuals within their organizations are their greatest source of competitive advantage. This is the logic that underpins the business case for diversity, which became popular near the turn of the 21st century. Companies began to invest considerable energy and resources into hiring people from different backgrounds, with the hope that they would bring different perspectives that could increase innovation and help to shape organizations of the future.

At the same time, leaders were beginning to acknowledge the critical role that HR should play as a strategic partner for the organization: not compartmentalizing the personnel or compliance side of implementing policies and routines, but really inviting HR into the C-suite as thought partners in trying to understand how human capital would serve as the vital and inimitable resources that would help organizations to thrive for years to come. So, the diversity and HR conversations both began moving in the same direction of strategic alignment.

After raising the profile of the business case for diversity as part of strategic HR activities, leaders began to focus on getting more diverse perspectives in the room. But the next set of questions – moving from representation to inclusion – quickly followed. How we can create organizational cultures where diverse perspectives would be welcomed?

DEI initiatives emphasized that it wasn't enough just to check the box because you've hired X, Y, Z people from a compliance and personnel standpoint, but organizations needed to really look at who was present within the organization and try to create a culture that would allow them to maximally engage from a position of strength.

Today's DEI agenda centres on building a company that welcomes and accepts the differences that people bring and helps them to show up at work every day with the feeling that they too belong in the organization and have valuable contributions to make.

We've come a long way in employment protections but we still have a long way to go in creating equal and equitable opportunity.

The conversation and history around diversity in HR varies by country and region. The history above and anecdotes below apply largely to approaches and regulations in the United States, but the case studies and practices later in the chapter are globally relevant.

In the early days of diversity efforts, HR's approach was largely focused on diversity based on representation in the categories outlined by legislature – ethnicity, gender, disability and so on. As mentioned in the Introduction, this is still the case for many HR teams.

When you examine how companies have embraced DEI, you'll find a range of methods, from a fully integrated embrace to outright resistance. Many companies viewed diversity efforts through a compliance lens. They built procedural and process milestones to certify their diversity efforts. It was often a 'check the box' effort aimed at avoiding lawsuits, dodging negative press and boycotts, and ultimately doing just enough to claim they were doing something.

Rather than viewing diversity holistically, it was often approached as a compliance-driven add-on to existing processes focused largely on hiring – driven in large part by the very people and institutions that were part of the problem!

This reflects why, today, DEI leaders in organizations, while oftentimes Black or People of Colour (PoC), have little power to effect real change. According to a global chief diversity officer survey, over half of chief diversity officers reported that they don't have the resources they need to execute new programmes and strategies (McGirt, 2019).

That thinking was a failure of imagination – and action.

Leading people teams today view diversity efforts through a much broader lens. They have better tools and terms to guide their work. At its core, they view diversity efforts not as a compliance-driven add-on, but an integrated approach embedded and integrated throughout their people programmes and practices.

The terms they use have broadened beyond 'diversity' and have expanded to representation, inclusion, belonging, equity and more.

As we pick up the banner of diversity we also have to be honest about our past. HR has not done enough. I'll go into that more deeply later in this chapter, but it's important that we have an honest conversation about what we've done – and what we haven't – to truly lead meaningful change.

This means we have to talk honestly about white privilege and systemic inequity. This point particularly applies to people who look like me – white men. For those not familiar with the latter term, 'systemic racism' means that we have systems and institutions that produce racially disparate outcomes, regardless of the intentions of the people who work within them.

Our systems and structures in work, as in society, have been built to cater to those in power – typically white men. Too often it fell to our marginalized and underrepresented colleagues to drive our diversity programmes. We supported these efforts just enough to exist, but not enough to make meaningful change.

We often couldn't see these systemic hurdles because they didn't impact us. We didn't understand because we didn't recognize there was something we should try to understand. We didn't get behind these efforts because we weren't willing to put in the work to really understand how the systems we built adversely impacted marginalized groups. Even when we observed discrimination, we weren't always willing to speak up for fear of retribution.

Perhaps reading this makes you uncomfortable. The provocation is the point. We have to reconcile our past in order to move forward.

Tara Turk is a friend and former colleague from my days leading recruiting at Ticketmaster. She's now the Director of People at Leaf Group in Los Angeles. Following the killing of George Floyd in Minneapolis and the subsequent protests that brought racial injustice to a new global awakening, I wrote a *Fast Company* story on what it's like to be a Black leader in HR at that moment (Schmidt, 2020). This was her response:

> As an HR professional – though I prefer 'People person' – this is the kind of change we hope to see in the world.
>
> For years we have all read hot takes, watched webinars, chatted in conferences about diversity and inclusion as a thing rather than a matter of survival.
>
> I know people keep change going, not departments, so I do wonder 'Why now?' I want it to stay forever and not be [a] fad. I want us to be heard and regarded every single day.
>
> I don't want us to be considered radical terrorists when we say our lives matter. I want to educate and not convince someone that my existence is equal to theirs.
>
> The actions we are witnessing now are actions a lot of Black folks have been dealing with since we were born. The resources we provide come out of our own experiences – as vast as they are, since there isn't just one Black community, but several Black communities. They aren't just slides on a social responsibility deck. Our resources have been born from self-survival and preservation.
>
> As a people professional, I'll continue to give because that's what I do. I just want to see these gifts finally change the world.

Our Black colleagues and friends have been fighting the battle for racial equity for generations. To truly move our organizations forward, all employees will need to work proactively to address the overt bias, unconscious bias, microaggressions, 'culture fit' and overt racism that permeate our organizations.

These systems make it emotionally exhausting for marginalized or under-represented employees to contribute at the same level as their white peers. Dr Laura Morgan Roberts describes it as the burden of fitting in:

> Workers who are in the numerical minority feel a greater burden or pressure to pretend that they buy into the culture wholeheartedly. They give the appearance that they go along with everything that the culture values and represents, wholeheartedly. Because if they deviate, the cost of deviance will be greater for them than it would be for someone who isn't burdened with bias and negative stereotypes about their competence or about their character just because of their differing group identity.
>
> In short, the people in power who shape the culture tend to shape it in their own image, so the culture tends to reflect white male patterns of behaviour. It's very comfortable and therefore easier for white men to fit into that culture. When white men deviate from the culture, people don't question their integrity, their loyalty, their commitment to the firm to the same degree as when people from other groups deviate from the culture.
>
> So the burden of fitting in is harder for underrepresented minorities on two levels. It's harder because they have to fit into a culture that isn't naturally theirs. Then it's harder because if they do it wrong, if they deviate from the culture, they're kind of stepping on a mine field. Somebody is going to say, 'Boom, I knew they didn't fit here anyway.' That kind of pressure creates a significant amount of anxiety and undermines people's ability to be truly authentic. It's cognitively taxing.
>
> If you're having to think about fitting in versus standing out, then you're not as able to easily immerse yourself into the work itself and just have a single-track mind – only thinking about the work project and the work output. You're also having to think about all of these other social dynamics too.

Coming to terms with our past is vital for charting our course to the future. DEI is an imperative for modern HR, so it's important we fully understand our past so we can avoid repeating history in our future.

The journey from diversity to inclusion and belonging

Building equitable companies starts with a mind shift from approaching it through a diversity lens to a representative or inclusionary lens. The term 'diversity' is too often a narrow and dated lens that conjures connotations of quotas and often focuses too narrowly on recruiting.

Building inclusive companies goes deeper. It means building cultures where everyone is welcomed and appreciated – not just represented. This doesn't happen by accident. You have to work proactively to build inclusive companies.

Imagine going to an interview and seeing no one who looks like you. Taking a tour of the office and noticing that there are zero employees who share your ethnicity. Or gender. Is that somewhere you'd want to work? Is that a place you feel welcome? Understood? How much extra work and emotional labour will you have to invest to make an impact?

Representation matters, and if you lack it, that shows.

PRACTITIONER SPOTLIGHT
Defining belonging

Katelin Holloway, Founding Partner, 776

If we believe above all else that human connection has the ability to change the world, what a powerful thing to be able to turn inward and say, 'How can we create that for our people? How can we create that for our team?' We do that through intentionally creating a culture of belongingness.

What makes people feel like they belong? What is the difference between a group and a community? People who show up to work every day versus people who are inspired to come to work every day and they are thriving?'

Belonging is like the difference between a house and a home. A house is a place where people simply gather. Whereas, a home is where people are bonded together. You come together because you have a sense of connection. You have a shared passion or mission. It's something that connects you so deeply through shared experiences that a group of people won't have.

The people that you commute in on the bus with, yes, you are all in the same place, you all have the same objective, you are all trying to get somewhere. But that does not make you a family. And so, really thinking more deeply about what a community is, and creating this culture of belongingness, is really around this kind of collective or shared identity that's created around mission or purpose.

Are you aiming for inclusion or belonging? The truth is you need both. A monoculture could have a deep sense of belonging and zero diversity. An inclusive company could have wide-ranging representation but no one feeling like they belong. When you marry them both, magic happens, as Katelin describes in the spotlight.

Why language matters

The words we use matter. Always. This is particularly true when discussing diversity and the vast terminology used within the field.

Earlier in the chapter I defined some of the key words that frame these progressive conversations on diversity.

The term 'people of colour' is defined by Racial Equity Tools as 'often the preferred collective term for referring to non-white racial groups'. In the traditional binary world of HR, we often categorized employees as 'white' and 'people of colour'. Some organizations even used 'white' and 'non-white'. Think about that for a moment. As you consider the concept of systemic inequity, this very framing assumes primacy around white versus everyone else. It makes this framing of inequity pretty clear.

Even using 'people of colour' is problematic to many, as it groups all non-white ethnicities and discounts the many differences among Black, Latinx, Asians, Pacific Islanders, Native American and indigenous, and multiracial employees. By turning a plural into a singular we diminish the experiences of each group.

The term 'People of Colour' (PoC) has broadened in recent years to a more inclusive and accepted Black, Indigenous and People of Colour (BIPOC). While the framing is more inclusive, the grouping effect is still problematic for some.

In 2020, the conversation around the importance of language was reinforced by a single letter. On Juneteenth (19 June) 2020, the Associated Press (AP), creator of the Associated Press Stylebook that most journalists and news outlets follow, updated its style guide to capitalize the B in Black (Daniszewski, 2020). John Daniszewski, AP's Vice President for Standards, described the reasoning for their decision: 'AP's style is now to capitalize Black in a racial, ethnic or cultural sense, conveying an essential and shared sense of history, identity, and community among people who identify as Black, including those in the African diaspora and within Africa. The lower-case black is a color, not a person.'

As the global conversation around racism and inequity continues to grow, it's vital that our profession pays attention to these trends and continues to educate ourselves on these terms.

It's important to recognize the ethnic and racial individuality of our employees. How HR teams approach this, both practically and legally, varies by countries and regions, so there isn't universal guidance on how to do this.

How do you know what will work best? You ask. Be sure you're calibrating your approaches with the range of employees they'll impact to ensure you're not adversely impacting different employee populations.

The struggle for LGBTQ+ equality

In June 2020, the United States Supreme Court ruled that employment discrimination on the basis of sexual orientation or gender identity is prohibited under the federal civil rights law. 'An employer who fires an individual for being homosexual or transgender fires that person for traits or actions it would not have questioned in members of a different sex. Sex plays a necessary and undisguisable role in the decision, exactly what Title VII forbids', wrote Justice Neil Gorsuch. Let that sink in for a moment. It's 2020 and these employment protections for LGBTQ+ employees have just been ensured by the Supreme Court.

As HR leaders it's our role to ensure these protections are infused throughout our operations. FundApps Head of People Pat Caldwell shares his perspective:

> At the heart of LGBTQ+ inclusion is a need for employees to have psychological safety and a genuine sense of belonging. As HR practitioners, we need to find ways to go beyond just diversity in our teams to build workplace cultures that recognize the unique experiences LGBTQ+ employees go through in their lives and the powerful impact it can have on our perspectives and voice in the workplace.
>
> The Supreme Court ruling on the Civil Rights Act protections for LGBTQ+ employees was a necessary step for the US to 'catch up' and provide basic security measures for LGBTQ+ employees. With legislation and policies in place, we must now turn to the day-to-day experience of LGBTQ+ employees and how to create psychological safety and belonging. We need to build curiosity and intelligence around concepts of gender and sexuality (particularly the taboo stuff). We need to define inclusive behaviours, especially leadership behaviours, and have the courage to hold people to them.
>
> We need to rewrite the HR playbook around the employee experience, from transitioning at work to gender-blind parental leave. And most importantly, we need to build a sense of community both within and across companies for LGBTQ+ people to come together and share experiences.

From the Stonewall Uprising in 1969 to this day, LGBTQ+ employees have been fighting for equality in society and in our workplace. The road to this historic Supreme Court victory is paved with advocacy and tireless offer-equality proponents.

More recently, Trans rights been in the spotlight as the current US admin-istration engaged in an effort to eliminate transgender rights (Fadula, 2020). At the core of their aim was to narrow the definition of sex as biologically determined at birth, and tailor civil rights laws to align with that definition. Fortunately, these efforts were struck down by the Supreme Court, but it illustrates the importance of continued vigilance for equality to this day.

More companies are embracing gender neutrality as practice in the work-place. From replacing *She/He* with *They* in employee handbooks to removing gender norms from parental leave, employers are rewriting their practices to make them more inclusive. This applies to pronouns as well.

Chances are you've noticed the increase in gender pronouns on social media profiles. You may have wondered why someone with an obviously gendered name would add them. To be honest, that was my first reaction as well.

I spent some time with friends in the LGBTQ+ community, asking ques-tions, and did additional research on my own to better understand terms that were new to me, like non-binary, gender-fluid and so on. I learned about gendering and mis-gendering and the massive obstacles these communities face just for wanting to be recognized as they see themselves.

It was then I realized that in many cases, adding pronouns to your profile was not necessarily about labelling yourself. It was about normalizing the practice so that those who do aren't alone. After learning that, I added pronouns to my profile.

If you've never worried about your own pronouns, they may not seem important. To others, it's a validation of their very being.

He/Him/His, She/Her/Hers, They/Them/Theirs. Creating an inclusive company isn't easy. It takes intention and effort. It also takes empathy and understanding.

Not sure what pronouns are preferred? Just ask (National Center for Transgender Equality, 2018). 'Can you let me know which pronouns you like for yourself?' or 'What are your gender pronouns?' If you assumed and got it wrong, apologize and move on. It's about respect.

Words hold power. To truly build inclusive companies we have to wield words in a way that recognizes individuals as they want to be seen. This is a significant shift from HR of the past, when we categorized employees by binary gender (male/female) and race.

Some employees conform to those traditional definitions, others do not. Building an inclusive company means taking the time and care to find out what your employees prefer and honouring that.

Designing your DEI team

In modern HR teams, most companies of a certain size have a dedicated DEI team or leader. These roles and teams come with different titles, but they're essentially responsible for leading the company's diversity efforts.

When is the right time to bring in a DEI leader? Like a lot of things, it depends. What's the executive commitment? Growth plans? Budget? Hiring plans? And a range of other subjective variables.

I asked my friend and HR Open Source co-founder, Ambrosia Vertesi, how HR leaders know when it's the right time to hire a DEI leader. Ambrosia has a unique lens here as she's built two tech unicorns (Hootsuite and Duo Security), both in markets outside Silicon Valley (Vancouver and Ann Arbor, respectively). Here's her view:

> There are two different pieces of feedback you hear from employees sometimes about a diversity and inclusion person coming in. One being on the side of why do we need someone to sit in HR and do this? This should be everybody's job. And is this the right hire for HR early stage? And then the second side saying, 'We absolutely need this person to make sure that it's integrated in all of our practices early.'
>
> I am in the second camp. I don't think that it's a vertical function. I think it's a horizontal function that happens to report to HR where it can make the most people impact. I also think it's really important to ensure that the business is ready for what that hire means.
>
> That means that for every practice, from the CEO's practices and how they show up and present themselves and interact with the world, down to how we do IT and how we build our remote programmes – that person has got their hands on it.
>
> Make sure you're thinking holistically and inclusively. That's a lot of work and it's a conversation that should be happening from the beginning, and they can be an asset in that.

It's much easier to scale good habits than rip out bad ones and start over. Investing in a DEI leader early means you'll be able to build a strong foundation for inclusivity that can scale and grow as your company does. It's really hard, and often fails, to ignore any proactive DEI work and then have to introduce it when your company is more established. Your bad habits already run deep. It's difficult to change them – to unlearn and re-learn.

One of the tools you need to drive change is data. If you really want to understand where you are as an organization, set goals, track progress and create accountability, you need to have a good grasp of your numbers. It's important to also recognize that even data, like people, can be biased. Be sure to calibrate accordingly when determining what and how to measure.

This isn't about diversity pipeline metrics. This goes much deeper. Culture Amp Director of Equitable Design & Impact Aubrey Blanche explains.

PRACTITIONER SPOTLIGHT
Bringing data to DEI

Aubrey Blanche, Director of Equitable Design & Impact, Culture Amp

Corporate diversity and inclusion (D&I) is really another iteration of what is basically the Civil Rights Movement. There are people who have been doing this work for decades. I think what was really interesting in tech in the early days is that there were a lot of people who were beginning to think about D&I in the tech context in a big way. They were not yet really basing all of that work in data, and in empirical research, which is funny for an industry that's so predicated on data and experimentation.

A lot of the early methods focused on just implementing a checkbox list of programmes, some of which have never been shown to be effective. And then, there really wasn't this thought around systems design, and research, and data, and impact driven. I would say that, especially over the past six years, you're seeing a big shift there, where I'm hearing more and more DEI leaders talk about using data in their work, which is powerful.

There are some downsides, but I would say that going to the impact-driven, data-informed approach to building equitable systems has benefited the work. Most of us in this field are aggressively under-resourced because business leaders do not treat this work like a business priority. So being able to do the most or have the maximum impact with the resources that we have is ultimately a good thing for everyone.

As more companies are investing in their DEI strategy and resources in 2020 and beyond, it's important that you build your capability in a thoughtful way, as referenced in this section. Embedding inclusive practices early is better than late, but it's never too late to start.

The problem with unconscious bias training

According to a report by McKinsey (2017), the United States spends $8 billion per year on diversity training. Yet despite that, very few companies have made meaningful change.

Too often we look at micro-solutions to address macro problems. For example, unconscious bias training has been a hot topic and investment for companies over the past several years in an attempt to address cognitive biases.

It's easy to write a cheque for training, but implemented improperly it can do more harm than good. Dr Laura Morgan Roberts explains:

> Executives and emerging leaders all need to understand the cognitive biases that lead us to jump to conclusions and make flawed decisions which can have very serious consequences. Sometimes the consequences are quite subtle, but other times these biases can lead to life and death consequences, like when we're talking about police forces, medical teams and even preschool educators who are more likely to suspend or discipline more seriously African American boys, or discipline them more seriously, than kids in any other racial category. These are very serious consequences that can result from implicit bias. So, it is really important that organizations are focusing on and raising awareness of implicit bias.
>
> My question is, are we doing this work in a way that is really pushing us to adopt new strategies that we might consider anti-bias? Are we pushing organizations to say, 'How are we engaging in implicit bias in our day-to-day practices within our own organization that may be creating internal disadvantages for us, or for our clients, or customers, or other stakeholders?' The risk is that people walk away from a session on implicit bias for instance, feeling, 'Well, we all have biases.' It normalizes bias and therefore doesn't push us to make any kinds of changes in our practices or in our power structures that would lead to a different set of demographic profiles to be represented at all levels of the organization – especially the most senior levels.

If you don't have a bias mitigation strategy, you risk normalizing bias. 'Well, we all have bias.' This is dangerous, as it presents bias as engrained and equal in everyone, without acknowledging its disparate impact and formulating a specific action plan to proactively address bias.

Studies have shown that poorly administered unconscious bias training can actually increase or activate bias (Dobbin and Kalev, 2016). Be mindful of this as you consider any training on this topic.

Dismantling systemic inequity

The 25th of May, 2020 was a day that rocked the world's conscience and shone a bright spotlight on racism, generational inequity, police brutality, and privilege. Two very different incidents came together to create a moral reckoning that's led to a global conversation on race and addressing systemic inequity. The incidents I'm referring to are the killing of George Floyd in Minneapolis and the confrontation in a New York park between Amy Cooper and Christian Cooper.

The death of George Floyd was caught on tape as three police officers watched a fourth kneeling on his neck for 8 minutes and 46 seconds as he repeatedly stated, 'I can't breathe', until he took his last breath.

The New York incident caught on tape involved a white woman wielding her privilege and 'weaponizing' stereotypes by calling the police and fabricating a story of an 'African American man' recording her and threatening her and her dog.

The protests again racism and injustice that followed began in the United States and quickly spread around the world. Hundreds of thousands of protesters, all races, all ages, all genders, standing up against systemic inequities designed to favour those in power.

What do these incidents have to do with HR?

These protests around the world are against systemic inequities that have plagued society for generations. These systems were built to favour those in power – typically white and male. Who leads most of our businesses? Typically, white men. Those same systemic systems of inequity are present in our HR operating systems as well.

These systemic issues have been hard for us to see, as our field is also predominantly white. Using Namely's 2019 HR Career Report (based on a sample size of 200,000 mid-market companies), let's take a representative look at the breakdown of our field today:

- Gender:
  - 71% Female
  - 27% Male
  - 2% Non-binary

- Ethnicity:
  - White (65%)
  - Asian (12%)
  - Latinx (10%)
  - Black (8%)
  - Two or more (4.4%)
  - Native Hawaiian/Pacific Islander (0.7%)
  - American Indian (0.2%)
- Average age:
  - Overall (35)
  - Non-managers (33)
  - Managers (39)
- Tenure (in years):
  - Overall (2.63)
  - Non-managers (2.21)
  - Managers (3.49)

To address some of the entrenched issues that favour those in power, we need to understand and own our past, then commit to antiracist agendas that proactively target some of the programmes that have supported inequity in our companies.

PRACTITIONER SPOTLIGHT
Why HR must be antiracist to drive change

Madison Butler, VP People and Culture, Sourced Craft Cocktails

Human Resources is broken. As a Black woman living in the HR world, I know first-hand the unwillingness to talk about real-world events, real-world trauma. Being Black in corporate America has its own long list of struggles, but being on a people team is hard right now. We are the people who are expected to raise morale, smile, and be the cheerleaders of our organizations.

How can I be a cheerleader when it feels like the weight of the world is collapsing on my shoulders? I made a decision a few years ago to bring all of me to corporate America and let the cards fall where they may. This means I am Black, out loud, every day. This isn't always easy or fun. However, it's a truth that the world deserves to see.

Too often we are taught to hide our magic and shy away from our greatness to fit into corporate white spaces and cultures. What we don't talk about is how taxing 'fitting in' can be. The emotional trauma is lasting, and the guilt that you carry, knowing you are helping to uphold systemic racism, is unbearable.

Oftentimes, organizations forget that Human Resources has the word 'human' in it. We are humans serving humans, uplifting humans, comforting humans. Some of these humans are Black, and it is important to recognize the real-world challenges that come with that.

As companies, we need to do a better job of having the hard conversations around diversity, not just the ones that make us feel good. We have to address trauma, fear. We have to be able to not only denounce racism but be fiercely antiracist.

How can companies drive real change to address systemic inequity when most of their executives and board members are white?

This is a real challenge that's often the limiting factor for DEI leaders' success. If the executive team is not fully bought in, diversity effort and outcomes are often superficial. If the executives have no shared life experience, building empathy is difficult. It's impossible without real and sustained effort and action.

As Dr Laura Morgan Roberts shared earlier in the chapter, despite all of our efforts, investments and programmes in DEI, the executive profile has remained largely the same. Beverly Carmichael is a mentor and friend. She helped launch my career when I worked for her at Ticketmaster. She's a Board Director and seasoned HR executive with experience leading people teams at Southwest Airlines, Ticketmaster, Cracker Barrel, Red Robin and others. She weighs in on the importance of representation at the board level and C-suite.

PRACTITIONER SPOTLIGHT

The imperative for diversity in the C-suite and the boardroom

Beverly K Carmichael, Independent Board Director

Despite a plethora of talent, not nearly enough African Americans are chief people officers (CPOs). It is one of the most critical roles in any organization and, now more than ever, the CPO should be the CEO's closest partner. The CPO must also be an advocate for diversity at the top, which includes recruiting African Americans (more than one) to serve on the company's executive team and its board of directors. If the CEO and the board do not understand why this is important, the CPO must be able to explain it and they should listen, learn, and make this a priority. If the organization rejects the notion of having African Americans at this level, the organization will be unable to recruit, and more importantly, retain talented Black leaders at any level.

Once in those important seats, Black executives and directors, irrespective of their function or expertise, should have the courage to speak up and speak out about the historic injustice and inequities that plague African Americans in every aspect of life. To be sure, their lives have been riddled with experiences that non-Blacks simply have not had. Sharing their perspective will educate and help the company prioritize, design and execute a sustainable DEI strategy for the organization.

The 2020 protests following the killings of more Black men and women by police officers set off a movement unlike anything I have ever seen before. The protests exposed to some, for the first time, how poorly Black people are treated in America. For others, the protests were a sober reminder of how poorly Black people have been treated for generations – including in corporate America. Across the globe, the blaring call for change came from people of all races, creeds, colours and generations.

With the seemingly newfound and widespread awakening of corporate America, I was struck by postings directed to corporate America. One stood out. 'Rather than post a corporate statement coiffed with a Black Lives Matter hashtag expressing your outrage about the discrimination and racial injustice that exists in America, show us your colours. Specifically, post a picture of your executive team and your board of directors.'

So what colour are they? If your executive team and your board of directors do not include the colour Black, you are contributing to the racial injustices that afflict African Americans, whether you knew it or not. Now that you know, you should dig deep to openly and honestly examine why Black people are absent at the top of your organization. Then commit to rectifying the issues you find – and commit to the sustained effort real change requires.

Corporate America – let the 2020 movement be a real awakening this time. It is not too late.

To rise up to this moment and affect real change requires bravery. As my friend and seasoned HR executive, Beth Steinberg, would say, 'Sometimes you have to know when to throw your badge across the table and walk out the door to stand up for what's right.'

Impacting real change in this moment requires courage and conviction. There will be moments where DEI work may be perceived as getting in the way of maximizing shareholder value. There will be companies that shrink DEI budgets under the cover of economic downturns. To effect real change requires the courage to stand firm in the face of these challenges.

Unfortunately, our track record in HR is littered with examples of the opposite. From #MeToo scandals to bad behaviour at high-profile companies, HR is usually perceived as protecting the interests of the company – not the employees.

Perhaps this moment is different? Perhaps, rather than a predominantly white field getting defensive about privilege, we can use that to effect real change? Eventbrite Chief Human Resources Officer David Hanrahan shares how his views on allyship and empathy evolved:

As I'd gotten deeper in my HR career, I felt like at any moment I'm going to fall prey to disenchantment – just seeing HR as a corporate entity that isn't here to do good. That doesn't take tough stands. That doesn't advance the needle on culture and progress within organizations.

This was reinforced by what I saw around me amidst diversity and inclusion conversations. I saw what I perceived to be relatively low-stakes takes from leaders and organizations. Things like changing to a rainbow logo for one month, and then never engaging again in a conversation around LGBT rights.

I saw myself getting disenchanted. It caused a lot of reflection and made me consider my role in D&I. I have to remind myself, as a cis white male, of my privilege. I have to remind myself that doing good things requires empathy. At times it's going to require taking courageous stands. I remind myself that I'm privileged. It means calling myself out when I might be nodding my head, but not actually doing anything. I have a responsibility to lean into the direction of doing the right things.

David Hanrahan's introspective look at his role in all of this is an internal dialogue we all need to be having. Together we can drive change. It's not going to be easy. It will require courage and conviction (and a few badges thrown across the table).

Part of the challenge of shifting systems of inequity is the difficulty we face having conversations about race in the workplace – a point Aubrey Blanche touched on in our conversation:

> The idea that we don't talk about these issues is actually a problematic idea. We must talk about them. One of the ways that racism has morphed to maintain itself in society is through this concept of colour-blind diversity.
>
> What you find is not that people aren't equipped to have discussions about race, but white people are not equipped to have discussions about race. Since they tend to be disproportionately in positions of leadership, those discussions don't happen. I don't mean that as a condemnation of white people, but they haven't learned how to deal with the stress of discussing race in the same way.
>
> There's a whole set of research about something called White Fragility. It speaks to that. Being 'colour blind' denies the life experience of non-white employees who don't have that luxury. If you really care about it, you have to deal with these categories because those of us who carry those particular identities know that they are real and impact our lives day-to-day. Talking about race, or talking about other types of difference, is not racist. What is racist is disparate impact.
>
> We can be well intentioned, but when we deny that those categories matter, or we don't grow our own facility for talking about them, we are actually passively allowing discrimination to exist. We've decided that our emotional comfort is more important than the equal opportunities of our peers.

If you're not familiar with the concept of antiracism, I've compiled resources that will help you learn more about this approach and how to apply them in the context of work, as well as other actionable diversity resources, in the website accompanying this book. You can view them at https://redefininghr. com/book.

The efforts around diversity and investment in our programmes are, by and large, not working. Sure, there are incremental increases and specific examples of success, but holistically HR's approach to diversity has failed. We have to go much deeper than hiring DEI leaders, investing in training and supporting employee resource groups (ERGs) if we really want to build equitable organizations. It will require introspection, education, and an active and sustained commitment to antiracist programmes and policies to truly drive change.

The next section and the case studies explore some of the steps you can take on that journey.

Moving the needle

Hopefully by now you're inspired to do more to support DEI initiatives within your company. This section is designed to provide ideas, examples and inspiration to help you get there.

There is a range of things you can do to further DEI within your company. There's no playbook, and what works for one company doesn't necessarily translate to another. I'm going to focus on highlighting examples and stories of actions that others have found impactful. Let's take a high-level look at just a few:

- Develop and publish a commitment to building a diverse and inclusive culture.
- Build (and fund) ERGs.
- Publish your employee diversity data.
- Publish your internal pay equity and promotion data by gender and ethnicity.
- Ensure your job descriptions and career site copy use gender-neutral language.
- Ban 'culture fit'.
- Design a structured interview process.
- Ensure representation on your interview teams.
- Invest in DEI early.
- Build an internal DEI resource library with articles, books etc.
- Conduct town halls and conversations on race.
- Make Juneteenth and Martin Luther King Jr Day company holidays.

- Celebrate multicultural holidays and consider allowing time off for Jewish, Muslim and other cultural events.
- Ensure representation on your career site and recruitment marketing materials.
- Demonstrate executive support for DEI initiatives.
- Review your dress code and 'professionalism' standards for inclusion.
- Partner with diverse suppliers, vendors and firms.

This list is far from comprehensive, but it provides a range of tangible steps you can take tomorrow to further DEI.

This chapter only scratches the surface of the topic of diversity. I wanted to include additional references for readers who want to go deeper and expand their understanding of this vital topic. I asked Sarah Morgan, an HR executive who regularly explores diversity on her blog TheBuzzOnHR and her podcast Leading in Color, for resources that go deeper, what books and resources practitioners should be reading (https://buzzarooneyllc.com/) to learn more about antiracism.

Some of the books she recommended include:

- *How to be an Anti-Racist* by Dr Ibram Kendi
- *Me & White Supremacy* by Layla Saad
- *White Fragility* by Robin DiAngelo.

Sarah Morgan included a range of other books and other learning resource recommendations that can be found on her blog post (Morgan, 2020).

So what does it look like when you're building out these practices? I asked leaders in the people and DEI space to share some of their journeys and case studies to close out this chapter.

One closing thought. If you're new to these discussions, don't let the desire to say the perfect thing prevent you from saying anything. Maybe this space is new to you. Maybe the heightened social consciousness of this moment has touched you in ways you didn't expect. We all have a lot to learn. We all have work to do. Accepting that is the beginning of this journey.

As HR leaders, we have a real opportunity to effect change. Let's rise to this moment – together.

I hope that after reading this chapter you have a better understanding of the history and complexity of diversity, and a deeper sense of how modern people teams are approaching this. I want to make it even more tangible with some of the practitioner spotlights and case studies.

Case studies

Aubrey Blanche has spent most of her career in the DEI space. Here she shares her experience of building the function from the ground up at Atlassian.

CASE STUDY
Building a DEI practice at Atlassian

Aubrey Blanche, Former Global Head of Diversity & Belonging, Atlassian

I think I was blissfully naïve about doing this work when I came into Atlassian. The thing that drew me to Atlassian was the conversations I had with people in the C-suite. After five years of working there, I still stand behind these beliefs that the leaders I talked to really genuinely wanted to create change as being correct.

They wanted to create these awesome outcomes for their people, which was important, but the gap was that they didn't know exactly why they weren't in the place they already wanted to be. Leaders say we want to create equitable outcomes, so in the first six or nine months a lot of my time was focused on re-education – lots of tough conversations with leadership.

I said, 'Let me help you understand that you've created the outcomes you're saying that you don't want. You own them and you're responsible for them. I'm not saying you intended for them to happen, but I'm saying that you caused them. Now here's a plan for how we un-cause them. We can't be successful without you all, as leaders, owning the outcomes, and me being your support player.'

I think the reason our efforts to drive belonging initiatives at Atlassian were successful was because the leadership was willing to do that really brave thing: to own their past and future. To say, 'Yep, we're accountable for this, we didn't authorize an imbalance, a gender imbalance, or a racial imbalance at Atlassian. But we didn't do enough to keep that balance as we scaled.'

A lot of what we did was able to pay down some of that diversity debt that Atlassian had. We worked to build a culture that was welcoming for everyone and help evolve the culture in a way that made that objective become more true and needed everyone to accomplish.

Pinterest was one of the first Silicon Valley companies to publish their diversity data for employees. They set what's now become a trend in the field, and led to a shout out from (then) President Barack Obama.

Publishing diversity data with Pinterest and a shout out from Barack Obama

Michael DeAngelo, former Chief People Officer, Mozilla

I was employee # 180 and one of the things I worked on with the leadership team was our diversity efforts. I had learned from experience with bigger companies that the longer you wait to really focus on this, whether that comes in the people that you hire or the types of inclusion practices you put in place, the harder it becomes. If you wait too long, you've lost.

It's very hard to turn big companies around. It's almost impossible if you get to 10,000 people and you're now trying to invest in diversity and build it into your DNA.

We started super early with all the work we did at Pinterest. Candice Morgan was my D&I leader and she's phenomenal – world class. She deserves a lot of the credit for the progress we made. We were probably in the top decile or top quartile in tech.

The crowning achievement, I'd say, is that we were the first company anywhere, I think, of any industry that I know of, to publish our D&I goals publicly. The coolest thing is that we got a shout out from President Obama the week after we did it. I have a picture from my team that everyone signed where it was him at the podium talking about our report. It was just a name-drop for Pinterest, but it was the culmination of probably nine months' worth of work. I remain very proud of the team and everything we did there.

As mentioned earlier in the chapter, ERGs can be an important way to support inclusion and belonging within companies. Asana has built some real rigour and structure around their programmes, as their Head of People Anna Binder shares below.

PRACTITIONER SPOTLIGHT
Building ERGs at Asana

Anna Binder, Head of People, Asana

Over half of our employees are members of at least one employee resource group at Asana. It's an active vibrant part of our community here. I'm so happy to see that a lot of companies have gone this route of creating ERGs and making them front and centre in their inclusion work.

One of the things that we've done in the last year is to professionalize that work. Each one of our ERGs has two leaders. In the past, I was feeling that people saw this as work on the side or extracurricular work. It was just something that you did 'after hours'. It was nice to have.

One of the things we wanted to do was shift it to be really more core to our work, so we did a number of things to professionalize our ERGs. We ran a recruitment process to identify, assess and select the leaders. We engaged managers to say, 'This is a wonderful opportunity; you should look for up-and-coming rising stars in your organization. This is an opportunity to give them a career opportunity.'

We got buy-in from the most senior leadership to support 20 per cent of their time going to this ERG work. We built a year-long set of capability workshops that would help those ERG leads be successful in their role, but also give them skills that would allow them to be successful after their ERG commitment ended and would allow them to grow their career. We increased their budgets. We taught them how to use those budgets, and how to think about connecting those budgets to the strategic goals of the ERG.

I think making this investment in the leadership and professionalizing it sent a message to the whole company. This isn't like this little thing on the side. This is core to our mission.

This chapter explored some of the shortcomings of one of the typical staples of diversity training – unconscious bias. We also explored the importance of language. Some companies are leaning into the latter to develop employee custom training on developing inclusive language. Dashlane Chief People Officer Ciara Lakhani shares their approach.

CASE STUDY
Building inclusive language training at Dashlane

Ciara Lakhani, Chief People Officer, Dashlane

Company: Dashlane
Region: Europe
Industry: Information and Communication
Company size: 201–500

What they did

We developed and rolled out inclusive language training

Why they did it

We wanted a more effective alternative to popular DIBs trainings such as unconscious bias training.

How they did it

Dashlane was founded in Paris and currently operates in Paris, New York and Lisbon. They wanted to formally roll out a diversity, inclusion and belonging initiative that would inspire the promotion of all three internationally. Because their goal was to encourage behaviour in a positive direction, they were cautious about the mixed results of research on the popular unconscious bias training. They didn't want to risk deepening the bias of those being trained, so they looked for other solutions.

They called upon their lead copywriter who proposed the idea of inclusive language training. After working with their people experience leader (who spearheads diversity, inclusion and belonging) for more than half a year and gathering feedback from key influencers in each of their three countries, their custom 'Building an Inclusive Culture Through Language' training made its debut in each of their three countries.

Their aim was to inspire people to expand their desire to respect co-workers to include the understanding of what identity language can mean to many people. They wanted to educate employees around emerging best practices on the topic of inclusive language. They reminded their team that they were not introducing rules but rather broadening their exposure and understanding.

They encouraged employees to integrate this knowledge into their culture of continuous feedback. They also reinforced that employees should be brave, not perfect, and try speaking to others and providing feedback if the language used isn't the language they prefer. Introducing the training led to a range of positive feedback and many thought-provoking conversations on diversity, inclusion and belonging among our team.

If you're reading this, chances are high you've bought something in the past year that came with a user guide – a detailed set of directions on how to operate the device. What if we built those for our employees? Axios Chief People Officer Dominique Taylor and VP People Operations Claire Kennedy share their approach.

CASE STUDY
Creating employee 'user guides' to drive belonging at Axios

Dominique Taylor, Chief People Officer, and Claire Kennedy,
VP People Operations, Axios

Company: Axios
Region: North America
Industry: Advertising, Arts and Media
Company size: 201–500 employees

What they did

To foster inclusion at Axios, we created 'User Guides' for our employees to fill out so they could capture and share with their teammates and managers how they work best.

Why they did it

We wanted to eliminate the guesswork on how to communicate, motivate and collaborate with one another and make inclusion possible for each employee from day one.

How they did it

Companies work hard to hire people from all walks of life but overlook that people need to know how to work together in a collaborative and productive way, especially if they're working with someone who's different from them in some way. Differences that can spark innovation can also spark frustration without the right framework.

As we made progress on building a diverse team at Axios (we went from 86 per cent white in 2018 to 63 per cent in 2020, and we are 58 per cent female and 18 per cent LGBTQA+), it was imperative that the team was supported during their experience here or else that work would be for naught.

We designed user guides so that Axions could quickly and efficiently learn about their colleagues. Our goal was to eliminate the guesswork on how to communicate, motivate and collaborate with one another.

Sample user guide

Name:

Pronouns:

Role:

Team:

List your top five strengths (we use the StrengthsFinder assessment tool):

What I value (What is important to you in your professional relationships? What are the hallmarks of a successful working partnership with you?)

What I need to be successful (What helps you do your best work?)

The best way to motivate me to do something (What motivates you/excites you? How do you make decisions?)

What I don't have patience for (What will you not tolerate in others? What distracts (annoys) you in a work environment?)

How to best communicate with me (How do you prefer to give and receive feedback? When do you like people to approach you and how? Which communication medium is best for what type of message(s); frequency and granularity?)

Your 'operating approach' (How frequently do you like to meet and how should meetings be scheduled and organized? How do you stay organized?)

How to earn a 'gold star' with me (What endears people to you?)

What people misunderstand about me (What do people misunderstand about you, and why?)

We launched this initiative at our company-wide retreat at the end of 2018. Every Axion answered these questions to create a user guide, including our founders, who shared theirs with everyone. Axions can add their user guide to their Slack profile and we ask them to share their guide with their colleagues and their manager. This is also part of our new hire orientation, and new Axions have 90 days to complete their user guides.

We have learned that it's important to have someone you trust review and edit your guide, as they can sometimes be written as more aspirational than accurate. And some Axions were more comfortable asking their best friend or current or former colleague to write their guides.

Now that you have a deeper grasp of diversity it's important to remember that this is not a stand-alone, isolated endeavour. To be successful, it must be integrated into all aspects of the employee experience.

In our next chapter, 'HR transformation', we'll begin exploring what's involved in transforming HR operations and capabilities.

References

Daniszewski, J (2020) The Decision to Capitalize Black, AP. Available from: https://blog.ap.org/announcements/the-decision-to-capitalize-black (archived at https://perma.cc/T95Z-DAVN)

Dobbin, F and Kalev, A (2016) Why Diversity Programs Fail, *Harvard Business Review*. Available from: https://hbr.org/2016/07/why-diversity-programs-fail (archived at https://perma.cc/PKW6-5HB3)

Equity Tool (2020) Definition of 'Equity'. Available from: www.equitytool.org/equity/ (archived at https://perma.cc/PH73-E8A2)

Fadula, L (20192020) Trump's Rollback of Transgender Rights Extends Through Entire Government, *The New York Times*. Available from: www.nytimes.com/2019/12/06/us/politics/trump-transgender-rights.html (archived at https://perma.cc/6P3Y-RYFF)

McGirt, E (2019) Chief Diversity Officers Are Set Up to Fail, *Fortune*. Available from: https://fortune.com/2019/03/04/chief-diversity-officers-are-set-up-to-fail/ (archived at https://perma.cc/75BG-U55G)

McKinsey (2017) Focusing on What Works for Workplace Diversity, *McKinsey*. Available from: www.mckinsey.com/featured-insights/gender-equality/focusing-on-what-works-for-workplace-diversity (archived at https://perma.cc/3FXF-C6ZK)

Merriam-Webster (2020), Definition of 'Diversity'. Available from: www.merriam-webster.com/dictionary/diversity (archived at https://perma.cc/73QM-TFCP)

Morgan, S (2020) #BlackBlogsMatter – the Miseducation of Whypipo, The Buzz on HR. Available from: https://thebuzzonhr.com/2020/02/11/blackblogsmatter-week-2-the-miseducation-of-whypipo/ (archived at https://perma.cc/FN6K-P9Q3)

Namely (2019) HR Careers Report 2019. Available from: https://library.namely.com/hr-careers-report-2019 (archived at https://perma.cc/YDH5-WD2G)

National Center for Transgender Equality (2018) Understanding Non-Binary People: How to Be Respectful and Supportive. Available from: https://transequality.org/issues/resources/understanding-non-binary-people-how-to-be-respectful-and-supportive (archived at https://perma.cc/YR4D-7PV3)

Racial Equity Tools (2020) Definitions of 'People of Color', 'Discrimination', 'Microaggression'. Available from: https://www.racialequitytools.org/glossary (archived at https://perma.cc/42S6-RNL5

Schmidt, L (2020) What It's Like to Be a Black HR Leader in This Moment, *Fast Company*. Available from: www.fastcompany.com/90515805/what-its-like-to-be-a-black-hr-leader-in-this-moment (archived at https://perma.cc/3962-ZL59)

US Equal Employment Opportunity Commission (2020) EEOC History. Available from: www.eeoc.gov/eeoc-history (archived at https://perma.cc/4FP2-TVZC)

04

HR transformation

Everyone loves a good transformation story. Hollywood was built on them. The seemingly irredeemable foil who changes their ways and saves the day. A slight gawky teenager who grows into a world-class athlete. The underdog fútbol team who find a way to play together under a washed-up coach and manage to win the championship.

Transformation stories connect because they're relatable. We root for the underdogs. We've all been there at some point in our own lives and careers: staring at seemingly insurmountable odds; our confidence wavering as feelings of doubt wash over us; perhaps a bit of self-sabotage for good measure and dramatic flair. Is it time for HR's redemption story?

As it relates to this chapter, the definition of 'transformation' can be big and little: macro-transformation or micro-transformation. All of the former begin with the latter: one change; one shift in approach; a pilot programme that eventually leads to a revolution in how work gets done. Giant leaps of progress begin with small steps, and transformation in HR is no different.

There are many factors driving the transformation of HR today – some macro and some micro. This chapter explores some of the key differences when you compare modern people practices with their legacy predecessors.

Policy for the many vs policy against the few

When you go back to the origins of HR, the function was largely driven by compliance and risk mitigation. How do we keep the company out of the headlines? How do we ensure employees don't get the company into trouble with bad behaviour? There was a default lean towards designing policies and procedures with risk aversion as a primary driver.

Given this focus, companies created complex employee handbooks, policies and procedures that ensured the company's interests were prioritized and protected. This fed the bureaucratic narrative that dominated early views of HR and laid the foundation for some of the current perception challenges HR faces. VaynerMedia Chief Heart Officer Claude Silver reflects:

> Prior to coming into the role of Chief Heart Officer, my perception was that HR was on the defensive all the time. They were protecting the company rather than protecting and working for the employees. That was a big shift that I wanted to make as I formed the team. I come from a long line of working in restaurants and bars in my earlier years, and I believe in hospitality. I believe in being of service. It was important to me to shape this team in that mould. We are here to serve. We are always going to be neutral, like Switzerland. We are not going to be in the 'no' business, and we're not going to be 'yes'. We are going to listen with intent and not be the judge and jury in any way, shape or form. We are here to guide, connect and serve the employees so that they may turn their ambitions into success for themselves and the company. That's the change I made.

In the early(ish) days of social media, I was a heavy user and leaned heavily on platforms like Twitter to drive our talent strategy at NPR. I vividly remember being asked to contribute a quote for an author who was writing about social media in the workplace for the Society for Human Resource Management (SHRM). I had never been in a book before and was really excited about contributing to my first book on a topic I was passionate about. I put a lot of thought into capturing some of my views on the benefits, value and potential of social media in HR and recruiting.

I believe this was the first HR book on the topic of social media. As the publication date approached, my anticipation grew. I was going to be in a book! I had a platform to share my excitement about social media in HR and recruiting. This is going to be awesome! Then I caught the title of the book: *A Necessary Evil: Managing employee activity on Facebook, LinkedIn, and the hundreds of other social media sites.* The cover literally included horns in the shadow of a tablet with a Facebook logo. Horns?!

As much as I liked the author, I was disappointed to see the governing body of my industry promoting this fear-based take on social media. I pictured stereotypical archetypes, old-school HR managers, grabbing their copies and seeing how they could craft a social media policy that protected them from the worst-case scenarios presented in the book. This compliance and fear-based approach of assuming worst possible scenarios and applying policies to prevent them for all employees was representative of this old-school view. Policies aren't necessarily bad; in fact, when applied practically they're necessary, as Eventbrite CHRO David Hanrahan shares:

> There was this interesting dichotomy of rules and objectivity and policies that sounded corporate. They don't sound rooted in progressive practices. In start-ups you keep trying to lean against putting rules in place. Some subscribe to the Netflix model of Patty McCord: 'Hey, we're all adults. I'm going to tell you how generally you should act, but I'm not going to put rules in place.' You can go that direction, or you can go in a direction of putting a bunch of rules and policies in place that people wind up not reading. There's that balancing act. I think I lean more towards trying to come up with guidelines and being clear around them in the culture of the company. Illustrate how we want people to act. Putting policies in place only when it feels as though it's going to improve experience. It's going to improve on an objective measure, like how we treat each other, as opposed to putting a policy in place just for the sake of putting a policy in place.

Modern people teams and leaders take a different approach. Rather than designing policies fuelled by preventing worst-case scenarios, they're rooted in the assumption that you're hiring capable adults who will generally make good decisions. Rather than defaulting to a 'policy against the view' approach, they embrace 'policy for the many' views that assume good intent and deal with bad behaviour as individual issues to be addressed individually.

Employees want to be treated like adults – responsible humans capable of making good choices. When given that respect, the benefit of the doubt, they can thrive. When burdened with bureaucratic policy and programme shackles that stifle innovation and impact, employees are less likely to feel empowered and impactful. Resist the urge to over-engineer policies and procedures and watch your employees (and organization) blossom.

Employee handbooks, guides and manifestos have come a long way since the compliance-driven versions of legacy HR. Much of this can be traced back to the now legendary Netflix Culture Deck developed by their former head of HR Patty McCord. Netflix's Culture Deck set a new standard for communicating organizational values and operating systems. It brought about a new era where HR teams had more licence to get creative in their communications. I'll go deeper on the impact of Netflix's Culture Deck in Chapter 9, 'Operationalizing culture and values'.

Netflix broke the mould of what employee handbooks and policy guides could look like. It raised the bar on how to clearly articulate your employee experience – shaped by the style of the CEO. What if your CEO was a former stand-up comedian? Former Twitter HR leader David Hanrahan shares the role of humour in employee handbooks:

At Twitter one thing we did was put a manager playbook together. It wasn't really policies, but more about how to handle these types of situations. We tried to imbue a lot of humour in it. Dick, the CEO, was a former stand-up comic. We had really funny routines at our recurring town halls. Humour wound up being something of a way to remind you of humanity and create interest in this thing that I'm reading from HR. It wound up being a very simple thing that we did to create interest.

Now we just need to broaden the influx of talent into HR with more stand-up comedians and take our handbooks to a new level.

Decentralize and empower over command and control

We work so hard to find exceptional talent for our organizations. Why do we diminish their value and impact with unnecessarily burdensome and complicated processes and procedures?

'The people have the power. All we have to do is awaken the power in the people' (John Lennon). It doesn't take a Beatle to understand the power in empowering your people. Yet that's a lesson that's taken HR a long time to learn. Legacy HR was built on a foundation that valued command and control and saw that as a path to power. We over-engineered systems and procedures, becoming a chokepoint through which things got done. In our quest for the proverbial seat at the table, we added layers of process and approvals that impacted most areas of the employee experience: promotions, vacations, benefits, hiring, firing, performance reviews and anything else we could control. HubSpot Chief People Officer Katie Burke shares the risks of micromanagement:

> Our founders rail against micromanagement. Most talented people hate being micromanaged. One of our core values is autonomy, so we care much more about the output of your work than the hours you spend. We don't believe in face time for the sake of face time. We believe in hiring great people and giving them great latitude to do big things.

The reality with this over-engineering process approach is that we shot ourselves in the foot. HR can't control every facet of every aspect of the employee experience – nor should they. It's not about authority through ownership, it's about engagement through empowerment.

Contemporary HR is more focused on providing strategic value to drive business outcomes. The focus is less on control and ownership, and more on understanding and aligning the people strategy to business goals, supporting and empowering the employees to do their best work. Provide the framework to maximize your employee's capabilities, then get out of the way and let leaders lead and watch your employees thrive.

A key element of moving the field of HR forward is actually letting go. A point AJ Thomas, Head of People Products, Strategy & Operations at X, the Moonshot Factory, reinforces:

> When it comes to being a transformational people leader, there's a moment where you cross the chasm and realize you cannot hold people accountable to the sacrifices your function makes that they cannot see. Whether it's layoffs, hiring the best talent, managing performance to drive the business forward, tough issues in the workplace – one rule still stands. Be compassionate always, and lead with purpose. That is true impact.

Focus on creating frameworks to enable and support success is often seen in the tech and start-up sectors where companies run leaner and often have less established process. In an industry that celebrates mantras like Facebook's 'move fast and break things', this bias towards speed and innovation sometimes comes at the cost of ensuring our leaders have the support they need to lead effectively. Michael DeAngelo weighs in on the impact of speed in tech:

> The strength in tech is you can move fast. People are more open to doing innovative things in the people space and testing. It tends to be a more open environment. There's higher tolerance for change because people's work and the industry change so much that the DNA is a little bit more change-minded. The downsides are there are areas like diversity and inclusion where we haven't made fast enough progress. We're still way behind. The one key difference is that the seasoning of managers or leaders is always harder in tech. People move so fast and they're going through promotion tracks so quickly, often they're not getting the seasoning of what it takes to be a really good manager or leader. It's not just judgement, it's going through mistakes and learning and getting the experience and wisdom of having some battles you've lost and you've learned from.

Rather than a vertical HR function that was often siloed from the business, modern people teams are integrated into the teams they support. You can trace some of this shift back to the creation of one particular position: the HR business partner. Rather than keeping HR isolated as a centralized team, this model embedded HR practitioners inside the business functions they support, allowing them to integrate more deeply into business units and support employees.

These embedded relationships allowed HR executives to have a much clearer view on an organization's people dynamics, organizational health, turnover risks and culture shifts – enabling them to be more proactive in addressing challenges and developing people strategies more closely aligned with the organization's mission and goals. We got closer to the business through these partnerships so we could be an additive resource in supporting them to implement their strategic plans.

Let's look at a few examples of this in practice from a *Fast Company* article I wrote titled 'The best HR is invisible' (Schmidt, 2018).

CASE STUDY
Square

In ultra-competitive Silicon Valley, the battle for talent is legendary. If hiring, talent development and retention aren't priorities for the executive team, you have little chance of success.

Few know this better than Bryan Power, a veteran HR executive who led global people teams at Google, Square and Yahoo. Early in his career, Power worked for a product executive at Google who assigned strategic HR outcomes to each of his direct reports – hiring to one person, talent management to another, employee communications to a third, and so on. This created a structure that made each leader accountable for the development of the global organization.

Later, at Square, Power implemented a similar ownership mentality as the company designed programmes and built processes to scale out of the start-up phase. Like most fast-growing tech companies, Square had many new managers who were quickly expanding into leadership roles for the first time.

Power understood that their success would be largely driven by his team's ability to get them trained as managers as quickly as possible. He also understood that for these new managers to take this development challenge seriously and invest the right amount of time and commitment, it had to be driven by the top.

So, Power and his team enlisted the company's top executives, including Square's CEO and key members of the executive team, to teach manager training modules. 'When executives think of these people challenges as their own issues to resolve, rather than issues for HR to solve,' Power says, 'that ownership and accountability transforms the organization.'

CASE STUDY
Mattel

What can an iconic toy manufacturer, founded in 1945, show us about progressive HR? Quite a lot.

In 2017, Mattel brought in a new chief people officer to transform its organization and modernize capabilities. Amy Thompson, an HR veteran with leadership roles at Starbucks and Ticketmaster, was lured from her position as TOMS's Chief People Officer to lead an HR transformation effort within the organization.

She brought with her a new leader-led model of HR, where managers are given the tools and support to evaluate the talent and capability health of their organizations and then develop the people strategy alongside their HR business partners.

This shift towards collaborative talent mapping put the planning focus on leaders as opposed to HR. The human resource team provided a general framework, then let the business design the organizational structure that best served that unit's goals and deliverables. They also translated their values into behaviours needed at each level of the organization.

Managers are then empowered to weave these behaviours throughout the employee-experience lifecycle. This shift put the onus on managers to own their employee's experience end to end and allowed HR to focus on more strategic initiatives to support the business.

'Especially in a creative industry like ours, talent is core and inseparable from our corporate and brand strategies, so we need our leaders to own both', Thompson says. 'This allows the HR role to become a more consultative function with a much higher business impact than in the past.'

CASE STUDY
Equinox

How does a human resources team at a high-growth company ensure employees in the field are supported? That's the daily challenge faced by Equinox SVP of People Services Kelly Rew-Porter.

As Equinox continues to grow (currently at 95 clubs across the United States, Canada and London), HR had to find a way to partner with field operations. The people services teams create the frameworks for HR services spanning compliance, recruiting, training and development, and then work directly with their general managers and field leaders to implement them locally.

One of the core advantages driving this adoption is that all of their GMs are hired from within, so their familiarity with the operational standards, culture, HR practices and programmes allows for autonomy and continuity.

'The perception of the role of HR is changing', Rew-Porter says. 'It used to be "Why is HR in the room?", now it's "Why isn't HR in the room?"'

Each of the examples above is distinct in its own approach towards HR transformation. What do they have in common? Letting go.

Modern HR leaders have a clear understanding that they and their teams can have the most impact by relinquishing ownership and integrating HR and people operations capabilities into the teams they support.

As more organizations shift towards a 21st-century model of HR, the very nature of the function will begin to blend and integrate more into the business itself. Relinquishing control may feel counterproductive to legacy HR, but ceding it may actually be the key to unleashing the people team's full potential – and impact.

Benefits to total rewards

Remember when benefits were simple? Time off, health insurance, dental insurance. Maybe a vision plan if you really wanted to take care of your employees. These were certainly much simpler days for HR teams.

Fast forward to the past decade and we became obsessed with sizzle: ping-pong tables, catered meals, onsite gyms and dry cleaning, beer on tap, small-batch kombucha. We felt these creature comforts would help us attract and retain talent. We leaned into happy hour and social activities on our career sites. In a quest to stand out, we obsessed over the wrong things and sold substance for sizzle. We're finally course-correcting to focus on broader benefits that add meaning to not just the work experience – but life experience.

Today's progressive people teams are dealing with a much broader array of total rewards aimed at supporting employees, boosting recruitment and retention, and differentiating. It's an arms' race of employee perks that goes way beyond ping-pong tables (thankfully).

Companies are getting much more creative with their benefits in today's market. From onsite childcare to unlimited vacation to more generous (and non-gender-based) parental leave programmes to mental health and fertility benefits, employees have never seen more variety in their benefits. Some perks demonstrate the values of an organization more than others. For example, if you work for Patagonia and get arrested for protesting, the company will pay your bail to get you out of jail. Talk about living your values!

Today's employees want more work flexibility. The dream of a 9–5 job has faded in many industries. Companies are experimenting with entirely remote structures (we'll explore this further in Chapter 8), four-day work weeks, on-demand talent and a range of other novel approaches to work. I'll go deeper on the shifting landscape of benefits and rewards in Chapter 8: 'The rise of employee experience (EX)'.

While not necessarily a new responsibility, today's HR teams also need to ensure that their companies are offering competitive compensation packages and addressing issues, from living wages to the gender pay gap. While the numbers have improved slightly over the past several years, in the United States women still earn $0.79 per dollar earned by men. That remains a significant gap that HR teams are in a position to impact.

PRACTITIONER SPOTLIGHT
Employee-driven benefits

Becky Cantieri, Chief People Officer, SurveyMonkey

At the tail end of 2017, we sent an annual survey to our employees. To be honest, it was a bit of an embarrassment of riches. We had high satisfaction ratings with all of our plans and programmes. People were delighted with our plan design and felt the cost share was fair and at market. It seemed that there was nothing glaring to focus on that year. Then we started reading the open-ended questions.

Reading the employee responses told a different story. I found mention of three or four janitorial service workers. They called them by name and asked if they had benefits on par with those of the troop (we refer to ourselves collectively as the troop). This comment set me back for a moment and made me pause. I knew the answer to the question was that they don't, right? We have rich competitive benefits and they do not benefit from the same.

So, we did just that. We set out a clear set of standards and decided to start with three of our primary vendors in our corporate headquarters in San Mateo. We went directly to those vendors and said, 'Here's what we're trying to achieve. We care enough about it that we're willing to contribute to additional costs associated with it, but are you willing to work with us to achieve this and make it happen?'

The response was frankly overwhelming. The vendors were really excited about the effort, couldn't believe that we were willing to contribute to it. They expressed that what had limited them in the past was their ability to navigate the world of benefits. That's when our broker agreed, on a pro-bono basis, to help them go to market and get plans or adjust their plans to meet our standards.

Expanding our benefits to partners has been probably the single best investment we've made in a long time in this particular category. Employees have been delighted by the impact that we've had on the lives of these partners. And I think they're really, really proud of us being a small company but a first mover in this category. This was illustrated at the end of 2018 when we determined the top 10 moments of the year. This was in a year when we had gone public, which is a hard milestone to beat. This initiative for our partners was ranked the number two best moment of the year in terms of what employees felt proud of.

As we enter a new post-Covid-19 world of work, total rewards will continue to evolve. Mental health and wellness benefits will move from fringe employee perk to mainstream. Employees will be more interested in areas such as employee benefits and corporate social responsibility rather than the flashy benefits and perks that have underpinned many companies' employer-branding efforts over the past several years.

Compensation creativity

For start-ups and small companies, compensation is often very ad hoc in the early days. This is often exacerbated by the rapid career growth and associated compensation changes that are common in high-growth companies. Asana Head of People Anna Binder shares her experience of designing their compensation as the company grew:

> In the early days in a start-up, compensation is done ad hoc. Each group does it in slightly different ways. Each manager might do it in a slightly different way. There are some data and there are some best efforts made. Compensation changes happen all over the place, all over the year, with very little rationalization, very little budget and very little analysis.
>
> One of the things that we've really overhauled at Asana was putting some structure around that. First of all, we mapped the jobs. We created a

levelling system. We bought some more robust data. We put in systems where compensation was reviewed at a cadence where all people were reviewed together multiple times a year. That gave managers greater confidence in the decisions we were making. The analysis and structure around it ensured we were making more equitable decisions, and that you could compare apples to apples in a more meaningful way.

I think a lot of people look at some of that more wonky operational stuff as it's not about culture, but it is actually everything about culture. Part of the people team's responsibility is making sure that everyone can thrive. It's making sure that you're paying people appropriately, and that you can explain why you're paying them what you are paying them. Putting structure around that is a really important step that you can take to ensure that you're thriving.

Let's be real – compensation is often one of the top drivers of employee satisfaction. We have to be thoughtful in how we're designing equitable pay practices to ensure we're able to attract, develop and retain talent. The prevailing legacy approach was basing compensation on an incremental increase on a candidate's current salary. That view sustained inequity legacy compensation structures that often disadvantaged women and candidates of colour. A range of US states now prohibit employers from asking about salary history. That's a good step, but we'll need more legislation, action and courage to really level the compensation playing field for all employees.

Some companies are taking the living wage into their own hands. Basecamp is a project management and communication platform. While they're headquartered in Chicago, employees can work anywhere in the world. As they compete for talent in highly competitive (and expensive) markets like San Francisco, they decided to base their compensation on the top 10 per cent of San Francisco market rates (despite not having any employees living in San Francisco at the time). This applies to any city their employees choose to live in, regardless of the cost of living.

The founders weren't comfortable with the pay gap between some of their highest-paid roles (software engineers) and lowest paid (customer and administrative support), so they decided to create a cost-of-living salary floor of $70,000. This means that no employee, regardless of role or location, makes less than $70,000 per year. They take their salary practices even further by publishing compensation ranges in all job descriptions, so that prospects had that data point when evaluating whether a role at Basecamp was right for them. Co-founder and CEO Jason Fried shares what went into their decision:

It's funny how companies that are about to hire somebody and work with them start off the relationship by hiding things from them. It just doesn't make sense. We want you to be a co-worker. We want you to be a teammate. Why would we ever want to start that relationship in a weird place? Why would we ever want to try to have leverage over you or have more information than you do about the role? What we do is we end up finding people who really appreciate the honesty and really appreciate the position and feel that the salary is fair for them. Maybe it's a huge jump up. Maybe it's a jump down for some. It depends what people are looking for, but at least they know where they stand, and that's the most important thing.

Basecamp's decision to raise the minimum salary was inspired in part by a similar move from another company – Gravity Payments.

In April 2015, Dan Price, CEO and founder, announced a $70,000 minimum wage for all employees. The announcement was covered in media outlets all over the country, including *The New York Times*, Today Show, Good Morning America, CBS This Morning and PBS Newshour. Some lauded the move as a bold step towards addressing the rising tide of income inequality in America. Others accused Dan of engaging in a publicity stunt to drum up attention for his company.

The pundits warned he was setting a bad example that would surely lead to his and Gravity's financial ruin. Five years later, their $70,000 experiment is still going strong. In September 2019, Dan announced that Gravity would extend its policy to all employees at its newly acquired Boise office.

Here are just a few examples of how their company, people and clients were impacted:

- In the year immediately following the $70k announcement:
  - Gravity received more than 30,000 resumés; before $70k, they received a handful of applications for any open position.
  - Employee commute time decreased a total of six hours a day. This freed up an extra 1,560 hours per year for their employees.
  - Ten Gravity employees gave birth to or were expecting a child, up from an annual average of 0–1 births.
  - Total 401(k) contributions increased by 130%.
- In the years following the announcement:
  - *Human impact:*
    - Before the $70k announcement, Gravity employees had an average of 0–2 babies per year. After $70k, an average of 7–8 new babies

have been born per year. This is an increase of roughly 400% per year, despite the headcount growing by just 75% in that five-year period. In 2019 alone, they had 15 new Gravibabies born! [Editorial note: I did not coin 'Gravibabies'.]

- Since the $70k announcement, they've had at least 20 team members, or more than 10% of the company, purchase a house for the first time.
- Between 2015 and 2019, the average individual employee $401(k) contributions increased 155%.

- *Business impact:*
  - Their headcount has increased by 70% since the living wage announcement.
  - Dollars processed (a key metric used to measure growth in the payments industry) has almost tripled from $3.8 billion dollars in 2014 to $11.2 billion dollars in 2019.
  - Their customer base has nearly doubled since 2014.
  - Customer attrition has maintained at 25%+ below the industry average.
  - Annual employee turnover has dropped from pre-70k levels of 40–60% to 16–30% (16% in 2019).
  - According to a company survey, 76% of employees report being engaged at work, compared to just 34% of workers worldwide.

Not all companies are in a position to create living wages and flexible benefits. At scale, the costs can be prohibitive. The most important takeaway for readers is to have a more holistic view of the support you'll provide to attract and retain talent in today's market.

Operating in a VUCA world

If there's one thing that 2020 reinforced, HR is operating in a VUCA world.

For those not familiar with this acronym, VUCA stands for Volatility, Uncertainty, Complexity and Ambiguity. The acronym was developed by students at the US Army War College to describe the global landscape following the Cold War.

The concept crossed over from military to business vernacular as executives and boardrooms navigated complex, uncertain business environments. As 2020 showed us, it's never been more relevant for HR and people practitioners.

The Arab Spring, Brexit, Covid-19, Black Lives Matter – all seismic events that have impacted our businesses, employees and societies. How does HR plan for a volatile, uncertain, complex and ambiguous world?

Covid-19 underscored the VUCA reality. In a matter of weeks, businesses around the world shifted *en masse* to remote work, cancelled business travel, closed offices and developed protocols to respond to the pandemic.

Many practitioners were caught flat-footed by the velocity of these events. In a matter of weeks, they had to re-engineer much of how they operate, from communications to operating rhythms to supporting the very real emotional toll this took on their employees. The very survival of their businesses was at stake.

That initial rapid action quickly settled into a VUCA reality that was mired in uncertainty around sheltering in place and safety protocols, economic volatility, furloughs, layoffs, quarantine zones, policy inconsistency across borders, return-to-work plans, how to support culture and morale, and more.

Our only certainty was uncertainty.

There's no way to know exactly where we'll be when the world has 'normalized' post-Covid. What we do know is that we'll be better positioned for it by designing our HR and people teams with agile approaches that can rapidly respond to whatever is next.

Some HR transformations are massive planned rethinking and re-engineering efforts about how we support our businesses. Others are responding to VUCA-related events. The key to optimizing our response to both is our agility and ability to adapt.

We need to be much more nimble and agile in our practices. As referenced in Chapter 1, shifting from command and control to decentralize and empower allows for more localized and rapid responses to some of the events our companies will face. Later in the book we'll explore agile approaches to HR. That flexibility and fluidity of approach is crucial to adapting and responding to the complex and volatile environment we're operating in now.

The concept of HR transformation is rooted in the idea that there is no one-size-fits-all playbook for HR. We can and should be questioning how and why we do things at regular intervals. We can't get locked into stagnant approaches based on legacy dogma.

If we embrace iteration and agile practices that regularly evolve, we might not even need massive transformation.

One of the biggest aspects of HR transformation connects directly to our thinking and approach on employee experience. We'll dig into that in more detail in Chapter 8: The rise of employee experience (EX).

Case study

The actual work of HR transformation is daunting. The level of pain and effort required for reinvention increases with the size of your employee populations. It's much easier to turn a jet ski than a cruise ship. Let's explore what this looks like in practice in some of the case studies below.

How do you drive HR transformation and innovation in enterprise companies? Like many large global businesses, Siemens AG grappled with that question. They approached it by creating an agile 'Future of Work' team to steer and influence HR innovation efforts across their global enterprise. Here's how they approached it.

CASE STUDY
Inside Siemens' Future of Work Initiative

Contributed by Caro Windenka, Head of Future of Work, Siemens

Company: Siemens AG
Region: Global
Company size: 100,000+

What they did

With the #FutureOfWork-Initiative at Siemens, we have created a strategic framework to deliver orientation and to enable the organization, as well as its employees, to realign and develop further in times of structural change and digital transformation.

Why they did it

Since Siemens is a pioneer regarding technology, products and processes in terms of Industry 4.0 in many of its business areas, it is important for us to constantly prepare employees for the challenges of future markets and coming transformations.
This means it's crucial to redesign all Human Resources topics in a new and innovative way, with a common holistic understanding across our global populations.

How they did it

In order to develop a joint understanding of the two most essential and existential questions regarding the future of work, we have developed a strategic framework around #NewWork and #NextWork. This framework considers all topics of how we will be working in the future and what our work will look like, in general as well as with regard to specific skill requirements.

Thus, we were able to provide concrete structures and orientation to a discussion that is typically driven by buzzwords or individual interpretations. Raising awareness around the topics linked to #NewWork (ie agile forms of organization and collaboration, leadership styles, flexible working conditions) and #NextWork (ie skills of the future, new learning approaches, upskilling and reskilling, recruiting and professional development) by using internal communication platforms to drive conversations and provide research and insights helped us to prepare our employees for future challenges.

We also launched an event series, inviting professors and scientists from different faculties to help us find co-creators from all disciplines and levels of hierarchy. Moreover, we interlinked these experts virtually in an agile, interdisciplinary and cross-hierarchical network organization of approximately 2,500 employees around the globe. The network organization has been supported by a core team within HR.

Having set priorities for what to focus on within this framework, the organization continuously developed new 'deliveries' for the future of work, such as new concepts for agile collaboration within teams and new formats for leadership development, as well as new approaches to identify future skill needs with a transparent view on how to tackle them.

The way we are now developing new concepts and deliveries differs compared to how we did it in the past. First, we're involving a range of internal stakeholders from the early beginnings, with HR hosting the process of joint co-creation with our employees. Second, we're designing an ecosystem approach, bringing in external partners such as researchers' expertise or early-stage solutions of HR start-ups, as well as the social partners' perspective. This allows the HR organization to be a driver and moderator of these co-creation processes and conversations for new future-oriented work structures.

Impact/ROI

Our efforts have shaped a sound narrative around future of work possibilities for our employees around the world, driven by a variety of projects tackling #NewWork and #NextWork.

You now have a deeper sense of *what* HR transformation looks like and *why* it's an important aspect of building modern people teams. The *how* is also an essential topic to explore.

'How?' is a topic that's long been a part of HR. The vehicles we use for learning the answers to these questions were largely dominated by membership and subscription-based associations and platforms. HR practices were often kept under lock and key, making it very difficult to answer those *How?* questions and stifling innovation.

To truly advance the field we have to unlock those institutional knowledge banks and find new ways to learn and grow. That's why open source is fundamentally reshaping the field, and we'll explain why in the next chapter.

Reference

Schmidt, L (2018) The Best HR Is Invisible, *Fast Company*. Available from: www.fastcompany.com/90264760/the-best-hr-is-invisible (archived at https://perma.cc/J94M-H7T5)

05

HR goes open source

The year was 2008. I was a VP Human Resources at Ticketmaster. I was recently promoted and tasked with leading several HR teams, including the creation of a new internal communications function. Four weeks into the new role we were told we'd be merging with LiveNation – our former biggest customer and (at the time) biggest competitor. It's complicated.

As the two companies came together for merger and integration planning, I learned that my newly developed internal communications skills would be a key part of this merger. That function did not exist at LiveNation, so I would be tasked with the global internal communication strategy for this $835 million merger. Me. The guy who had been figuring out how to do internal communications for a whopping month.

I won't lie – that night involved bourbon, stress-eating and enough self-doubt to last a lifetime. What were they thinking? How in the hell was I going to pull this off? Mergers are stressful enough when you're not tasked with ensuring everyone was dialled in to what was (and wasn't) happening. Now I was responsible for the dialling.

I woke up the next morning resolved to figure it out. I didn't know it at the time, but what happened next was my first (quasi) introduction to open-source shared learnings and network equity. While I had never done this before, I knew a handful of contemporaries who worked for companies that had recently gone through mergers. I knew they knew the people who drove internal communications for those mergers. A few called-in favours later and I had meetings with internal communications leaders from Fox, Warner Brothers, Disney and others. They were incredibly generous with their time, willing to share the triumphs, pitfalls, landmines and templates used for their mergers. Templates! It was all gold for me.

By tapping into the collective intellect and experience of these practitioners I was able to design and roll out a successful communications strategy for the merger. There is zero chance I could have done it without them. My deep appreciation of open source was born.

I'm not alone in owing much of what I've managed to learn and do in this field to open-source approaches. Katelin Holloway is a Partner at Initialized Capital and former People Executive at Reddit, Whil and Klout. She shifted into HR after spending five years at Pixar Animation Studios:

> I owe every single ounce of where I am today to the people who helped me get here and the sharing communities that exist. In my first people executive role the CEO asked me to start organizing things around talent acquisition, around policies, a handbook. I had never done those things before. I instinctively knew the direction I wanted to go and I'd had a few handbooks as an employee in the past, but if it had not been for the HR and people community that I very thankfully had access to, it would've taken me a lot longer to produce something. The shared thinking behind it was that we should be spending our time with people, not recreating and reinventing wheels that already exist. Rising tides raise all ships. I'm a huge fan of open source. I only wish that I could contribute more to those communities.

This chapter will spotlight my own journey towards open practices and collaboration, as well as how the field of HR is moving away from their traditional siloed mindset and opening their playbook, including recent examples of open source in the wild. I truly believe open source is the key to unlocking HR's future. This is why.

Before we get into the application of open source in HR, let's establish where open source came from. The concept originated as an approach to creating software by opening up source code for others to use, modify, enhance and so on. The idea was that you shouldn't have to write a line of code to do the same thing twice, and that by openly sharing source code you could rapidly accelerate collective capabilities. This 'collective' mindset transformed software and led to much of the technology and the platforms we use today. Could this communal thinking scale beyond software?

Tear down the silos

When I started my career in HR and recruiting 20 years ago, it was anything but open source. There was no Google. Your options for learning about new practices were limited to SHRM, a few other membership/subscription-based options and a handful of events. It was a lot harder to build diverse networks then, and even when you did, it was difficult to find peers willing to open up their playbooks and share. This made it really difficult for good ideas to spread and hindered the evolution of the field.

Look at the field today and it's a very different position. Google is our library and provides us with answers to most of our questions in seconds. There's a broad array of online and offline networks of practitioners sharing their approaches, work, templates and more (more on that later in this chapter). CHROs and people executives are presenting at conferences, posting on social media and blogging about their work: how they do what they do, what they're learning, tools they're using and so on. Even how they're failing!

Yes, failure is no longer verboten to share. It's a badge of honour! No breakthroughs in practices or approaches are journeys without failure – and today's HR and people teams are more likely to keep that real.

In Chapter 2 we explored the evolution of the CHRO and how more and more modern people executives are moving into those roles from other areas of the business. The rise of the open-source approach to sharing and collaboration is one of the things that make that possible. VaynerMedia Chief Heart Officer Claude Silver shares her experience:

> What I've learned from subject-matter experts, whether or not it's online or at conferences, is more of the compliance aspects of HR. How to do a performance improvement plan etc. Those things that actually need some form and structure. Open source has helped me discover more of the nuances of Human Resource programmes. How to create effective communications plans when you're doing a reorganization, how to do comp rollouts, what to look for in a performance management system etc. Those types of things have been topics I've reached out into the universe to find out who's doing it. Who's doing it in a way that I can beg, borrow and steal a little bit from? The great thing is that there's such a wide network on Twitter, LinkedIn etc where I can find you, and vice versa. It allows me to have a great dialogue with others that maybe I can offer a little inspiration to as well.

Having free access to all of this information is transformational for the field of HR. Why should knowledge, learning and templates be gated behind some pay wall or membership fee? Why should your budgets and resources be leading factors in your ability to make an impact? They shouldn't!

The rise of open-source approaches in HR is one of the keys to the transformation we're seeing in the field. This was a fundamental view behind the launch of HR Open Source (HROS.co) in 2015.

Working out loud: the origin of HR Open Source (HROS)

In 2012 I was introduced to someone who would have a profound impact on my career (and life). I was running recruiting and innovation at NPR in Washington DC at the time. There was an internal initiative called 'Generation Listen' aimed at connecting NPR with younger listeners. The founder, Danielle Deabler, built an incredible advisory board of young CEOs, founders and entrepreneurs. One of them, Azita Ardakani, insisted on introducing me to a 'fellow HR nerd', Ambrosia Vertesi.

At the time, Ambrosia ran the people team at Hootsuite in Vancouver. I didn't know it then, but our first conversation laid the foundation for a partnership and friendship that shaped the course of our careers. We spent two hours together opening up our HR and recruiting playbooks, sharing our struggles, asking for advice and lending our experience and perspective to each other's challenges. It was real, honest, vulnerable and profoundly helpful.

When I left NPR to start Amplify, Ambrosia brought me into Hootsuite to collaborate on employer-branding initiatives. In 2015 we were deep in planning conversations at the SXSW TalentNet conference in Austin, Texas. We were reflecting on our own journeys and the value our networks brought to our careers. We likened this network effect to 'the matrix' (fodder for all you Keanu Reeves fans out there): the ability to plug into a vast well of experience and insights at any moment and a near limitless supply of answers to help us solve whatever challenges our companies threw at us.

This access was a true differentiator for us – a privilege – but one that was limited to those who had robust networks and budgets and resources that allowed them to join conferences. What if we could open that up to everyone? What if we could find a way to democratize access to resources, templates, tools, case studies and ideas? We had to find out.

We had to start somewhere with a company willing to share their practices. We approached Hootsuite CEO Ryan Holmes with the idea and asked if he'd be cool sharing a detailed overview of some of the people/recruiting initiatives at Hootsuite. He was (thanks, Ryan!).

Over the next five months we published a range of case studies, spanning topics including the first global livestream employer brand initiative on Periscope, how to develop and execute a recruiting dashboard, becoming a B Corp, developing a global employer brand playbook, and more.

Four months into this pilot programme, at the time known as #HootHROS, we got word that we'd be giving one of the opening keynotes at LinkedIn's

Talent Connect Conference in 2015 (thanks, Mark Menke!). We were beyond excited by the opportunity to unveil HR Open Source to the world on such a big stage, but somewhat terrified of the work that needed to be done to get there.

We recruited our friends to contribute the first series of non-Hootsuite case studies. We also built out the full website and developed our presentation deck for Talent Connect. This all happened in the span of three weeks. It was exhilarating and exhausting.

HR Open Source was born.

Over the next three years, Ambrosia and I travelled the world meeting with practitioners, hosting meet-ups and seeing first-hand the enthusiasm around sharing resources and ideas. The (free) community grew to 10,000+ members in over 100 countries. We heard countless stories from practitioners who cited and leveraged HROS resources as guides for their own programmes. Good ideas spread. 'Department-of-one' HR teams now had more free resources to leverage and peers to share ideas with. It was magic.

The experience opened my mind to the struggles and barriers that practitioners face when pushing for progress. It reinforced the power of community and the impact of tapping into a collective intellect of experience to solve problems and advance the field.

Open-sourcing HR programmes can fundamentally change how practitioners work. In some cases, an HR business partner might be struggling to make a case to a sceptical boss to do something new or different. Being able to point to a case study with demonstrable ROI and impact measures as proof that it's doable can be indispensable. In other fields, finding quantifiable evidence to back up a proposed approach is easy and routine. In HR, it hasn't been.

Wondering how your competitor designs, implements and measures impact for a certain people programme? Why not ask? Unlike the race to corner a market, HR challenges are not zero-sum games. Sure, the talent market may be tight, and competition for certain in-demand roles even tighter, but the idea that another company's gain is your loss is dated thinking.

I understand that there are plenty in the HR world who aren't ready to embrace this kind of openness, but that approach only adds weight to the anchor that's holding HR back. This 'war for talent' mindset dictates that practices should be siloed and guarded as competitive advantages. They're mistaken. The reality is that collaboration and resource sharing isn't just useful, it's the only way sustainable innovation comes about.

PRACTITIONER SPOTLIGHT
It's not your grandmother's chilli recipe

Katie Burke, Chief People Officer, HubSpot

When we discussed releasing our Culture Code deck, I was surprised at the number of people who didn't want us to share it with the world. They felt like it was a grandmother's chilli recipe and something near and dear. They worried about our competitors or another company down the road copying it. One of the things we had to do was instil a sense of trust that what makes our culture special is not what we say about our culture – it's what we do.

We believe that the matching of the rhetoric to reality in culture is so hard that very few companies do it. It's still aspirational for us every day. What we have to believe is that our ability to close that gap and to continue to innovate and listen to our employees and make a great product that relates to our culture is significantly higher, better, faster than our competitors in this space for competing for talent. I really believe that. So, we try and actually share as much as possible about what we do here externally.

Part of that is because of our commitment to our value of transparency. The other part is because we know personally from experience how hard it is to make it all real and to live and breathe it every day. That's where the hardest work comes in. Creating the culture code is incredibly hard, but living it every day is the hardest work that we do collectively as a leadership team, and as a company.

As Katie referenced above, there tends to be a misplaced fear in opening up your practices – as if they're trade secrets or blueprints for success that your competitors might copy and hurt your business. Most of what we open-source in HR isn't necessarily new or novel, nor is it proprietary. Similar to my issues with 'best practices', the idea that someone can exactly replicate what others have found success with is pretty naïve.

Open source, #everywhere

Have you ever tweeted from a conference using the event hashtag? That's a form of open source.

Twitter has done so much to open up education and learning in the field of HR. I remember the early days of Twitter when I began building my online network through following hashtags like #HRevolution, #SHRM, #TalentNet and more. I couldn't afford to attend many conferences, but I could join the conversation on Twitter and follow along with what was being said and shared. Hashtags dramatically broadened the reach of the presenter's content and ideas. They allowed practitioners anywhere in the world to tap into the ideas and conversations that were happening.

Now you can add live-streaming to the mix. Live-streaming is another form of open source where conferences allow anyone to stream talks (typically limited to keynotes) for free anywhere in the world. You also have individuals live-streaming on tools like Facebook Live, LinkedIn Live, Periscope (Twitter), Instagram and other platforms, further extending the reach and audience of the content.

Another platform that more HR practitioners are using to work out loud and share their work is blogs. These are certainly not new, but with the ubiquity of blogging platforms like Medium and LinkedIn Publisher, more and more practitioners are taking to the keyboard to share their work, learnings, failures and results. When I'm preparing for Redefining HR podcasts, I usually do research on both platforms and it's rare that I come up empty. This openness, and ease, of sharing is having a transformative impact on the advancement of the field.

Google has its own version of open source with its re:Work initiative. It includes a range of searchable resources, templates and toolkits to help practitioners design and implement data-driven people programmes. Definitely worth a bookmark for anyone in the field.

COVID-19 demonstrates the power of open source

In early February 2020, I was noticing the conversation around Covid-19 escalating in some of my CHRO/CPO networks and communities. In mid-February, Coinbase, a cryptocurrency company based in San Francisco, open-sourced their Covid-19 Response Guide. It was a detailed account of the steps they would take based on certain triggers as the virus expanded. It was a golden resource – particularly as the situation that the global business (and HR) community was facing was unprecedented.

I wanted to boost their template, so I wrote a *Fast Company* article including a range of resources related to the challenges that the company would be faced with in the near-term future (Schmidt, 2020):

- Shifting to remote work
- Restricting travel
- Internal communication
- Supporting employees
- Increased xenophobia.

The article was viewed over 40,000 times in the first month, but I quickly discovered there was a problem. In the first week of March the situation was changing by the hour. A static blog post had no chance of keeping up. If the aim was to keep a current record of news, trends and resources, a different solution was needed – not something written or maintained by one person and posted as a static resource. Open source was the way.

Three days after the *Fast Company* article was posted, I created an open-source public Google Doc titled 'Coronavirus HR & Business Communications and Resources Guide'. The first version of the guide focused on detailing how companies were responding to the early days of the pandemic– restricting travel, moving to remote work, closing offices and so on. It was intended to be a guide so that HR and business leaders had a sense of what their peers were doing when developing their own plans.

After the first version was built, I called upon my network to help add news, updates and resources. As they added their own updates and shared with their networks, the document went viral. Within 24 hours it had been shared more than 4,000 times and within a month it had over 10,000 updates. The document evolved several times as the pandemic evolved. What really stood out to me as this evolved was the way that one act – Coinbase open-sourcing their pandemic plans – served as a catalyst for so much more.

Over a dozen companies shared their coronavirus response plans, many modelled off the Coinbase version, during the early days of Covid-19. In such an unprecedented global event, the ability for people and business leaders to model off what's already been built was a vital addition to their speed and planning efforts. As companies began planning their return-to-work (RTW) plans, the open-source model came into play again as companies open-sourced their plans and others used those for inspiration.

The benefits of open source during the pandemic were illustrated in a range of other ways as well. We've seen crowdsourced and collaborative documents on topics spanning:

- layoff and available talent lists;
- virtual/remote jobs listings;
- activities for children at home;
- school activities and learning opportunities;
- companies giving back and offering discounts etc.

The use case and value was proved again and again. Particularly in the field of HR where traditional knowledge and practices were walled off and siloed, Covid-19 demonstrated how learning and capabilities can be accelerated by opening practices and learning.

The Covid example above is one of many tangible and specific cases where the embrace of open source has had a transformative impact on the field of HR. As we continue to see open practices embraced and silos taken down, the evolution of HR will continue to accelerate.

There's no going back. The open-source genie is out of the bottle, and we're all better for it.

In the next chapter, we'll begin shifting into the recruiting side of modern HR with a chapter exploring lessons in hypergrowth and scale.

Reference

Schmidt, L (2020) How HR Leaders Are Preparing for the Coronavirus, *Fast Company*. Available from: www.fastcompany.com/90469161/how-hr-leaders-are-preparing-for-the-coronavirus (archived at https://perma.cc/SV6C-PBAC)

06

Building for scale

Surviving and thriving in hypergrowth

The first time I heard the phrase 'double-double' I got hungry. Literally.

You see, the Double-Double is a world-famous burger from In-N-Out – a renowned purveyor of delicious burgers based in California where I spent my early adult years.

Sadly, my reaction didn't quite align with the context of the conversation I was having. 'Double-double' in this context meant doubling the headcount of your company, and then doing it again in consecutive years. It's a euphemism for hypergrowth and scaling your business. It's common vernacular in Silicon Valley, but certainly not an experience limited to start-ups.

The field of HR is littered with tales of hypergrowth. From category-creating darlings of industry like Netflix to cautionary tales like Uber, the long-term success of hypergrowth is often dependent on the underlying people programmes that support it.

This chapter will explore some of the things you need to be thinking about from an HR/people perspective when building for scale. It's a collection of stories and perspectives from experienced practitioners with the scars to prove it, and considerations to help you build the right people foundation for scale.

All aboard: getting on the rocket ship

The analogy of a rocket ship and start-ups being deeply intertwined is hackneyed to the point of becoming a cliché. Like a lot of start-up vernacular, it's hard to trace the exact roots, but one of the more well-known quotes comes from Facebook Chief Operating Officer Sheryl Sandberg when she described a discussion with (then) Google CEO Eric Schmidt during her Harvard Business School commencement speech in 2012 (Yarow, 2012):

> So I sat down with Eric Schmidt, who had just become the CEO, and I showed him the spreadsheet and I said, 'This job meets none of my criteria.' He put his hand on my spreadsheet and he looked at me and said, 'Don't be an idiot.' Excellent career advice. And then he said, 'Get on a rocket ship. When companies are growing quickly and they are having a lot of impact, careers take care of themselves. And when companies aren't growing quickly or their missions don't matter as much, that's when stagnation and politics come in. If you're offered a seat on a rocket ship, don't ask what seat. Just get on.'

If you're offered a seat on a rocket ship, just get on. That is a compelling offer for many professionals – particularly in the start-up and tech sector where many employees are chasing the pay-out of an initial public offering (IPO) or successful acquisition. The key is how to pick the glory of Apollo 11 and avoid the disaster of Apollo 1.

Here's the traditional playbook in start-ups. You're a founder with a great idea for a new business. You get started on building a minimally viable product (MVP) and secure some angel funding to hire a few more engineers to build with. The product gets traction and creates some buzz in the industry, helping you secure your A-round of funding with a small cohort of colleagues.

This funding allows you to scale a bit more and shift some of your focus to recruiting. Most of your early hiring is from your networks, referrals from your existing team or introductions through your venture capital networks. Eventually you've hired all of those people, so you need recruiting support. Your first 'HR' support is your office manager or executive admin you've tasked with building out some basic people support systems.

Your company continues to grow. At this point you likely have a dedicated in-house recruiter and a junior to mid-level HR manager or business partner. You're still working off Excel spreadsheets and manual documents cobbled together and scaled as you grew. You continue to grow – 50, 75, 100, 150 staff – then the process breaks.

In the early days of the hypergrowth curve upswing, the people priorities are:

1 Recruiting

2 Recruiting

3 Recruiting.

That singular focus means that the underlying people infrastructure you're running on as a 150-person company is the same one you used with 10 employees. It evolved with Band-Aids and hacks. Now it's broken.

You decide to hire your first Head of People to guide you through your next phase of curve (you're still on that rocket ship trajectory). They lay out a plan for what's needed to build a progressive people infrastructure that scales, including HR systems and technology, headcount, programmes and time. After contemplating all the moving parts and gauging your ability to deliver, you green-light their plan.

They spend the next several months ripping out all of your outdated processes and programmes and rebuilding them from the ground up. They're implanting systems and lightweight processes to support the next phase of growth. These are a shock to the system for your team, as they've been operating without much structure up until now.

Hiring is impacted. Projects are delayed a bit. There's a brief stutter to the growth and business cadence until the new team and systems are integrated. Then, you're off and running again.

While the practice of *layering*, bringing a more seasoned people leader in for the next phase of growth, is common, it's not a hard rule. Many of today's leading people executives came to that seat from stretch engagements earlier in their career with CEOs who believed in them. Let's explore what that feels like in this example from Zynga's former Chief People Officer Colleen McCreary:

> If you had told me when I joined Zynga and we were 130 people, that at the end of my first year we would be 600 people, by the end of my second year we would be 1,500 people and at the end of my third year we'd be 4,000 people, I would have laughed in your face. We didn't know that was going to happen.
>
> You can't always plan for everything. You have to be reacting to the business and what's happening. We did twenty something acquisitions during that time and expanded all over the world. I would've never been able to predict any of that. I don't think our CEO would have been able to predict any of that. You have to make decisions with the information that you have in front of you at that time and trust yourself.
>
> There were a lot of times I doubted myself. Can I do this? Am I the right person for this? Many times I went to my CEO to say, 'Maybe you should bring in somebody who's more experienced than I am.' The best part is that I felt very supported by many people on our board and by my CEO. They insisted, 'If it's not you, who? You know this company. You've been here from the beginning. Who else is going to do this? There isn't anywhere we can go to. No one else has done this before.'

That thinking of putting off building a scalable people infrastructure is shifting. Companies are investing in people leaders much earlier. It's not uncommon to see a 50-person company hiring a Head of People. VC firms want a return on their investment and they've seen first-hand the struggles of their portfolio companies that neglect investing in people infrastructure early. The times are changing.

PRACTITIONER SPOTLIGHT
When to invest in talent

Matt Hoffman, Talent Partner, M13

So many companies don't think thoughtfully around their people strategy early enough in their lifecycle. They think it's something they can figure out later on, and they'll get around to hiring a Head of Talent when they're 75 or 100 people. I get why they do that, but then so many times they're already so far behind in terms of fixing bad practices that it becomes a barrier to the company working as well as it should in the beginning. And that's arguably when it's most critical, and when most companies are quite literally at a make or break stage as to whether they will survive or be successful.

I would never argue that you should hire a very senior Head of Talent as one your first five employees, but as a founder you should start absolutely thinking about talent as soon as possible. As a parallel, it seems obvious to say that any company that's going to create any traction in the world is going to need to have some fully fleshed-out go-to-market strategy. They're going to need to have a basic foundational tech and product architecture. You just couldn't imagine a company being successful without that basic foundation early on, but then it doesn't necessarily seem intuitive yet that you would want to have that on the people side. That's strange to me. Why wouldn't you? That's actually the most important part.

Early-stage companies absolutely need to think through their talent philosophy in order to build a healthy and robust foundation for the future. Who are the people they want to hire? Why do they want to hire those types of people? What are the types of behaviours they want to encourage? What are the behaviours they want to discourage? What values do they care about? Those things are just as important in the early stage of a company's lifecycle as is a tactical strategy around the go-to-market product to have... in some ways more!

> Companies pivot all the time in terms of product and go-to-market, but the foundation that you lay in your earliest stage around culture and talent is really, really hard to undo if it's bad. Those cracks in the foundation, or gaps in the alignment, will make you slower. It will become harder to innovate. You will move so much faster and smarter if you have at least a basic framework of how you want to build and grow your organization from the very beginning.

As Matt shares, investing early in a people leader ensures you're well positioned for the inevitable speed bumps and hurdles that accompany scale.

Thriving in ambiguity

Signing up for the 'rocket ship' that is hypergrowth is a serious commitment – and it's not for everyone. Hypergrowth is:

- Exciting
- Stressful
- Exhilarating
- Exhausting
- Rewarding
- Ambiguous.

The ambiguity shouldn't be dismissed. In hypergrowth, plans are often fluid and can change overnight. People leaders comfortable with operating on shifting sand can really thrive in these environments. There is generally a 'build' over 'buy' approach, so you can be stretched in ways that will dramatically accelerate your development.

If you need more structure, mentoring, direction or clarity, these environments may drive you crazy (or running for a more stable company). Because systems and processes are built on the fly, they may lack some of the tested-practice rigour you may find in traditional industries, and the environments can be a lab for experimental practices and thinking. It also means that the project you've been pouring yourself into for months might get scrapped if a founder doesn't like it.

Rockets do blow up from time to time, of course. Hypergrowth can also be an uneasy place if you need stability in your job. Losing a key client, a patent/intellectual property, or partner can send your rocket off course and send your organization down a death spiral overnight.

This point is illustrated by Colleen McCreary, former Zynga Chief People Officer, as she reflects on a moment that almost ended the company just as they were taking off.

PRACTITIONER SPOTLIGHT
Tales of hypergrowth @ Zynga

Colleen McCreary, former Chief People Officer, Zynga

This is a story that really resonates with me and is very truthful about what start-up life is like. I was working at Zynga in our early days. I think we were probably 600 employees. Most people who know our company know that we really foundationally grew as Facebook grew. We were on their platform. A lot of our games and success was based on that partnership.

We received some notice from Facebook on a Friday night that we potentially needed to end our partnership. On Saturday morning the entire board and our management team were in the office at 9:00 am figuring out what we're going to do. If we're off Facebook, what is our business? What do we go and do?

We spent the next three weeks as a company really rallying around building our own platform, our own network. People were sleeping on the floor and on the couches. We were there every single day. I was training my recruiting team how to be customer service agents to make sure the network was working.

We all lived through this whole three-week experience, working with the understanding that our business was at risk and we were going to have to do whatever it took to survive. Then it ended up that everything was fine and it didn't matter.

That's real-life start-up land, and the sort of the paranoia around what you are going to do to survive. I still look back at that as a really proud moment. As a company, we had a value around putting the company first. That was a big test of whether people would stop whatever they were doing on their games and do whatever it took to keep the company alive.

When you sign on to join a hypergrowth company, you're signing on for the journey – not the job – because it will likely evolve and change every 6–12 months. As an HR leader, you have to thread the needle of creating enough systems and processes to scale successfully – but not so much as to over-engineer and derail growth. It's a fine line.

As referenced to open this chapter, most companies don't grapple with these foundational process needs until they reach a couple of hundred employees. When you're all under one roof and known to each other, it's easy to work off understood protocols and practices – and if you don't, ask someone who does. The systems and processes that got you there are light-weight, and often flexible to an understood degree. Things just work.

As you scale and grow, the systems begin to strain and age. Customs and practices that worked smoothly at 50 don't quite fit the same at 500. You're no longer a mono-site company and have additional offices – perhaps spanning different time zones or countries as well. Lacking documented processes and 'how to's' was fine when you were small – now you're not and the systems are breaking down.

David Hanrahan is the Chief Human Resources Officer at Eventbrite. He joined Twitter in the early days of their hypergrowth through their IPO. He provides a window into that experience.

PRACTITIONER SPOTLIGHT
Scaling Twitter

David Hanrahan, Chief Human Resources Officer, Eventbrite

When I joined Twitter, it was about 600 people. I was just one of a couple of HR people on the broader people team. The recruiting team was quite big, but the HR infrastructure was not really there.

I remember I got lunch with my boss in the interview process. I'm like, 'Yeah, so what's my job going to be? What do you need me to do?' She responded she didn't even know – just to come on board and there's going to be plenty of opportunity. That certainly wound up being the case.

Almost immediately, our CEO (Dick Costolo) and the HR team were working together to put this manager training in. Dick owned and led the training for the next few years. It was a lot of reacting.

When you're in this hypergrowth mode, you're just reacting and trying to get your head above water on what you're thinking about, beyond the reacting. What are we going to need to put in place to have it ready next year? What's going to be the thing right around the corner that we're not even ready for?'

You're trying to constantly dig out, putting in your systems, putting in some basic policies, trying to figure out onboarding, trying to figure out these masses of people coming in. Then reacting to something the CEO wants or some other executive wants.

Eventually you get to the point where you realize you need a business partner model. You need to have some model by which you assign HR partners to teams or regions. Once you build in stronger skill sets in the HR team, then you're seeing around the corner a little bit further in advance. You start to slowly feel like you're digging out. Then the real proactive work begins.

One of the other challenges of leading people teams through hypergrowth is that you're building a people team to support a business model that may be pivoted or completely shifted on a moment's notice based on market conditions and opportunities. That requires business acumen to really understand the nuances of the business, market, threats, positioning, opportunities and more. Without it, you can't possibly build a people function that's built for the now and the next.

Agile thinking and foresight are invaluable to people leaders during hypergrowth. You can't just rely on a past playbook and 'build in a box'. Every situation is unique. You have to really invest in your understanding of the business and relationships with your executive peers to design and develop your people resources for maximum impact.

Ambrosia Vertesi is an Operating Partner at Operator Collective and former HR executive for two tech unicorns (Hootsuite and Duo Security). She's had a front-row seat for the trials and tribulations that come with the job. She weighs in on how people leaders should be thinking about this.

PRACTITIONER SPOTLIGHT
Proactive understanding and communication

Ambrosia Vertesi, Operating Partner, Operator Collective

I think from a people side of the organization, learning what your business perceives the customer challenges to be over the next few years and trying to stay as close as possible to the go-to-market will help you anticipate what your people growth needs are.

Learn what's going on with the business, as far out as you can see (and I know the smaller the company, the harder it is to see the horizon), but anticipating what the customer's going to experience will help you prioritize what the key differences are going to be in your growth trajectory because you are responding to the business.

Everyone who's going on that journey with you needs to know what's coming next in order to feel a level of certainty. If they don't, they can't attach to what you're building on the HR side.

The key difference in that early stage is communication about what you're going to be building and then bringing people along with you to share with them when things like merit reviews or performance reviews or leadership development are going to be coming in place, so that they're just not looking externally and going, 'Why don't we have this yet?' If you can do that, culturally you're going to buy yourself a lot of time.

When you get past 500 to 1,000, people will be able to know what to expect from you because you're going to have to build another roadmap that's going to be a bit different and it's going to be a bit more formalized.

From 500 to 1,000 you need to have a lot more structure and strategy around process, around compliance, that can show up as bureaucracy. People might not like that, but it has to be done.

Ambrosia's point about communication is so important – particularly establishing a cadence and rhythm to communication early. If you do that, your team and employees will be alongside you on the journey and not surprised by your actions. Neglecting this and 'dropping' new programmes and initiatives on them can lead to resistance and make adoption much more difficult. Transparency wins.

Scaling culture and values

How do you preserve culture through hypergrowth? That's a question I'm often asked by early-stage founders who want to retain their culture mojo as they scale – that special sauce that fuels late nights and deadlines and a deep sense of camaraderie within the team. The honest answer? You don't.

Culture is the manifestation of values and habits and a million small things done millions of times. It's shaped by behaviour – and behaviour is not static. As your company grows, anchoring on things like values and behaviours becomes your DNA. Your culture will be interpreted differently by each of your employees, but your values should be consistent. We'll go deeper on this in Chapter 9, 'Operationalizing culture and values'.

As you scale, particularly as you expand to new cities and countries, communication becomes even more important. We're all managing deep tech stacks for communication these days – Slack, Zoom, Google Hangouts, Google Docs, Microsoft Teams and more. Having platforms to communicate across borders is not our problem. Empathizing with our colleagues who aren't physically with us can be, as HubSpot's Chief People Officer Katie Burke explains.

PRACTITIONER SPOTLIGHT
Practising empathy at HubSpot

Katie Burke, Chief People Officer, HubSpot

As you scale globally, one of the things that start to break down is that notion of empathy. With nine global offices, time zones start to get into play.

You can imagine a scenario where you're working in the sales team in Sydney and I'm working on the product team here in Cambridge, MA. You share with me some customer feedback and I don't get around to responding first thing in the morning when I get in the next day. As a result, the story you tell yourself is, gosh, Katie doesn't care about any of our customers in Australia. She's not very collaborative. The company doesn't really care about being global first and that kind of thing.

So, one of the things we did was to say to people, the way we're going to scale this business is really by living and breathing empathy and assuming the best of our colleagues.

You can't be successful as a modern HR leader without empathy. There's just too much nuance and volatility to the human experience – not even mentioning that as an employee. The shared global experience of Covid-19 in 2020 really underscored this point. Employees were under immense stress and pressure. So were leaders trying to determine how to keep their companies alive in the market turmoil. Empathy became a superpower that allowed progressive HR leaders to shine by building programmes and support systems rooted in really recognizing the vulnerability of the experience for employees.

Setting yourself up for success

So, what's the best way to build your people team for scale? While there's no formulaic answer, as it really depends on the needs of the business and the aspirations of the founding team, there are some considerations that will steer your efforts.

Since we're talking hypergrowth here, you're going to need recruiters, possibly a lot of them. There's debate on ratios of recruiters to hiring needs, but again that's subjective based on what types of role you're hiring.

On the recruiting team needs front, one recommendation that applies in most situations is to hire an executive recruiter sooner than you think you need to. I realize this is a counterproductive recommendation as my firm Amplify does executive search, but for lean and fast-growing teams this can become quite an expensive line item if you're making all of your hires through head-hunters. If an in-house executive recruiter saves you 2–3 executive search fees, they've paid for themselves.

When it comes to building your broader people team, you have a range of factors to consider – business partners, operations, analytics, internal communications, employer branding, diversity and inclusion, compensation and benefits, and more. As a people leader you have to grapple with a lot more than 'who'. You have to contemplate 'why', 'what' and 'when'.

Ambrosia Vertesi had some excellent thoughts here on a podcast we recorded (21st Century HR Podcast, 2019):

> If I could have two key hires in the early days on my team, one would be a people operations person who works on how do we create simple practices for our employees so they know how to get things done and begin building infrastructure on the HR side of the business. The other would be a recruiting operations person.
>
> If you don't have someone building the recruiting frameworks and building the machine, then you end up having HR practitioners trying to do it. When you have an HR business partner trying to build an HRIS system or something like that, it's not their domain and the business sees HR business partners who are supposed to be with them, but the reality is that their HR leader drags them behind the curtain to do a bunch of building of programmes.

As your company scales and grows, your people team becomes more robust and dynamic to support the scaled complexity of the business. Let's take a look under the hood of a people team built to support approximately 700 employees with Asana's Head of People, Anna Binder.

PRACTITIONER SPOTLIGHT
Inside a modern people team built for scale at Asana

Anna Binder, Head of People, Asana

Let's talk about the people team structure to support heavy scale. It starts with recruiting. The size of the recruiting function is purely a function of how many and what kinds of people you have to recruit. What's your headcount growth? What's your attrition? How do you map that?

Our talent acquisition team includes functional recruiting, technical and business recruiting. It includes a sourcing team, a talent research team, operations, and then a candidate experience team.

We also have a diversity and inclusion leader who has a lot of dotted-line people. One-third is just people operations – compensation, operations, compliance, all the analytics, and that's a significant team.

We have what we call a growth and impact team. A lot of people might call this the HR business partners and talent development. We call it growth and impact because we think it allows people to grow and increase their impact.

We also have someone who is responsible for running our organizational strategy. At Asana, this includes the annual planning process, or the mechanism by which we come up with our annual plan, the financial plan, the objectives and the roadmap and how that all fits together. We have an employee communications person who supports employee engagement by thinking about what we are saying to employees. How are we connecting that to what we're saying externally?

In many of these chapters, my aim is to provide an intersection of research and interview-based ideas, stories from HR leaders and case studies from practitioners doing the work, in order to provide a three-dimensional view of the topic. Here are some specific case studies from hypergrowth.

Case studies

As shared earlier in the chapter, many hypergrowth companies struggle with how to preserve elements of their culture as they scale. This is how Snyk approaches this challenge.

CASE STUDY
Scaling culture with the business at Snyk

Dipti Salopek, VP People, Snyk

Company: Snyk
Region: Global
Industry: Information and Communications
Company size: 201–500 employees

What they did

Snyk, a leading global provider of developer-first security, put in place tangible actions to protect company culture as they hyperscale.

Why they did it

Snyk strongly believes that the deep foundation of their culture is a source of competitive advantage, and protecting this vector of their strength as they hyperscale is a key business priority.

How they did it

They firmly believe that the culture in which they operate – empathetic, supportive, collaborative – is a key reason behind their success. As a company going through hypergrowth on many vectors simultaneously (headcount, revenue, product etc), they were in an environment that could easily cause friction and conflict. They decided early in their discussions to be intentional about how they invest in their culture to prevent this friction from being a barrier to their success.

First, they put definition of their culture, and defined the two key areas that they believed were the essence of their strength – trust and collaboration. Then they put in place deliberate approaches to foster and support each of these:

- Trust: Their rapid scaling forced them to make frequent difficult organizational decisions that introduce tension and friction in an organization already under tremendous pressure. They aim to be intentional about investing in building trust, specifically to facilitate how these points of conflict are addressed in a constructive manner. They do this through operationalizing the approach of 'compassionate honesty' throughout their organization. It starts with a dialogue at their company-wide annual kickoff and is reinforced through management and leadership development programmes as well as individualized coaching for all Director+ leadership.

- Collaboration: Collaboration in their geographically distributed setup is held together through asynchronous communication and proactive transparency (eg online collaboration tools). However, the rapid scaling is forcing a rethink of information-sharing, transparency and decision-making structures. While transparency still remains a top priority, they now have to balance that against the volume of 'noise' in the system, as well as clarity on ownership and decision making. They are doing this through:
  - investing in their Slack infrastructure (in partnership with the Slack team) to design channels, best practices and separate environments that allow for prioritization of critical information;
  - rolling out and institutionalizing a framework for stakeholder management (eg RAPID), new to many of their employees accustomed to operating in a single-channel environment; and
  - strengthening interpersonal relationships through a deep investment in travel and bringing focused stakeholder groups together on a frequent basis.

Impact/ROI

Engagement survey – specific questions around trust and collaboration; attrition; exit interview feedback. Voluntary attrition <5 per cent annualized; engagement score 87 per cent as of last survey (February 2020).

One of the struggles that hypergrowth companies face is performance management and goal setting. A common approach found in tech companies is objectives and key results (OKRs) or key performance indicators (KPIs) in more traditional organizations. Here's a different take from Knotch.

CASE STUDY
Creating micro-goals to drive performance during scale

Garrison Gibbons, Head of People, Knotch

Company: Knotch
Region: North America

Industry: Information and Communications
Company size: 51–200 employees

What they did

They created micro-goals to track and support performance during scale.

Why they did it

Performance metrics have always been a challenge for hypergrowth companies, owing to frequent change and pivots, uncharted territory, small but mighty teams, limited managers or management experience, under-skilled or new to the workforce staff, and jack-of-all-trades vs specialist mentalities.

How they did it

It's hard to build a plane while you are flying, let alone attempt to map out the plane's course. Change is constant in a company that is experiencing hypergrowth. Performance management often seems like an impossible task. At Knotch, we attempted to enforce the popular performance metrics, like OKRs and KPIs. The issue is that these metrics were created for established corporations, not a company experiencing the early stages of hypergrowth. This led me to create and roll out 'micro-goals'. Micro-goals are weekly goals that take the form of a worm's-eye view instead of a bird's-eye view. By starting at the micro level you are able to embrace change in the moment, pivot as often as necessary, celebrate wins and acknowledge losses as they happen, and acknowledge the miscellaneous work outside of their job descriptions that is often done by employees in a start-up or hypergrowth environment.

There were things that I liked about OKRs and KPIs. OKRs provide a waterfall effect that trickles down from the company level to the individual level, encouraging visibility and transparency. The design of the OKRs demands specificity, which is lacking in other metrics. KPIs encourage a more black-and-white approach to performance, typically fitting into the SMART model – specific, measurable, achievable, relevant and time-based. After working for several hypergrowth companies that attempted to roll out OKRs and KPIs and seeing failed results, I created the concept of micro-goals, considering the pros of both practices. Micro-goals take the ideas behind OKRs and KPIs and make them more attainable and manageable for a hypergrowth company. Similar to OKRs, micro-goals waterfall from company level to the individual level. The target number is 3–4 weekly goals, encouraging more immediate feedback and embracing change or pivots. Similar to KPIs, they bring data into the equation and encourage employees to think more black-and-white. Micro-goals allow managers and direct reports to embrace wins or losses in the moment and acknowledge side projects and miscellaneous assignments. They are also easier for managers to track and manage, as they are micro in level and scope.

How do micro-goals fit into a larger performance framework? In a weekly one-on-one, direct reports and managers will discuss goals from the previous week and set goals for the following week. At the end of the quarter, managers and direct reports assess and review how micro-goals have tracked that quarter. Managers will discuss areas that need improvement, summarizing the conversation in a document or performance system. Once or twice a year, depending on the organization's needs, managers will conduct a formal review, taking the quarterly reviews into consideration and documenting the direct report's overall performance, opening the conversation to compensation review and promotion consideration as well.

Impact/ROI

Average Pulse Score of 3.8 out of a 1-to-5 engagement scale (5 being amazing and 1 being awful). In the first month, we saw an 80 per cent increase in direct report engagement with goal setting and submissions and a 250 per cent increase in manager review and response to goals set.

As hypergrowth companies scale, it becomes more difficult (and important) to successfully onboard and integrate new employees into the company. Let's take a look at how NextDoor approaches this with their 'Welcome Wagon' onboarding.

CASE STUDY
Setting up the Welcome Wagon with NextDoor

Bryan Power, Head of People, NextDoor

Company: NextDoor
Region: North America
Industry: Science and Technology
Company size: 201–500

What they did

They created a Week One onboarding experience for all new hires, called the 'Welcome Wagon'.

Why they did it

When bringing in a high volume of new hires which quickly becomes the biggest cohort of employee tenure, it's critical to create a consistent, focused onboarding programme that provides orientation, direct access to leadership and exposure to the company's values, culture and way of working.

How they did it

They had a few components in defining the experience:

1 Separate orientation (getting plugged in) from onboarding (getting up to speed). Orientation means employee paperwork (benefits administration), access (badging and identification) and systems setup (laptop configuration etc).

2 Access to leadership. Each leader on the executive team provides a 30–60-minute roundtable discussion on their area. This could be an introduction to the online advertising market from the Head of Revenue, company operating principles from the Head of People, introduction to the mission and values from a founder or a meet and greet with the CEO.

3 During the week, new hires introduce themselves globally with an introductory post on their internal version of NextDoor for employees. Typically, they share where they are from and their team and also a 'special talent' or something about their life away from work. They are also introduced live at the weekly all-hands during the first week, which closes out the first part of their 'Warm Welcome'.

Impact/ROI

They survey all new hires at one week, 30 days and 90 days. There is a lot of interesting impact; one key statistic is that over the last three quarters of 2020 (the entirety of the programme's existence), close to 90 per cent of new hires feel welcome at their new company.

Scaling a business, and people infrastructure, from the ground up is hard. Re-engineering an existing infrastructure for scale is much harder. That's the predicament that Delivery Hero Chief People Officer Jeri Doris found herself in when she joined the company in 2018. She inherited no existing people practices when she was tasked with taking them from 5,000 to 10,000+. This is how she did it.

CASE STUDY
Building a people-first foundation to scale the world's largest food delivery business with Delivery Hero

Jeri Doris, Chief People Officer, Delivery Hero

Company: Delivery Hero
Region: Europe
Industry: Information and Communication Technology
Company size: 10,001+

What they did

We built an employee first foundation to scale the world's largest food delivery business.

Why they did it

When I joined Delivery Hero in 2018, we had no people strategy at all – even though we were already 5,000 employees globally. If we were going to be a great place to work and also continue to scale, we needed to create a foundation to enable the business to do that. At the same time, we continued to focus on growing with purpose and staying true to our values.

How they did it

We took four key steps:

- We created a People Operations/Functional vision.
- We built key people processes around our values, which allowed us to scale our culture.
- We got the buy-in with the business owners on all key processes.
- We embraced an iterative approach.

The very first step in scaling a business going through hypergrowth was to focus on building a people-centric foundation. Establishing the intangibles that make a company unique, in addition to creating expectations for our employees, was key.

Therefore, the first step we took was to create a People Operations vision – to create an amazing employee experience. It became the barometer for everything we did. If it did not get us one step closer to fulfilling the vision, we did not do it. From HRIS technologies to key people processes, it became our North Star as we evaluated options for our employees.

With the vision as our cornerstone, we then focused on creating programmes, processes and key people foundations that centred around our values. We knew that if we were going to scale our culture, values were truly the foundation of how we were going to do that. However, one of the key components to a successful strategy is having the right stakeholders on board and their buy-in. So we focused on getting our leaders on board from the get-go.

We reviewed all initiatives that would impact our employees with our executive team. This way, our business leaders became advocates and champions for our key people processes, so it made the adoption of new processes faster.

In addition, it was essential to understand that as you build a foundation to scale a business going through hypergrowth, iteration is part of the process. Retrospectives became a natural part of every project. This step was probably the easiest we did, because it aligned directly with one of our values, which is to always aim higher. Therefore, we did not become complacent with our processes, and once it was available we were able to utilize data to identify opportunities for improvement.

Impact/ROI

Within two years, attrition rates decreased, engagement scores improved, our Glassdoor ratings improved drastically and we won the Great Place to Work award.

It's great to have an understanding of what hypergrowth looks like, and real stories and journeys from people leaders outlined above. As mentioned in the Introduction, one of my aims with this book is to go beyond theory and story and show *what* it really looks like. *How* does it happen? What's the *ROI and impact* to the business?

While this chapter is (mostly) focused on successful lessons in hypergrowth, the reality of scaling is often messy and difficult. It's full of soaring highs and crushing lows. If you've been through it, you know this. If you haven't, you will. Don't worry, there's no universal playbook in getting this right. You use your best judgement and call all the friends who've been there before you. You've got this.

Just remember, rocket ships don't have airbags.

In the next chapter, we'll go deeper into the fundamentals of modern recruiting.

References

21st Century HR Podcast (2019) Ambrosia Vertesi: Ground Zero to Unicorn, *21st Century HR Podcast*. Available from: https://21stcenturyhr.fireside.fm/ep12-from-ground-zero-to-unicorn (archived at https://perma.cc/LE6C-KRC8)

Yarow, J (2012) Sheryl Sandberg's Full HBS Speech: Get on a Rocketship Whenever You Get the Chance, *Business Insider*. Available from: www.businessinsider.com/sheryl-sandbergs-full-hbs-speech-get-on-a-rocketship-whenever-you-get-the-chance-2012-5 (archived at https://perma.cc/DQH2-EFVL)

07

Transformational recruiting

Remember when recruiting was just recruiting? A subset of HR focused solely on hiring? Well, technically the latter statement is still the same, but the methods sure have evolved.

I'm 'I used to recruit using a land line' years old in recruiting. Of all my experience in HR and people operations, recruiting is the function where I've spent the most time. Like most seasoned recruiters, I have the scars to prove it.

My path to recruiting was accidental, as I shared earlier in the book. I started my career in 1998 during the first dotcom boom, when I was recruited out of college by a technical recruiting agency called Pencom Systems. Only with hindsight do I realize how lucky I was to start my career there. The approaches I learned there would shape my approaches to recruiting to this day.

The majority of technical recruiting agencies at that time were commissioned head shops. They'd hire pretty much anyone on commission and throw them on the phones with little training. There was no risk to the business. If their new hires picked it up quickly and did well, they'd bring in revenue to the business and make enough commission to continue. If they didn't, well, let's just say recruiting agencies weren't exactly winning awards for employee tenure.

Pencom had a very different approach. Their model was based on relational recruiting and technical expertise. All of their newbie recruiters were paid enough salary for a modest recent-graduate lifestyle and bonuses based on hires/performance. They hired groups of 30–40 hires who would all join together and be based in their New York headquarters for six months of intensive training on technology, recruiting, research, relationship building and all the core skills recruiters needed.

They understood that every time one of their recruiters spoke to an engineer, that was a brand-building or brand-tarnishing moment. If their recruiters couldn't hold a reasonable conversation about programming languages, or moved aggressively into sales, that prospect likely wouldn't take a call from that agency again – and would probably tell their peers about the experience. They were thinking about their employer brand at least a decade before it went mainstream.

I distinctly remember one training session when we were working through mock interviews. We were presented with a scenario where a candidate we were representing had a competing offer that we knew was a better opportunity than the one we were representing. When asked what we'd do, most of us offered a range of sales pitches to try to elevate our client or diminish the competing offer. We all failed the test. The correct answer was congratulating the engineer on the other offer and letting her know that would be the best decision for her. Their view was that the loss in short-term gain (fee) would be offset by the gain of a long-term relationship that would likely lead to more referrals and placements in the long term.

Play the long game. Ethical recruiting. Relationships over fees. I was a recent graduate and didn't appreciate any of that at the time. Looking back, it's clear that the foundation of learning the domain, valuing long-term relationships over short-term gain and understanding the importance of doing the right thing would become foundational pillars of how I operated in this space.

After spending three years at Pencom, I was ready to take what I learned and move in-house. I never looked back.

Watching corporate recruiting evolve over the past 20 years has been fascinating. What started as a pretty singularly focused function with linear career paths has become so much more sophisticated. You now have a range of options beyond full-stack recruiter: sourcing, employer brand, recruiting operations, coordination, recruiting technology, executive recruiting, university recruiting, agile labour recruiting, recruitment marketing, and I'm sure several other disciplines by the time you're reading this.

The moral of this story is that the field of recruiting has become incredibly sophisticated. This chapter is designed to explore some of the foundational components of modern recruiting. It's far from comprehensive. There are many books dedicated solely to this topic, so I won't claim to cover everything here. (Also, you should read those books.)

I'm going to break this chapter down sequentially, like a recruiting funnel. We'll start with top-of-funnel activities like employer brand and recruitment marketing and work our way down. Throughout the chapter I'll include essays and case studies from leaders on the front lines to help you connect more deeply with the tangible practices, thinking and approaches.

We know talent is one of the most determinant factors in a company's success. That's why the demand for recruiters has continued to climb over the past five years.

FIGURE 7.1 What are the top concerns in your business?

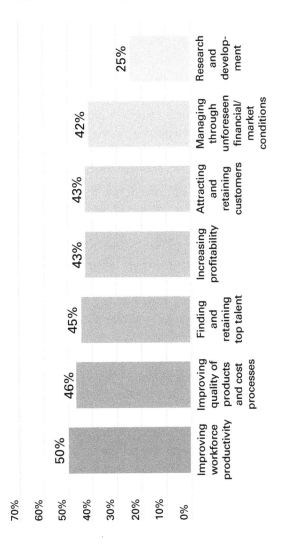

47%

of CEOs surveyed feel that talent-related concerns are their most important business problems

80%								
70%								
60%								
50%	50%							
40%		46%	45%	43%	43%	42%		
30%								
20%							25%	
10%								
0%	Improving workforce productivity	Improving quality of products and cost processes	Finding and retaining top talent	Increasing profitability	Attracting and retaining customers	Managing through unforeseen financial/market conditions	Research and develop-ment	

Greenhouse Workplace Intelligence Report, 2019. Reproduced with permission

The business value and importance of recruiting is clear. According to Greenhouse's 2019 Workplace Intelligence Report (Greenhouse Software, 2019), 47 per cent of CEOs feel that talent-related concerns are their most important business problem (Figure 7.1). You have very little chance of success as a business without the ability to attract and hire great talent. *How* to do that varies, but I'll be breaking down foundational components and examples throughout the chapter.

PRACTITIONER SPOTLIGHT
The importance of transformational (TA) leadership

Anna Binder, Head of People, Asana

In the first stages when a company is founded, your CEO or founders spend 90 per cent of their time pitching, and much of that time is spent pitching to candidates. Then you shift to the next stage, where you're a little bigger and you've got a small recruiting team and some hiring managers. You're trying to hire as many great people as possible, as quickly as possible.

Eventually you shift to a more professionalized recruiting function that looks a lot like a sales function. You have candidate marketing. You have a headcount plan. You map that headcount plan to resourcing, whether it's number of recruiters or number of hiring managers. You also map it to the number of interviews that you need, both phone interviews and onsite interviews.

You have a funnel. What is the close rate (the percentage of offers extended that are accepted) that you can anticipate, and let's build from there. Eventually, you move from a transactional relationship between recruiting and hiring managers, to a deeper partnership that works together on longer-term talent solutions.

Having someone leading the talent acquisition function who can think strategically and drive operational excellence can be transformative but very hard to find. For us at Asana, it's been game changing.

For example, our head of recruiting for people operations sits down with me on a monthly basis and has a series of questions: 'What's keeping you up at night? Let's look at your calendar. What are you spending time on? What are your monthly priorities?'

They're asking those questions because those things will give them hints of what I'm going to come and say I need to recruit for: X, Y and Z. She will sometimes come and say, 'Three months ago you talked about this. Is this still a problem for you or have you solved it?' When I say to her, 'Hey, now we're going to hire for this', she says, 'Yeah, I figured that based on our last conversation. I've already got a plan for how we might approach that. Here, what do you think about this?'

It's amazing. That's not transactional at all. She's asking me questions and gleaning in between the lines what she can anticipate, and then doing the work without me even being involved to prepare for that. That to me is deep partnership and anticipatory work that I'm so happy that our leaders here can benefit from.

Whether you're in hypergrowth mode (like Asana) or steady-state scaling, my aim is to provide actionable and practical tips to support your journey throughout this book.

The rise of employer brand

One of the biggest shifts in recruiting over the past decade has been the rise of employer brand. What began with tweets using #jobs has grown to a foundational element of most modern recruiting teams and capabilities. Some companies have come so far as to create internal employer brand agencies with animators, copywriters, videographers and designers.

Recruiting has become a creative field. Regardless of how you're resourcing employer brand or how advanced your capabilities are, these efforts allow you to extend your recruiting funnel outwards and reach more candidates.

A traditional recruiting funnel has a narrower top. You brought in applicants through direct sourcing, job boards, recruiting agencies, referrals and so on. Employer branding widens the recruiting funnel by adding more opportunities to influence potential candidates' awareness, sentiments and, ideally, affinity towards your company.

There are few people on this planet with more institutional knowledge on employer branding than Richard Mosley. We co-wrote a book on the topic in 2017 and it was impressive to see his encyclopaedic knowledge of the field up close. I knew I had to get his perspective on how the field of employer branding has evolved.

PRACTITIONER SPOTLIGHT
The evolution of employer branding

Richard Mosley, Chief Strategy Officer, Universum

I'm lucky enough to have been directly involved in the evolution of employer branding since it first started taking root around 20 years ago. After a number of years working in consumer brand marketing, I was given the opportunity to work on some major corporate brands, Unilever and Vodafone. This brought a realization that brands operate across many different stakeholder groups, not just customers and consumers. I became particularly interested in the relationship between brands and talent. It struck me that the most important brand in most people's lives at any given time is seldom a consumer brand, but the brand that people work for, their employer brand. This seemed to me to be relatively unexplored territory.

Looking for a new career adventure, I joined a small agency dedicated to this new idea. It was 2001. At this time, recruitment marketing was principally dedicated to hiring, rather than longer-term brand building. There were no employer brand managers or budgets, and few HR people had any training, or interest, in branding. By 2003 we were on the verge of going bust, but in a last-ditch effort to get our message across, we decided to write a book. Timing is everything.

The Employer Brand landed in late 2004 in a booming economy and global war for talent. The first wave of adopters was consumer goods companies, who naturally took to this new form of brand thinking. Coca-Cola picked up the phone first, then Unilever, PepsiCo and P&G. The banking industry came next. Then it seemed that everyone wanted to define their 'employer value proposition' (EVP). Within a couple of years, the major recruitment advertising agencies were all setting up brand consulting teams, and companies began hiring employer brand managers.

The next major development was the 2008 financial crisis and subsequent recession. Forward-thinking companies then, like now, began to recognize that having a strong employer brand, backed by authentic employee promises, was just as important in engaging and retaining talent as attracting them. Companies like Coca-Cola, with solid leadership commitment to the EVP we'd created, rode out the recession pretty well. They retained high levels of employee engagement even when cutting headcount and freezing wages.

Moving into the next decade, when the economy started picking up again, employer branding began to receive a lot more attention from corporate brand teams. It became increasingly clear that consumers wanted to get a feel for the people and the culture behind leading brands. In turn, corporate communications teams began to see the benefit of aligning themselves more closely with the human face of the business, the employer brand. This resulted in some internal tensions, but ultimately has brought a more positive alignment between purpose statements, core values (what's expected of employees) and EVPs (what talent can expect in return).

The rise of social media amplified this humanizing corporate trend over the course of the next decade, with an increasing focus on authentic, employee-focused storytelling in place of the 'manufactured' messaging that previously dominated recruitment advertising.

So where are we now? Well, Universum's recent global survey of HR leaders has confirmed the priority status of employer branding within most leading organizations, despite, even perhaps because of, the recent shocks to the global economy. Every organization depends on its talent to succeed, and if you want to compete effectively for talent, then developing and maintaining a strong employer brand is widely agreed to be a vital necessity.

The field of employer branding has come a long way. One of the more important (and recent) evolutions is our shift away from pure talent attraction to a more refined approach of attracting the *right* talent. Modern branding is not about sizzle.

The end of artifice

Let's be real about something. No one gives a damn about ping-pong tables.

In the early days of this digital iteration of the employer brand, companies went all-in on sizzle. Employer brand videos seemed interchangeable except for the colours and locations of the ping-pong tables. In an effort to stand out, we commoditized frivolous perks and built a sea of them.

We painted a utopian picture of work built on artifice. It was an arms race of corporate cafeterias and small-batch artisanal coffee. We leaned into our corporate highlight reels and clogged our recruiting pipelines with prospects. Prospects eventually became hires – hires who eventually experienced the other side of the coin that we shielded them from in our glossy employer brand campaigns.

You know what happens next. They leave. They share their true experience on Glassdoor, or, indeed, a range of other platforms designed to weaponize bad behaviour. This made it harder to attract and recruit future talent, as they saw through the veneer we had created.

As employer branding matured, we realized the error of these early ways and began to craft more honest views of the work experience. The goal isn't *more* candidates; it's more of the right qualified candidates who self-align with all you have to offer.

Repel to attract – radical (recruiting) candour

You don't want to be the company everyone wants to work for.

The legacy approach to building an employer brand was to create the sizzle that brought in as many candidates as possible. That was a mistake. We all have different drivers when it comes to how and where we do our best work. One person's dream job is another's nightmare.

Effective employer branding both attracts and repels. Do it right, and you'll have fewer candidates in your application funnel, not more. However, they'll be making more informed decisions about your organization, and that self-aligned nature means you're more likely to convert and then to hire – and ultimate make stickier hires. In this case, less really is more.

Be real with candidates. Don't be afraid to talk about some of the more challenging or undesirable aspects of the job or company – hours, pace, tech stack, resources, location, travel and so on. The better you can help prospects understand the highs and the lows, the more likely you are to have a targeted pipeline of talent.

I remember the look on a hiring manager's face when I suggested they add a section to job descriptions titled, 'Why You Shouldn't Consider This Job'. I analysed their recent hire turnover data and found some common threads about why new joiners were leaving. I suggested they own that upfront to bring more clarity to job seekers. Within a year they halved short-term turnover. It turns out that honesty is good for business.

Job descriptions don't have to suck

Let's be honest. Most job descriptions suck. The reason they suck is, in a sense, archaeological. The last job posting sucked. And the one before that. And the one before that. Job descriptions are often compliance-driven recycled relics dusted off from the last time that the position was filled.

The reality is that job descriptions are actually one of the most crucial employer brand assets you have. They often have the most traffic. They help inform and align prospects to your roles. They don't *have* to suck. They can sing! Okay, that's hyperbole – but my point is that even incremental advancement in job descriptions can feel monumental as the bar is so low.

Bring some design thinking to your job postings. Put yourself in the candidate's shoes. What would you want to know to be able to picture yourself in the role? Some things you may want to consider:

- **Write for mobile:** Assume your readers are doing so from their mobile devices and write accordingly.

- **Write for the audience:** Consider writing job descriptions in the second person: you/your/yours. Help the reader see themselves in this job.
- **Focus on outcomes and success measures:** Most job descriptions are infinite scrolls of bullets detailing responsibilities. Don't do that. Include what success looks like, what they'll accomplish, what they'll learn. How they'll grow.
- **Make it dynamic:** We're somewhat limited by the functionality of our applicant tracking systems on this one, but don't be afraid to add hyperlinks, photos, videos and so on to add more depth and context to your job description.
- **Be honest:** Per the points above on candour, don't be afraid to add some realness to the job description that might repel some applicants.

Do some research in performance reviews and exit interviews for hidden nuggets that might help you shape that job description in a more honest and authentic way. Talk to your employees in that role, especially recent hires, to get their feedback on what they enjoy and what's challenging, and bake that into the job descriptions.

The more data inputs you have, the better you and the hiring manager can craft a spec that help draw the right talent.

Business acumen + recruiting acumen

As the sophistication of recruiting teams and capabilities increases, so does the need for business acumen within recruiting leadership. Earlier in this book we shared how the CHRO role is evolving, and how the need for business acumen is bringing leaders from outside the field into the HR executive role. The same thing is happening in recruiting.

According to LinkedIn's 2019 Future of Recruiting report, more than one in three (35 per cent) current heads of recruiting came from a role outside of HR and talent acquisition, according to LinkedIn data (LinkedIn, 2019).

Outside of HR and talent acquisition, the most common previous functions for heads of recruiting are sales, operations and business development – areas with a clear and immediate impact on the organization's business goals.

I expect this trend to continue as the sophistication and complexity of recruiting continue to grow, particularly as we look at more agile workforces.

The rapidly evolving landscape and complexity of business is front of mind for recruiting leaders, as illustrated in Figure 7.2.

Modern people leaders want to know more than how you approach recruiting – they want to understand how well you understand the business. Anna Binder shares how she gauges business acumen in her hires:

FIGURE 7.2 Top priorities for recruiting over the next five years, LinkedIn (2019)

Per cent who say these will be one of their team's top priorities over the next 5 years.

Keeping up with rapidly changing hiring needs

#1 top priority over the next 5 years

65%

Keeping up with recruiting technology

52%

Showing business impact

43%

Leveraging data effectively

43%

Influencing business leaders

41%

LinkedIn Future of Recruiting Report, p 52. Reproduced with permission

I think of myself as a business person who happens to be having impact on the business through this function called People Operations. In order to be successful, not only do I need to understand those components of the business, but I actually need to really care and be interested in the product, the market, the competition. I need to engage and think about them, and think about how our people strategy supports and drives the business outcomes.

One of my common interview questions for People Operations candidates who come here to Asana is that they need to be able to explain to me the business model of the companies that they've been at. How do they make money? What are the gross margins? What are the risks? Who are the competitors? What are the growth rates? I'm not talking about headcount growth rates, I'm talking about revenue growth rates. If you don't know that, I don't know how you can really build people programmes to enable the company to achieve its mission.

Having a deep grasp of the business allows that to be a North Star when you're designing your recruiting and talent strategy. It allows you to proactively understand, and plan for, the dynamic needs of the business. You can't be a transformative talent leader in today's world without business acumen.

As recruiting operations have become more sophisticated, so has our ability to borrow practices from other functions and bring them into the field.

PRACTITIONER SPOTLIGHT
Borrowing business practices in recruiting

Melissa Thompson, VP Talent Acquisition, Nielsen

Over the past 20 years, I've had the opportunity to lead both US-focused and global talent acquisition teams. In that time, TA leaders have evolved strategies for finding and hiring the best talent. As CEOs publicly (and consistently) state, 'hiring top talent is a business imperative': the pressure is on TA to attract, select and hire that talent. In the past several years, I have borrowed the best practices from sales and business intelligence to reinvent how talent acquisition is done.

Sales concepts

It is not a new concept to have the recruiting funnel mimic the sales lead process. What is new for TA is finding ways to convert candidates effectively at the top and through the funnel.

Top of the funnel

Understanding and managing the experience before a prospect clicks apply is imperative to the candidate experience. One opportunity is to use your CRM's capabilities to capture prospects that abandon your application before completion. A simple review of your current applications could reduce your apply abandonment rate. 'Secret-shop' your application process to understand how long it takes to complete the application, what the communication looks like when you submit, and when you get outreach from the TA team. Using this methodology at McGraw-Hill, we revised the application time from more than 15 minutes to 2 minutes. As a result, our application abandonment rate dropped from over 50 per cent to below 10 per cent.

Funnel conversion

One measure of a good applicant tracking system is whether it allows you to review and understand candidate conversion at key stages in the recruiting process. For example, if you are trying to improve diversity hiring, it would be helpful to know the candidate mix at each key stage in the process – Apply/Screen/Interview/Offer. This data set could be evaluated at the requisition level, by the hiring manager or department. In my current role at Nielsen, we are using diversity throughput data to improve both our pipeline and our success at hiring diverse candidates.

Business intelligence concepts

In the age of analytics and dashboards, any savvy talent acquisition leader will tell you that data-driven solutions are the most effective. When I was asked to transform talent acquisition at Citrix, I shifted to a metrics-focused TA strategy:

Success metrics

This seems very general but is actually profound. There is a saying that goes 'if you can't measure it, you can't manage it'. For me, that means that if I add a new tool then it will be implemented with a measure that confirms the success or failure of the product. For example, we were an early adopter of a video job-posting tool. Success was defined as the impact of video job postings. For the pilot department, we saw an increase in candidates and the hiring manager specifically noted an improvement in the interview slate. At the same time, the time to fill those jobs went down by five days on average. Measuring those metrics allowed us to clearly understand the impact beyond anecdotal hiring manager satisfaction.

Net Promoter Score (NPS)

NPS is my favourite metric for the candidate experience because it is simple to implement but packs a powerful impact. A few years ago, my talent acquisition operations team piloted a one-question NPS survey for every candidate who came onsite to interview. In addition to scoring their experience on a 0–10 rating scale, we allowed for open-ended feedback. The results were quite eye-opening. We heard about candidates being left in the lobby, hiring managers texting during interviews, and overall poor candidate experiences. These specific concerns led us to design a comprehensive training for hiring managers called 'Passport to Recruit'. This training resulted in a +5 NPS improvement within the first year of the programme.

While there is no magic wand to identify what the future of talent acquisition will be, I do think continuing to review and adopt best practices throughout the organization is one tried and true methodology.

The need to broaden the skill set of recruiters to tailor to today's recruiting landscape is reinforced by the declining and ascending skills that recruiters are listing in their profiles (Figure 7.3).

FIGURE 7.3 More recruiters are listing these skills on LinkedIn, LinkedIn (2019)

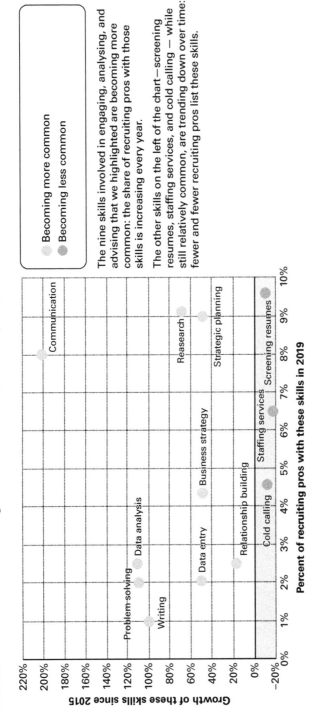

Becoming more common
Becoming less common

The nine skills involved in engaging, analysing, and advising that we highlighted are becoming more common: the share of recruiting pros with those skills is increasing every year.

The other skills on the left of the chart—screening resumes, staffing services, and cold calling — while still relatively common, are trending down over time: fewer and fewer recruiting pros list these skills.

LinkedIn Future of Recruiting Report, p 52. Reproduced with permission

This chart is a stark contract of legacy recruiting skills vs progressive recruiting skills. Unless you're in a 'smile and dial' volume recruiting role, you need these modern skills to be effective in today's world of recruiting.

Inclusive recruiting

According to LinkedIn's Future of Recruiting report, only one in three teams currently tracks the diversity of candidates (LinkedIn, 2019):

> Diversity metrics – such as the gender or ethnicity of candidates sourced, interviewed or hired – are rarely used today. While most recruiting professionals believe these metrics would be very useful, just one in three says their company currently uses them.
>
> That needs to change. While some recruiting leaders cite legal concerns around how to measure diversity, companies will need to solve those challenges if they want to see a meaningful difference in the diversity of their workforce. As Peter Drucker famously said, 'what gets measured, gets managed,' and that's particularly true for diversity.
>
> Diversity metrics don't stop at the end of your hiring funnel. To focus on outcomes, track the tenure of hires from underrepresented groups and monitor the overall makeup of your workforce.

We can't possibly build diverse companies without understanding our talent pipelines, and how we're maintaining or haemorrhaging diverse talent throughout our recruiting funnel. Modern recruiting teams understand their diversity metrics at each stage of the process. This allows them to identify any issues in their process, at any stage, that might be causing them to lose diverse talent.

Reverse-engineering how to build representative teams starts all the way back at talent attraction, employer brand and other top-of-funnel touch points. How are you positioning your company to attract diverse talent? Where and how are you showing up to diverse communities? How are you thinking about how your messages and positioning will be received by those you're trying to attract?

No more rock stars, ninjas and gurus.

Best-in-class recruiting teams closely monitor and measure diversity metrics at every stage of their funnel. They audit their job descriptions, career sites and recruitment marketing materials to ensure the copy is gender-neutral and inclusive. They have a proactive pipelining strategy to engage candidates of colour on an ongoing basis – not just when they're hiring. They're educated, informed, and armed with facts to influence hiring teams to prioritize diversity.

Most importantly, they understand that diversity must be embedded into how they operate – not just bolted on to a sourcing strategy.

It's vital to keep in mind that strong cultures are built on inclusivity and belonging. It's woven into much more than hiring, but it starts there. You have to be intentional, as HubSpot's Chief People Officer Katie Burke shares:

> If you have a really strong culture, one of your ethical obligations as a leader is to make sure that having a strong culture isn't an excuse to hire for sameness. You have to train people how to think about that and how to make sure they're building teams where not only is diversity a priority at the highest level, but you're really arming people with the tools to think about building diverse teams in that interview process. That's a skill.

Indeed, it's a skill. You have to give your teams the training and support in order to intentionally overcome bias in interviews. Without it, you risk building homogenous monocultures.

So how do you ensure your recruiting efforts are built to create diverse teams? Let's get under the hood on Asana's approach.

PRACTITIONER SPOTLIGHT
Building a diverse workforce at Asana

Anna Binder, Head of People, Asana

We recently looked at our work in D&I. We felt there's a recruiting element of it, and then there's an inclusion element of it once people are in the door. We looked at what a lot of companies do. Typically, there is a D&I team. It sits either inside of recruiting or inside of people operations. Sometimes it sits in a couple of other places.

D&I efforts with recruiting and inclusion are very different, particularly the recruiting piece. Recruiting is a specialized craft. It's very different from the work you do in inclusion. We felt that what makes sense is to take the recruiting portion of the D&I work and embed it more deeply into the recruiting team, so we moved our head of D&I out of recruiting. Recruiters have such difficult jobs. While they emotionally and spiritually support the concepts behind the diversity recruiting, it can feel like an effort that's making their life more difficult. What we wanted to do was to move the recruiting responsibilities around.

Building a diverse workforce means connecting it more intimately into recruiting and closer to the hiring manager. Make it a core part of their work. We've recently split that out, and we happen to have an amazing head of recruiting who wants this work to be core to her team's efforts.

Now our head of D&I is an advisor to that recruiting work, but she's not a recruiter and she's not a recruiting professional at all. She really focuses 90 per cent of her energy on the inclusion work, and just provides advisory support to the recruiting team on their work. This has had a powerful impact in terms of making people, both recruiters and hiring managers, feel like it's a deeper driver of our diversity efforts and it's more innate to their everyday work as opposed to this separate thing.

That anecdote is really important. No matter how impactful your DEI leaders are, these efforts must be embraced and owned by everyone to be successful. Building inclusive companies is a team effort and *must* be led from the top down. It's vital to approach it this way to set your DEI leader up for success. If you think you're hiring a saviour who's going to solve all your diversity challenges by themselves, you're setting them up to fail.

Sourcing 2.0

It's never been easier to find talent. It's never been harder to cut through the noise and get their attention.

Thanks to social media, LinkedIn, GitHub, Reddit and other online platforms, almost everyone has a digital footprint of some sort. Once limited to advanced Boolean search strings to find talent, recruiters and sourcers now have a range of powerful technology and other tools to find prospects and their email addresses.

The problem? Everyone has access to these same tools.

We talked about recruiters becoming marketers above. Now they're copywriters, too.

PRACTITIONER SPOTLIGHT
The evolution of sourcing

Carmen Hudson, Principal Consultant, Recruiting Toolbox

I started my recruiting career in executive search as a researcher in the mid-90s, an early version of a sourcer. It was the dawn of the internet. One night when I was working late, the general manager found me in my cubicle and asked me to research a name he had scribbled on a scrap of paper. Before this interaction we'd had only a few conversations. Fifteen minutes later, I'd pulled together a dossier on the mystery person with as many details as I could collect, including address and phone number. If his raised eyebrows were any indication, the GM was impressed with my research. In fact, I think I frightened him a bit.

I loved that job – identifying potential candidates for our clients' mid- to senior-level positions (what we called 'name gen') and occasional functional or industry reports; I loved the transactional satisfaction of finding what was needed. Since my time at the executive search firm, sourcing has evolved from its transactional roots. These days, good sourcers are pulled into work that includes deep market research, outreach and attraction strategy, technology implementation, digital marketing and content creation. I have sourcer friends who have such advanced skills that their employers ask them to help select new market locations or evaluate new business opportunities.

I'm disappointed, however, in the siloed nature of sourcing work. We help with specific positions or launching a CRM or doing the pre-work necessary to hire successfully at conferences and trade shows, but the work is not iterative. In most organizations, name-gen projects are abandoned after a few hires are made. We don't fully take advantage of candidate rediscovery and we're not (yet) helping our leaders identify global talent strategies.

As our methods and tools become more sophisticated, I believe that sourcing will become more than providing potential candidates as a need arises. Sourcers' ability to synthesize data and provide insight into talent markets could also help organizations proactively develop talent strategies, ahead of need, to support business initiatives and growth. I imagine that we will see the rise of sourcing pros who combine tactical search skills, data aggregation and recruitment marketing experience to advise and guide broader talent strategies. That's a job, had it been available back in the 90s, I would have loved even more!

To be fair, actually calling recruiters marketers or copywriters is a slight to professionals in those respective professions. We're just borrowing some of their techniques and practices to make our jobs more impactful – and let's face it – easier.

Digital marketing experts estimate that most Americans are exposed to around 4,000 to 10,000 ads each day (Simpson, 2017). Let that sink in for a moment. According to the latest Digital 2019 Report from Hootsuite and We Are Social, we're spending on average 6 hours and 42 minutes online each day (Hughes, 2019). That's almost 10 ads per every minute we spend online. That's what we're competing with when we're trying to get that data scientist's attention.

To cut through that noise-to-signal ratio means we have to provide a clear and concise message to have any shot at capturing a prospect's attention. It means personalization. It means directness. It means having a value proposition and call to action so that the recipient is not left to guess your intent – or made to fill in any gaps on their own. Direct. Concise. Actionable.

Are you (candidate) experienced?

Let's be honest – applying for a job is an exercise in vulnerability, and often full of stress. Changing jobs is one of the more significant life events in the human experience. It's often an emotional and uncertain exercise in opening yourself up to be validated (or not) by others.

In the age of Glassdoor and social media, a negative candidate experience is a couple of clicks away from your reputation as an employer. Though we've been talking about candidate experience for years, we haven't seen enough progress to shake the 'black hole' stigma – that candidates apply for jobs and then are never contacted again – that many job seekers place on us. Why is that?

While the conversations around candidate experience (CX) remain active, tangible steps and actions on enhancing CX remain elusive for many employers. Some organizations are trying to change that.

The Talent Board has been leading the conversation on CX for years through their CandE initiatives and awards. They partner with a range of employers around the world to survey and benchmark their applicants' feedback. In 2019 they surveyed more than 195,000 candidates who applied for jobs at over 175 companies for their Candidate Experience (CandE) Benchmark Report (The Talent Board, 2019). Some of their key findings included:

- Only 25% of all job candidates rated their candidate experience as great.
- Candidate resentment has increased 40% in North America since 2016.
- The candidate experience improves by 148% when candidates are asked for interview feedback.
- The candidate experience improves by 168% if an employer makes an offer within one week of the final interview.
- The candidate experiences improves by 29% if you reject candidates over the phone as opposed to by email or text message.

Are you surveying your applicants? Best-in-class teams are. Much like the diversity funnel awareness mentioned above, you won't know where you might have gaps or blockers that are costing you candidates if you're not collecting feedback.

When designing your CX survey, you'll want to consider when to send it and what to ask. There's no exact formula here. Some companies survey at each stage of the interview process, others just at the application or offer stage. I believe capturing feedback at the application and interview stages works well for most companies.

At the application stage, you'll want to learn more about how they found you and what they know or think about your company at that stage. Sample questions might include:

- How did you learn about this role?
- What were your thoughts on our company before applying?
- What websites did you use to learn more about us?
- Was the job description informative?
- Was the career site informative?
- What did you have a hard time learning or understanding about our company or role?

The answers to those questions are a gold mine in helping you tighten your external positioning. You can set this survey up as an automatically triggered survey from your applicant tracking system, or integrate with a third-party survey tool. Do *not* make it part of the application process, as it should be optional and you don't want to create unnecessary friction that might cost you applicants.

The interview survey will differ from the applicant survey. You'll want to ask questions that will help you gauge how your internal teams are managing the application process and (hopefully) building interest the deeper the candidates move into the funnel. Examples of questions you might ask here include:

- How long was the period between when you applied and when you heard from a recruiter or hiring manager?
- Did the recruiter help you understand the role and company?
- Did the description of the role align with your expectations based on the job description?
- Were all of your questions answered?
- Was the interview process professional (ie began on time, engaged interviewers, opportunities for you to ask questions etc)?
- Would you recommend your peers to consider jobs at our company?

The last question should be framed as an NPS question. It allows you to benchmark and measure trends over time. If those scores are dipping quarter over quarter, you know you have issues to address.

While all companies should be conscientious about candidate experience, it really comes into play for consumer-facing businesses where your candidates are likely your customers. A negative candidate experience can cost you more than a one-star review on Glassdoor – it can hurt your bottom line. Stitch Fix Chief People Officer Jevan Soo explains.

PRACTITIONER SPOTLIGHT
The business imperative of candidate experience

Jevan Soo, Chief People Officer, Stitch Fix

As a consumer company, when you're in high-growth mode and you are trying to get a lot of great talent to join you, it can be a double-edged sword. The wonderful thing about it is that you have a better shot at people quickly knowing you, resonating with you and having a relationship with you because you're a consumer brand out in the world.

Hopefully, they like what you do and what you are trying to create in the world. If they do, there's just a natural entry point for people to feel a deeper attachment and affinity. You start with an advantage in terms of that emotional connection.

On the other side, you're navigating two worlds at the same time. You're saying, 'I want to deliver an amazing candidate experience for you', but you're also navigating how candidates are experiencing your company in the broader world as a consumer. There are a number of other consumer brands that have shown how, when you have stumbles on either the people side or the consumer side, they end up affecting each other. Connecting those two worlds more deliberately is key.

For example, our PR team and my recruiting team are building even stronger connections now. They understand the fluidity of a candidate and a consumer journey in the world we live in and recognize there's both strength and challenge to that.

How do we best support our hiring managers and our recruiters to navigate that? Even if someone's not right for you as a candidate, who knows if their cousin is? Or their roommate? Or best friend? Any of whom could be ideal candidates.

It's my aspiration that every single candidate who spends time with us leaves as an advocate for the company, regardless of what happens in terms of their ultimate hiring decision. That is a very high hurdle, but it's a pretty good North Star to guide us all.

Many best-in-class companies also provide transparency and clarity about the recruiting and interview process up front. This ranges from detailed process overviews on career sites to auto-response FAQs covering most of the questions you know applicants will have about the process (timeline, steps, what to expect etc).

These steps may seem small, but whatever you can do to better support your applicants will pay dividends for your company and brand.

Recruiting reimagined: the rise of artificial intelligence

Could AI be the key to modernizing the recruiting process? Let's take a look at how AI *might* transform recruiting as we know it.

The resumé has been a staple of our hiring process for years. Candidates created chronological summaries of their employment history, job titles, responsibilities and education to impress hiring teams. Sure, we agonized over which paper stock would make the best first impression (pre-internet), or which font best says 'creative, but deadline-conscious (post-internet)', but the resumé has remained mostly unchanged (Schmidt, 2018).

For the most part, the same goes on the hiring side as well. Job descriptions have remained largely unchanged since they jumped from classified ads to online career sites and job boards. Some companies are jazzing them up with video, multimedia and hyperlinks – but, as mentioned earlier in this chapter, most job descriptions remain compliance-driven laundry lists of recycled responsibilities and qualifications.

Okay, but surely the application process has changed? Well, not really. Recruiters are now reviewing applications in their applicant tracking systems (ATS) as opposed to rifling through stacks of paper resumés, but it's still a human scanning a document to identify relevant skills and experience that may qualify the applicant for further human examination – each human with their own biases that steer and shape their assessment – even if only subconsciously.

On average, recruiters spend six seconds scanning a resumé to determine if they want to consider you for their company (O'Donnell, 2017). Six. Seconds. In the time it takes to have the internal debate on whether to upsize your soda, a recruiter is deciding your fate.

Even the best recruiters, armed with deep experience and efficiency honed by reading thousands of resumés, will miss great hires. Why?

There's a range of reasons, one of the more recent of which is that many career paths today aren't linear. We're still focusing our assessments on 'proven' experience and pedigree, rather than interest and potential. That's a very human mistake – and it's costing us candidates.

The antiquated case for 'fully baked' resumés

While recruiters run the interview process in most companies, the real decision making is driven by hiring managers – with lean teams, aggressive deadlines and pressure to do more with less. These factors drive an insatiable appetite for 'fully baked' candidates. Candidates who've worked in the right companies and went to the proper schools have the immediately transferrable responsibilities and vertically progressive career paths that position them into an instantly productive role. Those are really limiting, and subjective, criteria to use to make a hire.

That expectation of perfection is rooted in the ghosts of careers past – in the days of yore when careers were linear and everyone stayed on a vertical path of career progression within their specific field. That's just not how careers work today.

In George Anders' book, *The Rare Find* (2011), he coined the term 'jagged resumé' and laid a case for why today's careers (and resumés) don't look like those of yesteryear. As illustrated earlier in this book, many of today's careers paths often follow a lattice rather than a ladder. They pivot and shift and pause and reinvent. The linear vertical career paths coveted in the past are now being replaced by shorter tenures, stretch roles, entrepreneurial endeavours, time off work to spend with family, the gig economy and other 'work' constructs. Employees have changed their behaviour, but recruiters and hiring managers haven't reframed their thinking – and resumé expectations – to account for this shift.

Welcome to the (AI) future

Imagine a future where job descriptions and resumés no longer matter. Target candidate profiles are created by analysing massive amounts of data (pattern assessments of top performers, prioritized and weighted deliverables, application funnel history, performance data and more). Machine learning parses through all of these data to understand what experiences, traits, dispositions, career paths, and more, would allow for the highest odds of success in a role.

The resumé submission and application process will also change. Rather than sending a resumé, prospects would interact with a series of games and assessments that are custom designed to identify traits and profiles that best map to the profile of the job. The results are analysed by AI and matched to the position based on the likelihood of success in the role.

Career sites would be personalized based on your experience and interests, presenting jobs in your current discipline as well as other roles they deem your experience to be transferrable to. There would be AI career coaches who could map you to roles you might not even be imagining, send you training to bridge any gaps and validate your new skills and expertise.

We don't have to imagine these things because they already exist. AI and machine learning need a sizable dataset to add value, so most of these practices and tools are currently limited to enterprise companies. I imagine their use will be more widespread in the coming years.

As we embrace AI and other new technologies, we have to be mindful of their place in the greater landscape of recruiting. These tools should augment, not replace, human tasks. Johnny Sanchez, a seasoned recruiting leader with experience of leading progressive recruiting teams at Netflix, Hot Topic, Manduka and others, adds his perspective:

> As the recruiting industry was forced to embrace technology, much of the focus was on quantitative impact. While there is inherent value in this, it should never be the dominating factor. Advancements in the HR tech space should enhance and expand our opportunities for human interactions. Recruiting in the modern age is leveraging the right balance of design and technology that allows us to spend more time connecting and interacting with people. Building relationships and using our innate abilities to connect talent to the right opportunities. This is qualitative in nature, and just as important. The evolution of recruiting is all about leveraging technology to automate machine and manual tasks, and allow recruiters to do what they do best – engage with other humans.

Will AI replace recruiters? No. Is AI the key to removing all bias in hiring? No. Will AI become a ubiquitous part of our hiring technology in the coming years? Yes.

The future of recruiting will always be human, but it will be increasingly augmented by tools and technology that will benefit recruiters and job seekers alike.

Show me the ~~money!~~ numbers!

As the sophistication of recruiting has scaled, so has our ability to interpret and act on data. I'll go deeper in the next chapter on people analytics, but you can't have a chapter on modern recruiting without including our relationship with data.

A study by LinkedIn found that a slow recruiter who hires 10 high performers is far more valuable than one who efficiently hires 25 poor performers (LinkedIn, 2019). The report goes on to add:

> Tactical metrics – like time to hire, candidates per hire, or offer acceptance rate – track the immediate actions of your recruiters. That's a good starting point, but the future of recruiting will revolve around strategic metrics: those that measure the business outcomes of your team's efforts – not just the actions they take.
>
> The role of recruiting is rising. Shaping your business's talent strategy will be just as important as executing it. To do that well, you'll need to track the metrics that really matter.

The two most impactful metrics of the future are both strategic, results-based measures. Quality of hire and sourcing channel effectiveness – a measure of which sources produce quality hires – both account for the business impact of the people your team is bringing in.

Most recruiting teams still aren't tracking either, but the metric with the biggest gap between usefulness and actual use is candidate experience, a measure that we expect will become more commonplace in the near future.

Metrics are only useful if they're accurate. Data integrity is crucial to building data-driven recruiting programmes. It's also really difficult when you consider all the individuals touching data and making updates throughout your recruiting ecosystem.

Microsoft was spotlighted as a leader in this space in LinkedIn's Future of Recruiting report. They shared their tips for ensuring accurate metrics with LinkedIn:

1 Focus on one or two metrics at a time. At Microsoft, recruiting leadership selects just a few data fields to focus on every month or so. Recruiting managers communicate clear expectations to their teams so everyone's aligned on the proper way to record those metrics.

2 Track how well they're recording that data. Next, leaders will see which manager teams are doing the best job of tracking that month's metrics. Since they're only looking at a few data fields, it's relatively easy to audit accuracy and completion.

3 Source best practices across teams. Top-performing manager teams will share what they're doing differently to help everyone improve. 'The individual acts aren't that hard', says Chuck Edward, Microsoft's Head of Recruiting. 'It's more about building the habits and not skipping steps.'

As recruiters we've always had data, metrics and reporting. How we use them and how those data shape our strategy is one of the elements that distinguishes traditional versus transformational recruiting. In the next chapter on people analytics, we'll go deeper into what that looks like and where to start.

Becoming talent advisors

A talent advisor is the pinnacle of a recruiter role. It's a transcendent level of recruiting based on deep levels of trust between recruiters and hiring managers, informed by insights gleaned from data and market intelligence, and powered by clarity and mutual understanding.

The concept of talent advisors was influenced by industry veteran John Vlastelica. John is a veteran recruiting leader with experience of running global recruiting teams at Amazon and Expedia before launching his training and consulting firm, Recruiting Toolbox. He explains the evolution of the recruiting role.

PRACTITIONER SPOTLIGHT
Becoming a talent advisor

John Vlastelica, Founder and Managing Director, Recruiting Toolbox

The role of the corporate recruiter is evolving. It's moved from 'the hiring manager is my customer' to much more of a peer-to-peer relationship, where the *company* is my customer. It's no longer about 'taking the order' and accepting unrealistic target candidate profiles, unrealistic salary ranges and bad interviewing practices. It's moved to something more akin to a strategic partner.

Today's modern recruiters are true talent advisors. They bring external and internal insights into expectation-setting conversations, co-build realistic and diverse target candidate profiles with the hiring manager, recommend salary ranges, coach the hiring manager to play a leadership role around the interviewing and selection process, and engage the hiring manager as a key player in the closing process. Diversity is embedded in their approach. Not because of compliance, but because they know that talent is equally distributed across people, but access and opportunity are not. To improve diversity, they ensure hiring managers don't depend on candidate pedigree as a signal for quality, look outside of their homogenous teams for referrals, build interviewing teams that reflect the diversity they seek, and make fair, transparent, bias-free hiring decisions.

Great talent advisor recruiters recognize the opportunity to help individual hiring managers improve speed, quality and diversity. That's what hiring managers want and need. They approach their strategies and processes with those outcomes in mind: 'How am I helping this hiring manager define quality, find and assess that quality, and do it quickly to ensure we're building diverse teams?'

The very best talent advisors recognize the opportunity they have to impact the whole company and culture. They see their role as more than helping hiring managers recruit great talent... they see their role as making hiring managers better at hiring and creating a culture of recruiting. It's a dynamic role. They're part-trainer, part-coach, part-accountability partner. They know that the single biggest ROI impact they can influence is to build a culture where recruiting is a core capability required of every people manager. Hiring is not a bonus skill, or something top hiring managers do as a favour for recruiters.

Tools that talent advisors leverage include funnel metrics, speed metrics, quality of hire metrics, candidate experience feedback and diversity metrics. The insights from these tools allow them to diagnose strategy challenges, adjust processes and identify hiring manager skill gaps, and then partner with departmental or regional leaders to align hiring teams on what great looks like and the overall hiring plan.

One of the key characteristics of a talent advisor is their ability to influence and train hiring managers to be effective networkers, interviewers, closers and diversity champions.

If you work in a company where you're not yet operating as a talent advisor, don't worry. Most hiring managers actually *want* you to play a more strategic role; there is *pull from the business*. We've worked with thousands of hiring managers, hundreds of companies, in 20+ countries, and during our focus group conversations – where hiring managers share what they want more of from recruiters – almost all recognize that they need a strong partner, want more insights and are ready to improve their strategies and processes *if* you can show them how it gets them what they want: speed, quality and diversity.

As you can see, the way talent advisors approach recruiting, and the impact they have, is significantly more involved than transactional recruiters. Want to gauge where your recruiting team sits on the talent advisor spectrum? Use the Recruiting Toolbox eight-point checklist to gauge your ability to deliver as a talent advisor (Recruiting Toolbox, 2020):

1 **Hiring manager engagement:** We engage hiring managers so that they see recruiting top talent as a core part of their day job and view us as a partner, not a supplier. We effectively engage them in pre-funnel workforce planning, community engagement, passive candidate conversations, EVP development.

2 **External insights:** We leverage insights into market realities – talent availability, market salaries, target company offerings, target geos (location-based advertising for recruiting), immigration and relocation challenges, diversity availability etc – to set expectations with and make data-informed recommendations to our hiring managers and execs.

3 **Internal insights:** We establish our credibility and confidently help our hiring managers optimize speed, quality and diversity by leveraging historical sourcing, time in stage, funnel, offer, and diversity ROI data from prior internal recruiting successes to shape our strategy and process recommendations.

4 **Kickoff, not intake:** We leverage a quality, two-way conversation pre-sourcing to convert job descriptions into hiring criteria, align on the target candidate profile, strategy and process, and set expectations on trade-offs needed, our roles, and timeline expectations. We do not simply 'take the order'.

5 **Sourcing strategy:** We build and communicate a pragmatic sourcing strategy that leverages the highest ROI sources for each role or job family. We co-create the employer value proposition and messaging that will speak to our target candidate motivators and help with diversity. We effectively engage the hiring manager in networking/referrals and selling activities.

6 **Interview strategy:** We co-build and recommend an interviewing plan and process that includes the right type and number of interviewers and aligns our interviewing team on hiring criteria, focus areas and the sell. We create a brand-worthy, inclusive candidate experience that helps us appeal to the best talent.

7 **Decision making:** We facilitate transparent, rigorous, evidence-based hiring decision-making processes to ensure we're making fair, objective hiring decisions. We're prescriptive around our process to avoid groupthink, to assign proper weightings to our hiring criteria and to avoid both false positive and false negative hiring decision mistakes.

8 **Closing strategy:** We know that top talent is interviewing us as much as we're interviewing them, so we effectively engage our hiring teams to help us close top talent. We pre-close candidates, hiring managers, compensation/HR to ensure our offers are competitive, and we don't lose quality talent at the bottom of the funnel.

So where do you stand on that talent advisor diagnostic checklist? Five out of eight? Two out of eight? Very few companies are rocking a perfect score here, so don't feel bad if you have some work to do.

Let's take a look at a few companies building some of the practices we discussed in this chapter.

Case studies

Veterans are a large, highly skilled and trained workforce that is often untapped by employers. In our first case study, CVS shows how they partnered with the United States Department of Defense to tap into this talent pool with great success.

CASE STUDY
Building veteran recruiting programmes at CVS

David Lee, Director of Military Community Initiatives, CVS

Company: CVS Health
Region: North America
Industry: Healthcare and Medical
Company size: 10,001+

What they did

They developed a partnership with the Department of Defense SkillBridge programme to train and hire veterans.

Why they did it

To provide training to transitioning service members to help reduce post-service unemployment.

How they did it

Transitioning to post-military careers can be a challenge for thousands of veterans and their families. Veterans face unemployment rates over 40 per cent in the first three months after service and still over 30 per cent after nine months. At CVS Health their Workforce Initiatives team is currently using the Department of Defense SkillBridge Initiative at four military bases: Fort Bragg and Camp Lejeune in North Carolina, Norfolk Naval Base in Virginia, and Schofield Barracks in Hawaii to provide training to service members in their last six months of service and expanding to other locations.

Members of the military who are transitioning into civilian life connect with a CVS Health colleague to learn about job opportunities and explore how their skills can translate to a career within the company. Participants receive classroom and online training and complete a 12-week externship at a nearby CVS Pharmacy. Following the completion of their service, veterans are eligible to apply for any position at CVS Health.

In addition to CVS Health's participation in SkillBridge at Fort Bragg, the base hosts their company's Talent Connect Center (TCC), a training and employment facility. The TCC guides veterans and their spouses through CVS Health career opportunities nationwide, providing assistance throughout the application process, including support with resumés and virtual interviews.

Since 2016, they have trained 175 service members in their store manager training programme, which is run in part by CVS Health colleagues who are also veterans. In 2019, they expanded their training through the Hire Our Heroes Fellowship programme to a total of 10 bases, including Fort Bliss, TX; Shaw Air Force Base in South Carolina; Joint Base McGuire-Dix in New Jersey; and the USS *Carl Vinson*, a US Navy ship that ports in Bremerton, WA. Since 2015, they have hired over 18,000 colleagues with military experience and more than 7,000 military spouses.

Impact/ROI

These programmes save the Department of Defense unemployment expenses and provide the service member a chance to gain training and experience before leaving the military, while providing CVS Health colleagues who tend to have longer tenure with the company.

The vast majority of recruiting is done in real time. Transactional processes ramp up when a requisition gets approved. The ability to build and regularly engage prospects to have a ready pool of on-demand talent is a key differentiator for best-in-class corporate recruiting. In the next practitioner spotlight, Daniel Harris from Mott McDonald shows one way to approach this.

PRACTITIONER SPOTLIGHT
Building a talent pipeline model at Mott MacDonald

Daniel Harris, Head of Talent Acquisition, Mott McDonald

Throughout my career, I have led talent acquisition teams at some of the largest design consultancies in the world. Traditionally, a consultancy business model is to hire top talent and then charge clients a fee per hour for gaining access to this talent. It is critical that these consultancies access the talent they require in real time – not 30, 60 or 90 days later.

Many companies (not just consultancies) set their recruitment teams up to be reactive to requisitions as they come up, establishing a target time-to-fill from the moment a vacancy is created. This approach does not fit a consultancy business model, as time-to-fill is essential. Every day that goes by with an empty seat will cost the business money.

Over the years, I've supported numerous talent acquisition teams as they evolve their delivery to a talent pipeline model. This moves away from the traditionally reactive full-lifecycle recruiter and puts emphasis on pipelining and candidate experience over requisition management. A talent pipeline model splits the role of a full-cycle recruiter into two, the recruiter and the advisor.

- **The recruiter** is responsible for proactively going to market to source, engage and nurture talent. In addition to hiring talent, they're responsible for managing the pipeline of talent, creating engaging content and running a series of events for their pipeline. They generally spend their time facing the external market and engaging with the talent. The skill set required here is of both a recruiting detective, uncovering talent, but also a marketer, creating engaging content that will resonate with their target audience.

- **The advisor** is responsible for managing direct applications and ensuring an excellent candidate experience. They create engaging job copy, set up interviews and manage the onboarding. The skill set here is very different from a traditional recruiter, as the advisor is required to create copy and offer excellent support to the candidate and hiring manager. It's a blend of customer service and copywriting expertise, but doesn't require the 'in-front' nature of the recruiter.

Both the recruiter and the advisor work in unison and move candidates through a cyclical flow. As the recruiters identify talent in their pipelines, they feed them to the advisors once they move into a recruitment process. The advisor then manages the candidate through the process to a completed hire or feeds them back to the recruiter as a silver medallist to continue the relationship in the talent pipeline.

The main benefits of a talent pipeline approach are that you are setting up the organization to become the experts at identifying and delivering the talent to make their business successful, and that you are getting better talent faster as you are already in contact with talent before a need is required.

There are very few companies that can honestly say they've met their diversity goals. The reality is that almost all companies carry diversity debt. In this case study, Help Scout's Director of Talent Acquisition, Leah Knobler, shares their approach to turning it around.

CASE STUDY
Turning around diversity debt at Help Scout

Leah Knobler, Director of Talent Acquisition, Help Scout

Company: Help Scout
Region: North America
Industry: Science and Technology
Company size: 51–200 employees

What they did
We built an inclusive, diverse, 100+ person remote company.

Why they did it
We fell into a hole of diversity debt and needed to climb out authentically.

How they did it
In 2016, it was easy to look around at Help Scout and notice which identities were well represented and which were missing, but it was important to us to learn how people on our team self-identify so that we don't make assumptions. So, we launched our first demographic survey to see what the data said and to inform our goals.

Once we had data that showed our team was overwhelmingly white and male, especially on our engineering and design teams, it was clear we needed to be intentional. I became our first in-house recruiter and exclusively sourced people from underrepresented groups, while bringing in more unconscious bias training for hiring teams. We also moved to structured interviews and listened to and made changes from the feedback we received in candidate feedback surveys.

We also had to make sure Help Scout was an inclusive company where people of all identities could feel safe and supported. We wrote a company code of conduct that lists our values and beliefs around inclusion, and all new hires read and sign off on it.

We created dedicated, private Slack channels for different demographic groups (like ERGs but remote-friendly) in order to build community. Our parental leave policy used to allow different amounts of leave time for 'primary caregivers' versus 'secondary caregivers', so we changed the policy to be gender-neutral and more inclusive of all new parents. Our marketing team audited the content on our blog to remove ableist language and created a content style guide with guidance around inclusive language use on public-facing sites.

We have quarterly guest speakers come talk to the company over Zoom about topics relating to diversity and inclusion to help everyone learn and grow. We also went through the rigorous process of becoming a B Corps company, which means our purpose is not only profit, but a positive impact for employees, communities and the environment.

Impact/ROI

Data are taken from our demographic/inclusion surveys as well as our engagement surveys conducted twice a year:

- In 2016, Help Scout was 70% men, 30% women, and 82% white, 0% Black, 3% Latinx, 11% Asian.
- In 2019, Help Scout was 50% men, 50% women, and 75% white, 7% Black, 9% Latinx, 5% Asian.
- In 2016, Help Scout's Engineering and Design team was 90% men, 10% women, and 86% white.
- In 2019, Help Scout's Engineering and Design team was 60% men, 40% women, 76% white, 7% Black, 9% Latinx, 4% Asian.
- As of today, Help Scout's leadership team is 67% women (including women for VP of Engineering and VP of Product).

In 2020, our overall engagement score using Culture Amp's engagement survey was 91 per cent, and when filtered by the demographic of women, it's 93 per cent.

Ninety-three per cent responded agree/strongly agree to 'I feel like I belong at Help Scout.'

The role of a sourcer has always been difficult, but the challenges were certainly magnified in 2020. The founder of the Talent Agency, Stacy Zapar, explains how she adapted.

PRACTITIONER SPOTLIGHT
Sourcing in Covid times

Stacy Zapar, Founder, The Talent Agency

A sourcer's job is never easy. We need to identify highly sought-after professionals and convince those gainfully employed top performers to consider making a career move. This is tough even in normal times.

Now layer on all of the incredible circumstances we're dealing with during 2020: global pandemic and quarantine, record unemployment, many employees working from home for the first time (with kids!), uncertainty around childcare and schooling, record unemployment, racial injustice and inequality demonstrations (raising important issues that also impact hiring), financial worries, grief and a politically charged election year for those of us in the United States. Whew! We're all feeling overloaded and drained. Yet we're still expected to step up to the plate and deliver qualified candidates to our hiring teams.

There is so much uncertainty, but one thing that *is* clear is that fewer employees are voluntarily leaving their jobs and, as such, our job as sourcer has become exponentially harder. These were some of my best tips for sourcing in 2020. Your mileage may vary. :)

1 **Diversity sourcing** is more important than ever. Set measurable goals tied to the representative population from which you're sourcing. Hold hiring managers accountable. If you see issues, speak up. Not just because it's some new initiative or KPI, but because it's the right thing to do.

2 **Layoff lists** (such as those found at layoffs.fyi) are plentiful and a great resource for sourcers. But don't stop there, as the competition for that talent is fierce and saturated with recruiters. Use these lists to identify the companies and industries that are unstable and/or laying off, and source prospects who are still employed but likely have concerns around job security. As is always smart in sourcing, go where the competition isn't.

3 **Empathy** is a core theme in everything we do as sourcers, especially in 2020. Put yourself in your prospects' shoes as you're identifying candidates, crafting your outreach messages, conducting interviews, making offers and creating a stellar candidate experience. The idea of joining a new team (virtually) under a manager you've never even met in person is a scary prospect. For many, it feels safer to stay put and ride it out. What can we do to make people feel safe, get them to talk to us and even consider making a move right now? Approach everything you do with empathy.

4 **Referral sourcing** is a strategy that's worked very well for me. Use LinkedIn to source the connections of your current employees (former co-workers, classmates etc) to proactively drive referrals. Already knowing someone on the team can make a career change less scary. Involve your hiring team members and empower them to be advocates and ambassadors. (Caution: Be careful that this doesn't discourage a diverse pipeline! Use in conjunction with other sourcing methods.)

5   **ATS sourcing** is a great way to identify warm leads (former interviewees and applicants) who've expressed interest in joining your company in the past. These people are much more likely to consider your opening than a cold-sourced candidate.

6   **Patience and flexibility** are essential in our current work environment, not just with candidates and hiring managers, but also with ourselves. Practise self-care and take breaks as needed. Set realistic expectations. Be understanding when people are late to interviews or no-show to meetings. Everyone is carrying incredible burdens right now, so a little understanding is essential these days. Forgive others and forgive yourself when things go sideways. Because they will.

I imagine many recruiters are hitting the end of this chapter with a feeling of 'I wish you covered X' or 'I wish you went deeper on Y'. I hear you. As a recruiting wonk myself, it's such a dynamic time in the field and there's so much to cover these days. Confined to a chapter of a book, I tried to hit the key foundational elements with enough depth to frame how we should be thinking about recruiting. Here are some of the key takeaways from this chapter:

- Truly understand the business to effectively support its recruiting efforts.
- Embrace authenticity in your employer brand efforts – great programmes repel and attract.
- Scrap the traditional job description templates.
- Embed inclusive practices throughout the recruiting lifecycle.
- Personalize your sourcing efforts.
- Be cognizant of your candidate experience.
- Embrace data and become metrics-fluent.
- Strive for talent advisor relationships with hiring managers.

So now that you've worked so hard to bring exceptional talent into your company, how do you keep them? The next chapter is an exploration of the blossoming field of employee experience to help you build people programmes that retain talent.

References

Anders, G (2011) *The Rare Find*, Penguin, New York

Greenhouse Software (2019) Workplace Intelligence Report. Available from: https://grow.greenhouse.io/ (archived at https://perma.cc/CH4J-NYH3)

Hughes, M (2019) Study Shows We're Spending an Insane Amount of Time Online, *The Next Web*. Available from: https://thenextweb.com/tech/2019/01/31/study-shows-were-spending-an-insane-amount-of-time-online/ (archived at https://perma.cc/3H9Z-GNA4)

LinkedIn (2019) The Future of Recruiting: 7 Ways Your Role Will Change. Available from: https://business.linkedin.com/content/dam/me/business/en-us/talent-solutions/resources/pdfs/future-of-recruiting-report.pdf (archived at https://perma.cc/G6M7-JYH2)

O'Donnell, J T (2017) If Your Resume Isn't 6-Second Worthy, Studies Reveal Recruiters Will Toss It, *Inc*. Available from: www.inc.com/jt-odonnell/if-your-resume-isnt-6-second-worthy-studies-reveal-recruiters-will-toss-it.html (archived at https://perma.cc/XL4P-PQPU)

Recruiting Toolbox (2020) Talent Advisor Diagnostic Tool. Available from: https://go.recruitingtoolbox.com/talent-advisor-diagnostic-tool (archived at https://perma.cc/MC4H-RC4T)

Schmidt, L (2018) A Glimpse Into The Future of Recruiting, *Forbes*. Available from: www.forbes.com/sites/larsschmidt/2018/01/31/a-glimpse-into-the-future-of-recruiting/#5754aec03f2f (archived at https://perma.cc/4DR9-X3GA)

Simpson, J (2017) Finding Brand Success in the Digital World, *Forbes*. Available from: www.forbes.com/sites/forbesagencycouncil/2017/08/25/finding-brand-success-in-the-digital-world/#7efac244626e (archived at https://perma.cc/9859-76FE)

Talent Board (2019) Candidate Experience Benchmark Report. Available from: www.thetalentboard.org/benchmark-research/cande-research-reports/ (archived at https://perma.cc/89UA-NUCH)

08

The rise of employee experience (EX)

Remember when Human Resources was all about employee relations, compliance and employment law? I suppose technically that's still a core focus for some teams, but in progressive people functions it's a facet in a much larger portfolio of capabilities.

Today, we're more focused on the idea of employee experience – a more holistic way of grouping a range of initiatives that impact employees on a day-to-day basis.

When we talk about 'employee experience', we're covering a broad range of topics spanning physical work space, benefits, office configuration and amenities, workforce, hours, compensation, remote work, and much more. I'll explore some of those elements in this chapter. Others I'll cover more deeply later in the book.

'Employee relations' is a term that evolved from 'industrial relations' back when the function was largely focused on navigating the interrelations between employees, employers, trade/labour unions, employer organizations, and state and local organizations.

Technically, in this context employee relations is still a relevant and current component of HR. My view in this chapter is that the purview for modern people teams has grown much broader.

In this chapter, I want to examine some of the components comprising that broadened scope of employee experience. Some are common practices. Others are nascent fields I expect we'll see more of in the coming years.

Setting the foundation

If you're considering this through a Simon Sinek lens, you're probably starting with *why* (Sinek, 2009). Strong employee experience components have a direct correlation to your bottom line. Consider the analysis below from LinkedIn's Global Talent Trends report.

The business impact of employee experience

Companies that rated highly on:	Saw:
Compensation and benefits	56% lower attrition
Employee training	53% lower attrition
Purposeful mission	49% lower attrition
Flexible work arrangements	137% higher headcount growth

The business value may be clear, but the holistic idea of employee experience can feel overwhelming. Think about all the stages of the employee journey and segment them so that you can evaluate, assess and optimize each stage individually.

The 4 P's of employee experience (Figure 8.1), courtesy of LinkedIn's 2020 Global Talent Trends report, is an easy way to think about it (LinkedIn, 2020). It breaks down employee experience in a way that captures the entire journey and makes it manageable.

Josh Bersin is one of the leading minds in HR. He's been at the forefront of innovation in the field and has a finger on its pulse like few others. His insights are drawn from a mix of his deep data surveys and reporting, his robust network of CHROs and HR tech companies, and an ability to identify future trends. In a recent report on employee experience, Josh presented a roadmap on how HR teams can influence employee experience (Bersin, 2019):

Design thinking – this really matters: It's time for you to 'empathize' with your employees, follow them around, survey and interview them, and sit down with them in workshops. They will tell you what bugs them at work, and you'll hear all sorts of little things that make work difficult.

Start with the basics: Look at the common 'moments that matter' at work first, and flatten these issues completely. Onboarding, job changes, relocation, and all the little things can really bog people down if they're difficult. Every company can look at these topics and map out better solutions.

FIGURE 8.1 The 4 Ps of employee experience

People

The who
- Relationships with managers, teams, and leadership
- Interactions with customers and suppliers

Place

The where
- Physical work space
- Flexible work options
- Work–life balance

Product

The what
- The work itself and how stimulating it is
- Match between tasks and skill level

Process

The how
- Rules/norms for how gets done and is rewarded
- Degree of complexity in tools and technologies

LinkedIn Global Talent Trends, p 10. Reproduced with permission

Partner with IT and Finance: As I discuss in the Employee Experience Platform report, none of these problems is HR's alone. Bring Finance and IT into the team immediately, they are going to be part of the solution.

Practise co-creation: Every solution you develop should be 'co-created' with business people and leaders. There's no way to improve the employee experience without employees being involved. We have to work with them to fix old and broken processes, design new systems, and make work easier. Job shadowing is a good practice to use.

Look at new tools: The ERP and HCM platforms may not help as much as you think. Every client I met with in Europe told me their big HR systems project did NOT necessarily improve the employee experience. In some cases they did, but only if they looked at the platform project as an 'employee experience project.'

Practise process simplification: Every 'process harmonization' project I uncover comes down to one thing. We have a tendency in business to make things too complicated. As your company grows, acquires, and changes, people keep tacking on new steps, approvals, and branches to everything.

Segment the workforce: We can't possibly fix every employee's experience in every way at once, so we need to segment the workforce. After we take care of the basics (i.e. core HR practices, IT), we can move into specific strategies for the workforces or personas that matter most.

These are all important steps that must be considered collectively to enhance employee experience. Design thinking, in particular, is an approach that's quickly gained traction in designing HR and talent programmes. If you're not familiar with design thinking, it's an iterative process that seeks to understand the user and redefine problems in an attempt to identify alternative strategies and solutions. The reverse-engineering of processes, starting with the issue from the user's perspective, helps uncover solutions that might not be obvious based on our initial understanding of the challenge.

It's an empathy-led process, as it's driven by the perspective of the individuals it will impact – not forced upon them like many legacy HR approaches.

As the focus on employee experience grows, the need for HR leaders in this space grows with it. Since 2015, there's been a 240 per cent increase in HR professionals with 'employee experience' in their title (Figure 8.2).

FIGURE 8.2 Employee experience roles are rapidly growing, LinkedIn (2020)

Number of LinkedIn members whose current job titles include the phrase 'employee experience'.

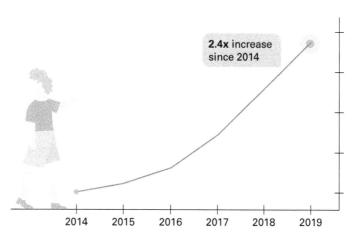

2.4x increase since 2014

2014   2015   2016   2017   2018   2019

LinkedIn Global Talent Trends, p 11. Reproduced with permission

As you now know, the field of EX is quite broad (and could easily be its own book). To properly set expectations, this chapter will focus mostly on organization and workforce design and structure – the how, what and why behind strictures that make (or break) our organizations. Let's dig in.

Career lattices and new organizational models

Remember career ladders? Those linear career progression maps based on well-defined job families with roles of escalating responsibility and titles? Back when the only way to progress someone in their career was usually vertically? Those were simple days. Those days, at least in the sense of linear progression being your *only* option as an employee, are gone.

Employees today don't want ladders, they want lattices, options. They want opportunities to grow and develop linearly and horizontally. Opportunity equals retention.

This shift happened within a generation. Most of us GenX employees inherited a system built by the Baby Boomers before us. It was predicated on a tiered system of roles and a set hierarchy of the organization chart. We played that game to start our career, willing to 'pay our dues' to advance one rung at a time up the corporate latter.

[Editorial note: I'm usually not one to focus on generational differences because I think it's lazy thinking to apply a set mould of archetype characteristics to a broad population, so when I use terms like Boomers and GenX I'm speaking more to age ranges than traits ascribed to them.]

Okay, Boomer. Younger generations aren't interested in corporate ladders. According to a Deloitte (2018) survey, 43 per cent of millennials plan to leave their jobs within two years. Only 28 per cent plan to stay beyond five years. This is the generation that will be 76 per cent of the global labour pool by 2025. If you're not designing organization structures that align with their needs (see 'Tours of duty' later in this chapter), you're going to struggle to attract and retain talent.

Our thinking needs to go deeper than ladders and lattices. In the 21st century, the traditional organization chart hierarchy began to give way to new forms of governance. Let's go deeper on a few of these new approaches.

Hello goodbye, holocracy

In 2015, the holocracy model of non-hierarchical self-governance, 'no job titles, no managers, no hierarchy', was thrust into the spotlight after Zappos embraced it. As one of the renowned trailblazers for progressive HR, Zappos' move caught the attention of many in the industry and they pondered whether self-governance could really work. Could this be the future of high-performing teams?

Within a year, 18 per cent of Zappos employees opted to take a severance package and leave the company. Many cited the lack of role clarity as a reason for their departure. They've since moved away from pure holocracy to more of a hybrid model (Groth, 2020).

Other companies, including Medium, adopted holocracy practices for a period of time before abandoning them for more traditional organization structures. There are still some companies operating under this model, but most of the tech world saw more friction than value.

Embracing agile

Agile practices quickly rose to favour as an efficient model built for scale. Companies like Spotify, Google, ANZ, IBM and others have adopted agile teams with names like squads, chapters, tribes and guilds. Rather than relying on traditional siloed corporate functions, agile models create fluid cross-functional teams designed around projects and specific work to be delivered. The idea behind agile is that it allows companies to innovate, adapt and evolve more quickly by avoiding traditional and cumbersome hierarchical models.

PRACTITIONER SPOTLIGHT
Embracing agile in HR

Mike Clementi, Unilever EVP, Global Markets

Agile practices have been getting a lot of attention over the past 24 months. This has been fuelled in 2020 by the pandemic, as many companies, knowingly or unknowingly, were forced to work in new ways, breaking traditional cultural norms and behaviours and working in real time to reinvent policies, practices and processes.

At the heart of agile working is mindset. It is about focusing on what matters most, which is value through the eyes of the consumer/customer, in essence, the end user, and then deliver value as fast as possible – what is known as a minimal viable product, an MVP. To do this, you institute rituals or ceremonies that are dedicated to ensuring that all team members are focusing on value and speed to the consumer.

Rather than working on several projects at once, something we have all got used to over the years, ruthless prioritization is key. Once priorities are known, simple tools, like working in sprints and squads with regular, short stand-up meetings, kanban boards, retrospectives and demos, are all necessary to build new muscle and rigour.

Covid-19 has helped companies focus on value, working on short-cycle teams, learning, failing fast, reiterating and working in collaborative ways that many of us only started to test pre-Covid. As HR professionals, we need to ensure that we retain the positive learnings that have come from Covid as we build cultures and norms that are fit for purpose in today's fast-paced world.

Agile shares some DNA with holocracy in the sense of aiming to minimize bureaucracy and rigid hierarchy. However, rather than stripping away all titles/structure, agile processes implement minimal viable bureaucracy with an aim of balancing high alignment with high autonomy.

Spotify's version of the agile manifesto is based on five core principles (Kamer, 2018):

Continuous improvement: At Spotify, part of my work is to look for ways to continuously improve, both personally, and in the wider organization.

Iterative development: Spotify believes in short learning cycles, so that we can validate our assumptions as quickly as possible.

Simplicity: Scaling what we do is key to Spotify's success. Simplicity should be your guidance during scaling. This is as true for our technical solutions as for our methods of working and organizing the organization.

Trust: At Spotify, we trust our people and teams to make informed decisions about the way they work and what they work on.

Servant leadership: At Spotify, managers are focused on coaching, mentorship, and solving impediments rather than telling people what to do.

Their embrace of agile coupled with their commitment to autonomy, trust and career development seems to be working. Spotify brought in $7.44 billion in revenue in 2019 and now stands at over 3,600 employees (Schneider, 2019).

The agile approaches provide some clear advantages to tech companies that are regularly delivering software or shipping products. Could it work outside that space?

My first experience with agile was during my time running talent acquisition and innovation at NPR. Our engineering and development teams used scrum (a framework of agile) and held quarterly workshops for new employees to learn about the practice. I was curious about applying agile practices to our HR team, so I joined a training session and was quickly hooked.

My idea board and project wish list were all over the place. I turned my whiteboard into a scrum board and mapped out my stories (ie projects) and categorized their sub-projects (deliverables) into: To Do, In Progress, Done. That gave me and my team real-time visibility of progress, dependencies and delays. I was hooked, and got more done that year than in the prior two years. Agile, for the win!

PRACTITIONER SPOTLIGHT
We've got it wrong about agile

Perry Timms, Founder and Chief Energy Officer, People
and Transformational HR

If you read some of the business press of late, it's a mixture of lauding agility (in light of the Covid-19 responses) in working from home and adapting to social distancing and PPE for key workers and agile, the way of delivering tech products in sprints. In the latter, the narrative is that it's overused and probably dead as a 'methodology'. Quite what is in its place I'm yet to see.

I've been interested in, and eulogizing for some years now about, the dawning of a wholeness-based workplace – where you come alive through your work and have economic exchanges and build meaningful relationships.

Agile, holocracy, Teal, self-managed squads, design thinking, impact mapping, networked teams, Rendanhayi, Cynefin. All around us are amazing pearls of wisdom, and yet, many are being ignored in favour of the inculcation of what we know is making us unwell. By unwell I mean the categorization by the World Health Organization that burnout is an officially recognized condition of ill health.

The demonization and fetishization of work has us caught in a paradox, yet there are a lot of spaces between hating work as suppressing the masses and romanticizing work, with it your only thing in life, ignoring friends, family, love and the wonders of the world.

Agile is – I believe – a big part of the answer to closing this paradox and building more inclusive, participative and fulfilling workplaces, whatever the industry or size.

Agile – as a method of developing tech products that came from the Agile Manifesto of February 2001 – has been at the heart of developing software. It has arguably seen us move from huge lumbering programmes, which often became bloated, slow and ineffective platforms and applications, to nimble, iterative, fast-paced development that has seen the software giants of the world amass huge spread and, with it, wealth.

Since 2010, I've been experimenting with it in HR, Organization Design (OD), Learning and Development (L&D), and Change. And I enshrined my thinking behind it in the creation of a new model for HR – the Transformational HR model – with four zones, not three functions: People Performance & Development; People & Programme Support; People Strategy & Partnerships; and People & Organizational Transformation. Not four functions, but overlapping and episodic movement around these zones pertinent to the needs of the people and the business.

Without agile, it's my assertion that HR would be in serious trouble. As we head towards a post-pandemic recession or even depression, we will see businesses need to pivot constantly to meet needs, deal with a lack of financial resources and a still-increasing pressure to be a safe-house employer, be an ecological guardian not a destroyer, and mean more to communities and society.

So the reports of agile's demise are premature. Maybe tech has a new way to get its products user-friendly and to take over the world, but in HR, OD, L&D and Change, we're only just getting started and, I believe, we will show why agile truly was conceived.

People-powered change.

Is agile right for your company? Maybe. The truth is that there are a range of variables that determine what models best support a company's organizational structure, goals and growth plans. I'm not here to pitch one over another – just to plant the seed that new ways of thinking just *might* get you to those goals faster.

Internal mobility

The importance of talent mobility is now clearly understood by the C-suite. A Deloitte study in 2019 found that 76 per cent of executives responded that internal mobility is important, with 20 per cent rating it as one of their organization's top three most urgent issues (Volini, Indranil and Schwartz, 2019). While the imperative is there, there are blockers to be overcome. The survey listed roadblocks to internal talent mobility, including:

- lack of process to identify and move employees (49%);
- availability of internal employees to fill roles (48%);
- current manager's resistance to internal moves (46%);
- lack of information for employees on available roles (45%).

This deserving executive focus, illustrated above by Deloitte, reinforces why we need to rethink how we approach mobility.

If we accept that today's workforce is more fluid than ever and that talent mobility is crucial, we have to shift how we approach developing, engaging and retaining our employees. This includes helping guide them out of our companies when their aspirations and interests no longer align.

Internal career coaching and development has long been a component of Human Resources. Often, it was focused on 'high potential' employees and succession planning to ensure continuity in leadership roles. What if we adapted our thinking and created a dedicated workforce coaching team that was entirely based around the development of an individual? Coaches aimed at bringing the best out of each employee around their individual goals and aspirations, *not* the company's? What might that look like?

Imagine your company has a dedicated team of career coaches. They may or may not sit directly in HR. These coaches are tasked with being dialled into external market conditions and trends in the workforce, technology, emerging markets, digital branding and so on. They have semi-regular meetings with each of your employees to talk about their career growth plans and aspirations. These conversations aren't limited to jobs within your company.

The coaches are tasked with creating individualized development plans, including resources and budgets to support each employee's growth. They're empowered to provide counsel and advice that prioritizes outcomes for the individual – not the company. This means that when the aspirations no longer align with internal opportunities, the coaches steer them towards external opportunities that do.

Yes, the coaches direct them to leave your company.

As a recruiter, even typing that feels counterintuitive, but think about it. If you can build a company with an earned reputation of being an absolute developer and incubator of talent, what will that do for your ability to back-fill those employees with more exceptional talent? You will have alumni singing your praises about the development they received while they were there, and the impact that their time in their role with you had on their career. They'll be lifelong fans and advocates.

Other companies will cherish your alumni as they know the development invested in your employees. The money invested in your career coaches could pay for itself a few times over in reduced recruiting costs.

Play the long game and reap the results.

PRACTITIONER SPOTLIGHT
Navigating career options

Jevan Soo, Chief People Officer, Stitch Fix

Employees have so many career options, both externally and internally. That can become overwhelming in the same way that tyranny of choice with consumer products can overwhelm people.

One of the things that I have seen over the past several years is people saying, 'I don't want to go back to the time where I had a career track that was prescribed to me and that was the only thing I could do. Where you just had to put on your blue suit and your red tie and grab your suitcase and sign up for the next 30 years.' I don't think anyone wants to return to that, but they're also saying, 'Look, this new world is really challenging! There are so many things available to me, even just within this company, as well as over the broader course of my career.' How do they navigate this?

I think it's a real competitive advantage to build an organization where leaders are equipped to handle those conversations and help talented people navigate those choices. When I think about my own career and some great managers I've had as well as people I've managed, some of the most powerful moments have been where we've had conversations that weren't as scripted. It wasn't straightforward in saying, 'This is the career path, here are the next two steps, do these things' and so on.

Instead it was: 'You have a diversity of interests. You have a diversity of talents. You could actually do three different things. How do we think about that? What are the personal things that attach to that in terms of trade-offs for you? How would this fit into the broader life that you want to have? What are the different ways that we could shape your work over the next coming year that would give you that optionality?'

Those conversations I think are more thrilling and more fulfilling for people, inspire them and make them want to stay on teams and at companies. They're also damn hard. For managers, they're not the same conversations that you had to have 30 years ago. It's somewhere I want to lean into, building that capability and mindset in our leaders.

Some companies are already embracing this thinking and building fluid internal mobility programmes that allow employees to opt into internal mobility hubs that list their skills and interests, and allow them to be contacted for internal roles – giving employees more ownership over their own career development.

In 2020, France-based energy management company Schneider Electric introduced an internal mobility platform – Open Talent Market *(note: I'll go deeper on this in a case study at the end of this chapter)* (Anderson, 2020). The aim was to create an 'internal gig economy' for their 135,000 employees in 100+ countries supported by AI matching technology and including postings, mentors, training opportunities and part-time work. The platform was put to heavy use in 2020 with the impact of Covid-19. It allowed their talent team to match employees with excess capacity with managers with labour shortages.

I asked Schneider Electric's VP of Talent Digitization, Andrew Saidy, what was the genesis and drive behind creating the Open Talent Market. He said: 'If you're doing your day-to-day job and nothing else, you're not acquiring new experiences. We want to create new opportunities for employees to acquire new experiences and skills. We've always told our employees that they own their careers, that they are in the driver's seat. The open talent marketplace makes that a reality.'

Creating new experiences and skills can do wonders for retention – and ultimately your bottom line. Before launching Open Talent Market, nearly half of departing Schneider employees cited lack of opportunity as their reason for leaving. A 1 per cent reduction in attrition could represent millions of dollars in savings – not to mention the brain drain that comes with regrettable turnover.

Obviously, you need to have a certain level of scale for a platform like this to work, but the advantages are clear. When you create internal opportunities and remove internal bureaucratic restrictions on talent mobility, everyone wins. Upskilling and training can be focused on work and skills needed for company initiatives – or it can go beyond that.

The ability to re-allocate on the fly was demonstrated again during Covid-19 when Bank of America built their coronavirus crisis response team by temporarily converting more than 3,000 employees from a range of banking positions and temporarily putting them into roles supporting the onslaught of calls from small business and consumer customers (Ungarino, 2020).

Basecamp, a project management and work productivity platform, takes a novel approach to all things work, including training. Their co-founder and CEO, Jason Fried, explains why:

> It's about creating an environment where people can do the best work of their lives and they feel supported by the company, and the company can help them be better versions of themselves even outside of work.
>
> Something we do at Basecamp, for example, is pay for continuing education beyond your trade. If you're a designer, maybe companies will send you to a conference or a design conference. If you want to learn how to fly a plane or you want to learn how to be a better cook or you want to learn how to throw pots on a wheel or you want to paint, we'll pay for those classes for you too that have nothing to do with your career. They just are supportive of you as an individual because we want you to be able to do things and be a more interesting person and pursue things and get a little bit of help from a company that you dedicate your day to.
>
> That's what is really interesting about HR, and of course there's also the other side which is mental health and helping people through problems and helping people who are struggling. It's the human part.

We have to guard against losing that *human part* in our quest to evolve the field and optimize our impact. We can't reduce the humanity of our employees down to headcount figures, organization charts and succession plans. We must keep that in mind as we develop, engage and grow our teams.

Tours of duty

Every now and then, I'll read a book or article about work that gets seared into my brain and reshapes how I view the field. That was how I felt after being introduced to the concept of 'tours of duty' by LinkedIn Founder Reid Hoffman's 2014 book *The Alliance: Managing talent in the networked age* (Hoffman, Casnocha and Yeh, 2014).

I'm old enough to remember the *Tour of Duty* television show and young enough to have played the *Call of Duty* video game. Reid's version speaks more to a construct between employee and employer based on candour around alignment, expectations and duration – an honest discussion about creating win–win job partnerships based on short- to medium-term mutually understood goals. The book describes the tour of duty alliance as:

> In an alliance, the manager can speak openly and honestly about the investment the company is willing to make in the employee and what it expects in return. The employee can speak openly and honestly about the type of growth he [sic] seeks (skills, experiences, and the like) and what he will invest in the company by way of effort and commitment. Both sides set clear expectations.

Rather than open-ended employment that lacked clarity and direction beyond the immediate role you were hiring into, this Tour of Duty approach focused on the impact you'd make, what you'd learn/how you'd benefit, and the duration for those things to happen (usually 2–4 years).

I've collaborated with LinkedIn extensively over the years and have many friends there. I've seen them move between (entirely different) teams, relocate around the world and reinvent themselves based on their understanding of the employment alliance and expectations they have.

Reid and his co-authors Ben Casnocha and Chris Yeh described tours of duty to the *Harvard Business Review* (Hoffman, Casnocha and Yeh, 2013).

FROM 'TOURS OF DUTY: THE NEW EMPLOYER–EMPLOYEE COMPACT'
Harvard Business Review

The tour-of-duty approach works: The company gets an engaged employee who's striving to produce tangible achievements for the firm and who can be an important advocate and resource at the end of his [sic] tour or tours. The employee may not get lifetime employment, but he [sic] takes a significant step toward lifetime employability. A tour of duty also establishes a realistic zone of trust. Lifelong employment and loyalty are simply not part of today's world; pretending that they are decreases trust by forcing both sides to lie.

Why two to four years? That time period seems to have nearly universal appeal. In the software business, it syncs with a typical product development cycle, allowing an employee to see a major project through. Consumer goods companies such as P&G rotate their brand managers so that each spends two to four years in a particular role. Investment banks and management consultancies have two- to four-year analyst programmes. The cycle applies even outside the business world – think of US presidential elections and the Olympics.

After reading *The Alliance* I began thinking of my own career in terms of tours of duty, keeping my horizon at 1–2 years at a time. What is my focus this year? Will this [project, client, conference etc] further that? Can I add unique value to help them further their goals? It made me rethink the very nature of employment. If you haven't yet, I highly recommend you read it.

Remote work goes mainstream

March 2020 was the month that remote work went mainstream. As Covid-19 quickly spread from China to Europe, North America and the rest of the world, what was once a somewhat isolated practice suddenly became the default for millions of employees. It was a turning point and retired the notion of remote being a 'future of work' pillar. That future was now.

As Covid-19 raced across the globe, the world of work was turned upside down. It started with conference and business travel cancellations, and seemingly overnight broadened to a full shift to remote work. There's never been such a radical and sudden shift in the workplace.

To be clear, this impacted a segment of the overall workplace. Many front-line workers and those in positions not suited to working from home continued to work as usual – this doesn't apply to them. Not yet at least.

As the pandemic unfolded, HR and IT departments scrambled to ensure continuity. They were developing new playbooks on the fly. On the HR side, people leaders looked to each other and moved away from the function's siloed past to embrace open-source practices.

This seemingly overnight shift was shocking in its seamlessness. Sure, there were adjustments for companies that were dominantly office-centric, but the velocity of the change necessitated by the global pandemic forced even the most stalwart 'office' types to reconsider their views.

One of the biggest perceived knocks against distributed work has been a perception that its remote workers can't be productive. That should have been laid to rest two months into the pandemic when most organizations continued to maintain operations and deadlines – despite the pandemic.

This 'no going back' perspective is shared by GitLab's Head of Remote, Darren Murph, during our conversation on the 21st Century HR podcast: 'This remote ball is rolling. This is what remoters have understood for a really long time. Many people that have had their identity tightly tied to the office so it's been difficult for them to envision working remotely. When Covid-19 broke down that belief where there was no physical office happening in their life every day, it gives them that freedom to ask those questions' (Murph, 2019).

Let's also be honest about what was happening at this time. This isn't 'optimal' remote work. This was 'I'm now a home school teacher wrapping up my 10th Zoom meeting of the day and trying to meet deadlines while stress-eating half a box of doughnuts for dinner' remote work. These are the worst suboptimal conditions that could possibly exist – yet most employees were still getting it done.

Many CEOs came forward during the early months of their newfound remote structure, expressing surprise at the maintained productivity levels and minimal disruption they saw in the shift. Others admitted that their aversion to remote was driven largely by their own personal struggles to be effective outside the offices, and the assumed or inherited correlations that if they couldn't be productive, their employees couldn't either. Even the staunchest advocates for 'we all need to be here' approaches are forced to rethink that dogma during these times.

While Covid-19 was clearly an accelerant for remote work, the sentiment was already shifting that way. In Greenhouse's 2019 Workplace Intelligence Report (Greenhouse, 2019), 70 per cent of surveyed employees agreed or strongly agreed that they would be open to working remotely (Figure 8.3).

As regions around the world began phases of reopening, companies were then faced with a decision on whether and how they would return to an office. What that might look like? How would they determine who would return, and when?

FIGURE 8.3   I am open to working remotely

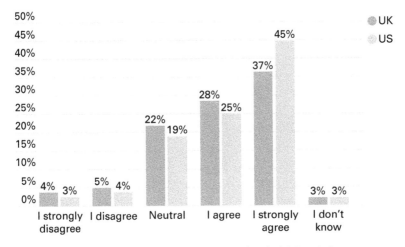

Greenhouse Workplace Intelligence Report, 2019. Reproduced with Permission

The complexity of safely returning to offices is massive. A question many CEOs are currently grappling with is: Is it worth it?

The likelihood is that most of them will land somewhere in between. One of the first major companies to take a public stance on this question was Twitter. They sent waves through the tech sector after CEO Jack Dorsey notified employees that those who preferred remote work could choose to remain to do so 'forever'. He's far from the only CEO with that view.

The most important term in that announcement wasn't '*forever*'; it was '*choose*'. Some employees couldn't return to an office fast enough. Others were wracked with anxiety at the thought of public transport, commuting times, childcare, underlying health conditions and a range of topics that make the thought of going back into an office a nightmare scenario.

By notifying employees early, even while California – where most of their team resides – remained under shelter-in-place orders, Twitter removed the uncertainty and allowed employees to have one less stress to navigate during their day. Employees want choice. They want the flexibility to decide how and when and where to get their work done.

At this point in time, that model of distributed work had already been proved by (largely tech) pioneers, including GitLab, Automattic, InVision, Elastic, Zapier and more. The majority of companies that embrace *remote* are actually hybrid models where they have populations of employees in offices and pockets of remote employees spread around the world.

Many of these companies were remote from day one, as GitLab's Head of Remote Darren Murph recounts:

> GitLab was remote from day one. The first three employees were in three different countries, so they had no choice but to be remote. There was this brief moment of time when the company came to California and went through Y Combinator (a US company that provides seed funding for start-ups). You get an office coming out of Y Combinator, so for a brief period we had one. It lasted three days. The people just stopped showing up and the work still got done and they just let it go. So we sort of serendipitously fell into being remote. It was really beneficial that the founders understood the recognition of documentation very early on. They wrote everything down. If you have a vision for scaling up, writing things down when there's not a lot to write down is going to pay massive dividends.
>
> Now GitLab is over 1,200 people and we still benefit from what was written down in month one. The amount of knowledge leaks that we've prevented, because we were heavy on documentation, is amazing. So, start writing stuff down today. Build a company handbook. Start it as a FAQ, just answering some basic questions that people have across the remote landscape. In six months, you'll have a shocking amount of content written down.

Entirely distributed models can offer a range of advantages, from commercial real-estate and operations savings to being able to tap into a truly global pool of talent. There are also disadvantages. Building interpersonal work relationships, trust and culture is difficult when the majority of your interactions are via screens. Navigating time zones and cultural differences may be an added layer of complexity to navigate versus an organization where everyone is under one roof.

So how to do you get remote right? Let's go back to GitLab's Darren Murph for a crash course in designing remote for the long haul.

PRACTITIONER SPOTLIGHT
Designing remote for the long haul

Darren Murph, Head of Remote, GitLab

The key is to implement as many remote-first practices as you possibly can – not just because this helps people who are remote now, but because it will help you be more effective and efficient as you transition back to the office.

Let's say you have five or six people in an office boardroom and then five or more people were joining in remotely. The right way to do this meeting is to have the six people in the office all open up their individual laptops and look into individual webcams so that you create a level playing field for the entire meeting party. This is going to feel awkward for the people in the room, but that's entirely the point.

I want the people in the room after the meeting to look at each other and say, 'How many hours did we spend commuting to do this in this room when clearly it wasn't necessary?' This is kind of the mental unlocking of, 'Can this really be done from anywhere? Does it really require us to be in an office?'

You're seeing that myth break down. You've always been told that your job can't be done remotely, or this element of the job can't be done remotely and then all of a sudden, it turns out it can – even in the worst of circumstances.

This isn't the 'future of work'; this is now just work. There will be parts of your company that remain remote – and in many cases already were. If you have an office in Singapore and an office in London, those subsets of people have always been remote to each other. Implementing remote-first practices will help you thrive as a company even if you have both of those subsets going back to the office.

Distributed work is democratizing. To do remote right, what you should do is get all of the executives out of the office for a meaningful amount of time, at least a month, ideally a quarter. Force them to have all of their meetings on Zoom. Force them to document things that they may just verbalize to someone, to really put discipline and intentionality behind the things that they're doing. You'll start to see communication gaps – things that don't funnel up to the top or funnel back down to people who need this information. Document what those issues are.

When you're not in the office, there's no Band-Aid solution. You have to be intentional about making sure that your communication is rock solid and seamless all the way up and all the way back down. Covid-19 broke down the barriers for executives who were unsure about remote. It allowed them to understand the mentality of the remoter, and how things work and how things are different.

As more companies shift to remote and/or hybrid models, HR teams will need to determine how the policies and programmes might have disparate impacts on different populations. Do you have 'office policies' applied to remote employees? Should you consider 'remote policies' for in-office employees? Perhaps a hybrid model?

If your company expects to have a large percentage of your workforce remote, or at least having the option to choose, you may want to consider building remote-first policies and programmes. They tend to be more equitable for all employees, regardless of location, as they don't penalize employees who aren't coming into the office on a regular basis.

Work becomes 'work'

The very notion of what it means to work is evolving. Once, the terms we used to talk about workers were fairly limited: exempt, non-exempt, full-time equivalents (FTEs), contractors, consultants. Most companies had reasonably static headcount plans and budgets, and teams built for long-term projects.

Many large companies of the past were built on a 'throw headcount at it' approach. This led to bloated and overstaffed organizations that made it difficult to nimbly shift or reskill when market opportunities arose that didn't align with their existing capabilities.

The past couple of years have begun to extend and redefine our definition of work. The rise of the gig economy, whether by choice or necessity, created a new category of on-demand dynamic talent. Platforms like Upwork, Fiverr, 99Designs and others allowed companies to augment their internal teams with freelancers and consultants around the world. Companies now have alternatives to the traditional approach of investing large amounts of time and finances looking for full-time employees. They can stand up a team of specialists in a matter of days to solve problems and get work done.

Let's look at some of the key numbers from Upwork's 'Freelancing in America 2019' report (Upwork, 2019):

- Fifty-seven million Americans freelanced in 2019 (as much as 35% of the US workforce).

- Younger generations are more likely to freelance: Gen Z (53%), Millennial (40%), Gen X (31%), Baby Boomers (29%).

- Freelancing contributes nearly a trillion dollars to the US economy (almost 5% of GDP).

- Fifty-one per cent of freelancers say they will not go back to a traditional job.

These numbers are hard to ignore. They also present a real opportunity for savvy organizations to scale faster and more efficiently than traditional methods (note: just be sure you're compliant with local labour regulations).

As the Covid-led shift to remote gave more employees their first experience with the freedom and autonomy of distributed work, expect the pools of freelance talent – and even teams or guilds or independent employees – to be relied upon more as a talent pool for companies.

A 2016 report by Accenture, 'Liquid Workforce: Building the workforce for today's digital demands', saw this coming. It detailed how legacy businesses were moving away from traditional models to embrace more agile approaches for their workforce. The core premise is the shift from today's model for building companies, based on static workforces organized around specific skills and functions, to tomorrow's approach of agile and adaptable workforces organized around projects with embedded training and skill development.

For example, the report details how industrial-age-founded GE launched *FastWorks*, a programme aimed at embedding lean start-up practices into its workforce and accelerating their pace of change. This includes upskilling and reskilling employees to retain and redeploy employees to better align with business needs (Accenture, 2016). The new *FastWorks* methodology allowed GE to build a new regulation-compliant diesel engine that shipped nearly two years ahead of their competitors.

So, what are the barriers to employee experience? As LinkedIn's graphic in Figure 8.4 illustrates, they are many of the components that align to modern HR as outlined in this book.

As we think about optimizing employee experience, we should be mindful of the mindset of where employees are today. We've experienced a range of once-in-a-generation events triggered by Covid-19 and social justice consciousness. Every one of your employees has been impacted by these events in some way. Many still are.

These events have caused introspection and a reassessment of values and priorities for many of our employees that directly impact employee experience – work–life balance, remote work, flexible hours, mental health, financial health and more.

As this chapter shows, the conversation and focus on employee experience had been building for years, but as we build and navigate what's next, it's gone from important to critical. As HR practitioners, it's vital we're listening and paying attention to what our employees need, while recognizing that those needs are not static.

FIGURE 8.4 Parts of employee experience that need fixing, LinkedIn (2020)

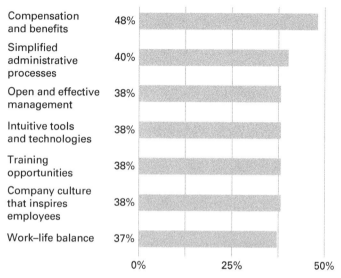

Percentage of talent professionals who say their company
should improve the following:

Compensation and benefits	48%
Simplified administrative processes	40%
Open and effective management	38%
Intuitive tools and technologies	38%
Training opportunities	38%
Company culture that inspires employees	38%
Work–life balance	37%

LinkedIn Global Talent Trends, p 15. Reproduced with permission

The roadmap is there. We just need to prioritize and commit to the initiatives and programmes our employees are asking us for.

Case studies

Let's take a look at how some of these approaches to employee experience are being implemented.

Earlier in this chapter I shared the ground-breaking work that Schneider Electric is doing with their Open Talent Market. Here's the story behind it.

CASE STUDY
Creating an internal talent market with Schneider Electric

Andrew Saidy, VP Talent Digitization, Schneider Electric

Company: Schneider Electric
Region: Global

Industry: Energy
Company size: 100,000+

What they did

Our mission at Schneider Electric is to ensure that *'Life is On, everywhere, for everyone and at every moment'* – a promise which certainly starts with our own 144,000-strong workforce. To ensure this, we embarked on a transformative experiment to create an internal opportunity marketplace: *Open Talent Market*.

The Open Talent Market is an internal platform acting as a one-stop-shop for career development and internal mobility by creating an internal talent market powered by AI to match the supply and demand of talent throughout Schneider Electric.

By uploading their profile to the Open Talent Market (or connecting it to their LinkedIn), employees get AI-suggested development and career opportunities based on their skills, competencies and future ambitions.

Why they did it

With a large globally distributed workforce, we know that retention is a crucial component of our long-term success. We analysed our exit interviews and identified that 47 per cent of leavers cited a lack of internal opportunity as their reason for leaving. We coupled that with external skills-based benchmarking, including:

- The half-life of learned skills is roughly five years.
- Software engineers must redevelop skills every 12–18 months.
- Average job tenure is four years.

How they did it

We worked with an AI-powered platform created by Gloat to build an internal marketplace for opportunities, projects and development of employees. We wanted to make sure it was user-friendly and intuitive in order to drive adoption. Some of the core features we were designing for include:

- reducing attrition and turnover;
- allowing our employees to own their careers and develop to their fullest potential within the company;
- giving employees the opportunity to acquire a portfolio of diverse experiences and skills;

- supporting leaders in finding diverse talents faster and building the best teams;

- creating networks of expertise throughout the organization and enabling greater diversity on teams across the organization;

- guaranteeing more transparency around available roles and projects.

The initial focus of the platform was driving internal mobility of employees interested in finding their next full-time role. This was later complemented by the addition of part-time projects (gigs) and mentorships through AI-powered connections.

This shift towards projects and gigs has been especially expedited in light of the current health and economic crisis, as the need for talent agility and workforce rebalancing is bigger. We initially launched the platform to all 2,300 HR employees globally, followed by a few geographies (UK, Singapore, the United States and France) and a global launch after that. Forty per cent of connected employees have already opted-in and they have access to a variety of new opportunities added every day.

As adoption continues to grow in the coming years, we'll be adding more AI functionalities, such as career pathing, succession planning and workforce insights.

ROI/Impact

While we're still in the early days of the Open Talent Market, some of our early impact measures include:

- Employees have participated in more than 1,000 projects.

- Collectively, the market has unlocked 48,000 hours, where full-time employees have participated in side-gigs at no extra cost.

- We've started to see attrition decrease in areas where the market has been available for a longer period of time.

- Improved organizational agility and engagement.

Upwork is a technology platform that connects professionals and agencies to businesses seeking specialized talent around the world. As you might expect, they also engage in some of the flexibility practices their platform enables, building scalable and dynamic teams focused on solving current projects and challenges. Here's what that on-demand talent model looks like.

CASE STUDY
Build on-demand agile teams at Upwork

Zoe Harte, SVP Human Resources and Talent Innovation, Upwork

Company: Upwork
Region: North America
Industry: Human Resources and Recruiting
Company size: 501–1,000 employees

What they did

Leveraging their technology platform, Upwork Enterprise, they developed an internal team within HR focused on building a home-grown solution that would enable their teams and clients' teams to quickly access, scale and safely engage independent talent.

Why they did it

In order to take advantage of the global talent who offer their services on their platform, they needed a centralized process for engaging freelancers within the organization that was safe and maintained compliance.

How they did it

'Upwork's mission is to create economic opportunities so people have better lives' – it's central to their work and it's an integral part of how they engage across their workforce. With hundreds of full-time employees and more than 1,000 contingent workers from the United States and around the world, fostering that culture through change and massive growth over the past few years – including a rebrand and their initial public offering (IPO) – has been a challenge.

Leveraging their own technology platform, HR built an internal 'talent innovation' team focused on developing a home-grown solution that would enable their teams to access a global pool of talent quickly and at scale while maintaining employment compliance.

In 2015, they launched their 'Talent Innovation Program' (TIP), which sits within the HR function. The team was responsible for creating a centralized process and in-product solution to engage independent talent internally. Every department within Upwork today engages independent talent (ie social media moderators, designers, copywriters, engineers etc). They ensure that employees engaging independent talent on their platform are doing so properly and within compliance.

The TIP team makes sure that onboarding goes smoothly, that new workers have access to the right systems and that they're integrated into their internal communications. They have a centralized repository of information because people need an easy way to access information. They have technology that supports collaboration and they find ways to make personal connections.

TIP brings an intentional structure to their people practices. They start by asking: What is the work to be done, and what's the best way to do it? The optimal resource isn't always an employee; top talent can add expertise and perspective when and where we need it. Ultimately, they want the best people for each unique project.

In addition to leveraging the solution for internal purposes, Upwork's TIP has helped inform the product offering for Upwork Enterprise clients. The Upwork Talent Innovation team plays a major role in helping Enterprise clients who are using the Upwork Enterprise compliance offering are properly and safely engaging their independent workforce.

Impact/ROI

Today, every single function within the business leverages a hybrid, distributed team. Since 2015, their team has engaged approximately 2,800 independent professionals across all areas of the organization. As a result, their speed in bringing contributions back to the business is far faster than competing for corporate employees in hiring hotbeds like the San Francisco Bay Area and Chicago.

As you can see from this chapter, the considerations around employee experience are vast and dynamic. That will likely increase as we continue navigating how we'll be constructing work in the new post-Covid landscape.

Another determining factor in how we consider employee experience is how these programmes align with our culture. Different companies will prioritize different employee experience initiatives based on how they align with their values and support their unique culture. In the next chapter, 'Operationalizing culture and values', we'll cover what makes culture real and how to scale it as you grow.

References

Accenture (2016) Liquid Workforce: Building the Workforce for Today's Digital Demands. Available from: www.accenture.com/fr-fr/_acnmedia/pdf-2/accenture-liquid-workforce-technology-vision-2016-france.pd (archived at https://perma.cc/7BLA-9449)

Anderson, B (2020) 6 Tactics Schneider Electric Used to Amp Up Internal Mobility, LinkedIn Talent Blog. Available from: https://business.linkedin.com/talent-solutions/blog/internal-mobility/2020/schneider-electric-internal-mobility (archived at https://perma.cc/L3AY-LM4Y)

Bersin, J (2019) The Employee Experience: It's Trickier (and More Important) Than You Thought, JoshBersin.com. Available from: https://joshbersin.com/2019/03/the-employee-experience-its-trickier-and-more-important-than-you-thought/ (archived at https://perma.cc/SM2Q-2HWR)

Deloitte (2018) Deloitte Find Millennials' Confidence in Business Takes a Sharp Turn: They Feel Unprepared for Industry 4.0. Available from: www2.deloitte.com/global/en/pages/about-deloitte/press-releases/deloitte-finds-millennials-confidence-business-takes-sharp-turn.html (archived at https://perma.cc/F9XJ-ZWPS)

Greenhouse Software (2019) Workplace Intelligence Report. Available from: https://grow.greenhouse.io/p/1 (archived at https://perma.cc/CT3S-B9TD)

Groth, A (2020) Zappos Has Quietly Backed Away From Holocracy, QZ.com. Available from: https://qz.com/work/1776841/zappos-has-quietly-backed-away-from-holacracy/ (archived at https://perma.cc/DMR5-2VLN)

Hoffman, R, Casnocha, B and Yeh, C (2013) Tours of Duty: The New Employer–Employee Contract, *Harvard Business Review*. Available from: https://hbr.org/2013/06/tours-of-duty-the-new-employer-employee-compact (archived at https://perma.cc/W8YB-WH9C)

Hoffman, R, Casnocha, B and Yeh, C (2014) *The Alliance: Managing talent in the networked age*, Harvard Business Review Press, Brighton, Mass.

Kamer, J (2018) How to Build Your own 'Spotify Model'. Available from: www.linkedin.com/pulse/how-build-your-own-spotify-model-jurriaan-kamer/ (archived at https://perma.cc/9EW6-YLQA)

LinkedIn (2020) Global Talent Trends 2020. Available from: https://business.linkedin.com/talent-solutions/recruiting-tips/global-talent-trends-2020 (archived at https://perma.cc/3W5K-5UHK)

Murph, D (2019) Ep56: GitLab Head of Remote, Darren Murph, 21st Century HR. Available from: https://21stcenturyhr.fireside.fm/ep56-gitlab-head-of-remote-darren-murph (archived at https://perma.cc/8B25-6XLJ)

Schneider, M (2019) Spotify Increases Paid User Base to 124M, Reports $7.44B Revenue in 2019, *Billboard*. Available from: www.billboard.com/articles/business/8550174/spotify-earnings-2019-paid-user-totals-financial-results-q4 (archived at https://perma.cc/M7E7-YMKH)

Sinek, S (2009) *Start With Why: How great leaders inspire everyone to take action*, Penguin, New York

Ungarino, R (2020) Bank of America Shifting Some Employee Roles Amid Coronavirus, *Business Insider*. Available from: www.businessinsider.com/bank-of-america-shifting-some-employees-roles-amid-coronavirus-2020-4 (archived at https://perma.cc/2MLY-5KDQ)

Upwork (2019) Freelancing in America 2019. Available from: www.upwork.com/i/
  freelancing-in-america/ (archived at https://perma.cc/S3BD-R446)
Volini, E, Indranil, R and Schwartz, J (2019) Talent Mobility: Winning the War on
  the Home Front, *Deloitte Insights*. Available from: www2.deloitte.com/us/en/
  insights/focus/human-capital-trends/2019/internal-talent-mobility.html (archived
  at https://perma.cc/75YK-GZG9)

09

Operationalizing culture and values

'Be your best self.'

'Dream big.'

'We put the customer first.'

'We put employees first.'

'Synergy.'

Everyone has seen these posters on the wall. We've all been indoctrinated into organizations that mask buzzwords as culture. When the onboarding jazz hands settle, we find ourselves feeling more like that cat in the *Hang in There* motivational poster than the climber triumphantly summiting that peak just in time for an epic sunrise.

Culture is not posters. Culture is not swag. Culture is not even what you proudly state your culture to be.

Culture is a thousand things, a thousand times

One of my favourite definitions of culture is from Airbnb co-founder and CEO, Brian Chesky: 'Culture is a thousand things, a thousand times. It's living the core values when you hire; when you write an email; when you are working on a project; when you are walking in the hall.'

In essence, culture is the lived behaviour of the organization. It's not what you say, it's the cumulative (and dynamic) result of all that you do.

The best way to convey this tangibly goes back to Airbnb. During the Covid-19 crisis their business was decimated as travel screeched to a global halt. Like many businesses during this time, Airbnb laid off a significant portion (25 per cent) of their team. Unlike most, their approach was a master class in living their values.

These were some of the steps they took to support their laid-off employees:

- **Severance**: US employees received 14 weeks' severance plus an additional week for every year of service.
- **Equity**: They accelerated vesting schedules so that even employees who were there less than one year would realize benefits.
- **Healthcare**: They covered healthcare continuation costs for all US employees for 12 months.
- **Outplacement**: They pivoted their internal recruiting team to become their Alumni Placement Team. They also launched an opt-in public-facing website with their alumni that was promoted heavily to potential employers.
- **Equipment**: They allowed all impacted employees to keep their Apple laptops to use for their job search.

They didn't have to do many of these things. Yet they did. In the middle of a global pandemic... that most dramatically impacted their sector. One moment a high-flying unicorn racing towards a much-anticipated initial public offering (IPO), and now this. It was a clear example of a company being true to their values.

What got even more attention than the mechanics of their layoff was the heartfelt, empathetic and transparent letter from their CEO to all employees. It will stand the test of time as a master class in leadership. Here are just a few excerpts that stood out (Chesky, 2020).

Context on the decision

> Let me start with how we arrived at this decision. We are collectively living through the most harrowing crisis of our lifetime, and as it began to unfold, global travel came to a standstill. Airbnb's business has been hit hard, with revenue this year forecasted to be less than half of what we earned in 2019. In response, we raised $2 billion in capital and dramatically cut costs that touched nearly every corner of Airbnb.

His message starts with an honest framing of the current external circumstances impacting the business, including specific financial impact and hardship caused by the crisis.

Clarity on how they approached the decision

> It was important that we had a clear set of principles, guided by our core values, for how we would approach reductions in our workforce. These were our guiding principles:
>
> - Map all reductions to our future business strategy and the capabilities we will need.
> - Do as much as we can for those who are impacted.
> - Be unwavering in our commitment to diversity.
> - Optimize for 1:1 communication for those impacted.
> - Wait to communicate any decisions until all details are landed – transparency of only partial information can make matters worse.

He was clear that their values guided these decisions and transparently defined how they would guide their approach to layoffs.

Transparency on the decision-making process

> Our process started with creating a more focused business strategy built on a sustainable cost model. We assessed how each team mapped to our new strategy, and we determined the size and shape of each team going forward. We then did a comprehensive review of every team member and made decisions based on critical skills, and how well those skills matched our future business needs.

This level of detail into how the decision framework was designed and executed is rare in layoff announcements. Employees are often left to wonder how their name made it on to a list of layoffs. By addressing this proactively, they demonstrated empathy for that plight.

Empathy for those impacted

> I am truly sorry. Please know this is not your fault. The world will never stop seeking the qualities and talents that you brought to Airbnb... that helped make Airbnb. I want to thank you, from the bottom of my heart, for sharing them with us.

This closing section also jumped out at me for the consideration of what employees who were impacted were feeling. It's human nature to wonder what you might have done to be made redundant. I've been there and I can vividly recall that experience even 20 years later. By addressing this and explicitly stating it was not their fault, Airbnb showed an empathy and understanding for those emotions their employees were surely experiencing.

Layoffs are hard under the best of circumstances, let alone during a once-in-a-generation global pandemic and recession. These words don't remove the pain those impacted employees experience, but they recognized their plight.

Empathy isn't always enough

Several months after the layoffs *The New York Times* published an article, 'Airbnb was like a family, until the layoffs started' (Griffith, 2020). It detailed some of the disenfranchisement of employees who were let go and the survivor's guilt of those who remain. The story aired frustrations, from their treatment of contract workers to the sense of betrayal some of the laid-off employees felt towards the company.

The Covid-related layoffs, and the resulting fissures in the perception of Airbnb's culture, will certainly be a test for them. My guess is they will weather this storm and rebound because of the strength of their values and leadership.

In the end, Airbnb's actions during these difficult economic times represented their values. There is no perfect way to make these difficult decisions. Brian Chesky's message was consistent with the culture they had built on belonging and humanity.

You can't fake that, and you won't find it on a poster.

The problem with 'culture fit'

Chances are that if you work in any aspect of HR you're more than familiar with the term 'culture fit'. What began as darling term of the tech set quickly became common hiring vernacular in many industries.

Look back at the past decade and you'll find 'culture fit' as a foundational component of many hiring practices. It was integrated into interview processes, embedded in career sites, plastered on job descriptions and touted as a competitive advantage for many organizations.

Check out our ping-pong tables! Did we mention our office has a slide? Our open bar hosts a happy hour in days that end in 'day'.

Do you like kombucha? We have three artisanal blends on tap!

This isn't culture, but for a while this is what many companies reduced it to in their hiring practices. Now they need you to 'fit' into this. What exactly is 'this'?

As the race over corporate perks heated up, the term 'culture fit' took on more of a tribal meaning. People who *work* like us. People who *live* like us. People who *think* like us. People who *look* like us. Like. Us.

The result was a homogenous culture of like-minded, like-schooled, like-privileged and often like-ethnicity and like-sex (ie white men). In short, 'culture fit' became a weaponized antidote to diversity. Silicon Valley is still climbing out of the lasting hole which that caused.

One of the problems with 'culture fit' is that it's often used as a nebulous catch-all to affirm bias. Hiring processes that allow this term as a reason for exclusion are full of bias. The term is often wielded as a lazy weapon by interviewers to reject candidates who don't align with their view of the ideal candidate. Without training and support, most interviewers are more likely to hire people like themselves and discount others who are different.

If your company still allows 'I don't see them being a good culture fit' as a reason for declining candidates, I challenge you to respond with, 'What exactly do you mean by that, specifically?' Press and probe. Perhaps it's innocuous. Maybe there's a valid concern and they just haven't found the words to articulate it. It's your job as a talent professional to find out – and not accept generic reasons.

Creating a representative and inclusive culture doesn't happen organically. Inclusivity takes deliberate effort, time and commitment. Removing 'culture fit' from your recruiting language won't eliminate unconscious bias, but it sets a clear expectation that an unqualified 'no' is not acceptable.

PRACTITIONER SPOTLIGHT
The right questions reveal your culture

Matt Hoffman, Partner, M13

One of the things I'm most impressed with is when I see companies be very thoughtful and intentional about culture early on in the process. I really believe thinking deeply about culture and values as a founding team is key:

- What kind of company do we want to be?
- What do we stand for?
- What are the types of people we want to hire?

- What is our talent philosophy?
- Do we want to hire quickly?
- Do we want to hire slowly?
- Do we want to fire quickly?
- Do run want to fire slowly?
- Are there certain behaviours we won't tolerate?
- How important is diversity early on and why do we think that's important?

You don't have to have everything laid out from an operational perspective, but you should be at least thinking about this question very early on, and hopefully having conversations with your founders about the topic on a regular basis. I would argue that once you get beyond the founding team, your first non-founding employee, you're starting to create an actual culture. Whether you want to or not.

So, you may as well start thinking about it. As you get bigger, it gets much harder for founders to change the culture because, by definition, every time you hire another person the founder influence itself gets diminished. So how do you make sure that you're hiring people who are going to be consistent with the founder's vision, and add to it and create better scalability rather than worse? Those are things worth thinking about.

What are the types of attributes and the types of people you're looking for in your interview process? Maybe you're not ready to build a full interview pre-brief or debrief interview kit, with structured interview questions and so on at only 3–5 people. But you should at least be thinking about who are the types of people we want and why:

- Do we want people who are exactly like us because they're easy to find in our network?
- Do we want to find different people because that will create a more varied and diverse and better perspective set?
- Do we want to hire for specific skills or do we want to hire for talent and potential because we know that in six months our company's going to look very different anyway?

Those are the things that are worth thinking about at the very earliest stage. Having that framework for how to think about people, how to think about culture and how to think about talent is time well spent by an early-stage team, just as much as a go-to-market strategy, the product strategy, the social media strategy and everything else.

Codifying culture

In 2009, Netflix Chief Talent Officer Patty McCord, along with Founder and CEO Reed Hastings, penned one of the more influential documents ever written in HR – 'The Netflix Culture Code: Freedom and Responsibility'.

Netflix's Culture Code was heralded by Sheryl Sandberg as one of the most important documents that ever came out of Silicon Valley. It's inspired countless other decks around the world to this day.

The core tenant of the culture deck is based on personal responsibility and accountability. Treat employees like adults. From one of the first companies that got rid of formal vacation policies to their 'Act in Netflix's Best Interest' expense policy, they trusted their high-performing teams to do the right thing. The made a deliberate choice not to stifle their employees' ability to make an impact with unnecessary and burdensome policies. Don't over-engineer HR. Simplify it.

It placed an emphasis on focusing your recruiting efforts on hiring top talent and acting decisively to move on when the skills of the individual no longer align with the needs of the business. While many founders were using flowery mantras such as 'we are a family', Netflix embraced a 'we are a high-performing team' approach – and they meant it. Netflix was playing to win (McCord, 2014).

Is that culture for everyone? No. Should any company be for everyone? No.

The fact that Netflix embraced their high-performance culture and shared those aspirations publicly helped candidates self-identify whether they aligned – or not. Both of those outcomes are good when you're scaling and you need employees who share your vision.

One of the culture decks that was inspired in part by Netflix was HubSpot's *Culture Code*, initially created by HubSpot Founder and CTO Dharmesh Shah and updated extensively by HubSpot Chief People Officer Katie Burke and her team. She shared some of the thinking that went into it with me on the 21st Century HR podcast:

> One of the things I hear from founders is that in their process of codifying their culture, they essentially wait until every employee or every leader is happy with every element of the deck. They wordsmith it to death. What you end up with is this really stale, boring document. I've never seen a CEO who says 'We want to attract average people with average interests and average passion'. That's just never going to happen. One of things I always say to people is that if you're doing your culture code right, it is as important for the people it keeps out as those that it draws in. You have to be willing to have a point of view.

Some companies go to extreme lengths to keep employees who don't align with their values and culture out.

Zappos is renowned for its quirky and unique culture. Dozens of articles and books on it have been written, so I assume that if you're reading this you're familiar with their story. One of the unique ways they built and preserved that culture was by paying new hires to quit. In the early days of this programme, new hires went through a four-week training period that immersed them into all things culture, strategy and their absolute commitment to customer service. One week into this programme, new hires were offered $2,000 to quit on the spot. This offer extended through their employment and increased by $1,000 every year until it reached $5,000 (Taylor, 2008).

The aim was to make it easy for employees who didn't want to be there to leave. Actively disengaged employees kill culture. By providing new hires and existing employees an easy exit, you're helping them *and* your business. Win–win.

Amazon agrees. After acquiring Zappos they tapped into this approach for their own pay-to-quit plan. They began a yearly programme of offering employees in their fulfilment centre $5,000 to leave the company. Those who take the cash can never work at Amazon again. Similar to Zappos, their pay-out scales from $2,000 to $5,000 based on tenure (Umoh, 2018).

PRACTITIONER SPOTLIGHT
Creating a culture of belonging

Katelin Holloway, Partner, Initialized Capital

I've been thinking a lot recently about how we have actually deconstructed this notion of belonging to build and develop actual programmes, things that are tangible that people can feel and see. I've actually been able to parse this out from a people perspective and from a programmes perspective through three different layers that we need to address.

The first is the company identity. The company identity is that extra external or outward-facing, 'Oh wow. You work at X company. That's awesome.' This is your sense of pride for where you work. It means, generally speaking, you are a place that has a strong brand. It's a place where you have a strong mission that people can talk about. People want to feel that pride. It doesn't matter if you're

5 people or 5,000 people, having that really strong sense of external identity is important to people. Now we go further in on that layered sense of belongingness.

The second layer is your shared identity. This is the part of the identity that is the connection to your peers, connected to your job. When you feel the work you are doing has an impact. When you feel you have a responsibility and a commitment to your colleagues. When you feel very loyal to what it is that you are building and what you are putting out to the world. This is your actual work. That's having that sense of shared identity internally. Your policies, your practices, your meeting cadence. You're able to give your colleagues the benefit of good intent and assuming the best in one another because you have this connection that is outside of yourself and your own.

Then there's the third layer, the part of the identity we're really careful to help nurture: the individual identity. It's no longer good enough to say, 'Wow, I work at company X and I'm proud to be there. And I feel my role has an impact. And I love my colleagues. This is a good job for me. I feel like this is my home.' We are now asking people, and people are asking us, if they can bring their whole selves to work. There are things that we share that are going to impact our ability to show up at work in a certain way. By really addressing this kind of true identity, all together, it helps us to develop these relationships and the sense of belongingness.

Operationalizing values and culture

So, you have real, tangible, C-suite led and lived values. How do you actually operationalize them into your company? That's the art.

Culture manifests itself in different ways. Some organizations deliberately engineer their recruiting practices to enhance culture. Some companies simplify this to an individual trait – like decency. Mastercard Chief People Officer Michael Fraccaro explains:

Every organization wants the best talent. You recruit and retain people who are smart, capable, have relevant experience and can relate well with each other. So, the IQ and the EQ component are well represented. Taking that notion a step further, our CEO coined the term 'DQ' (decency quotient), recognizing that as society shifts, corporations need to take a bigger role and responsibility in responding to social issues – so organizations also need to shift. The way we see it, the fabric of Mastercard and what sets us apart are all the things we're able to accomplish as an organization, balanced through this lens of decency. In our corporate objectives, we refer to 'Driving a winning culture with decency at its core'. We still want to compete. We still want to ensure that we've got the best products and services out there. But we want to do it with a heart and we want to do it in a way that treats people with respect and dignity.

Whether focused on traits like decency or other core values, if they aren't rigorously reinforced in all aspects of your people programmes there is a risk that these just become posters on the wall or empty slogans. Your values should be infused into how you hire, fire, promote, reward, incentivize, develop and communicate across the organization. Your employees have to know you walk the walk when it comes to living your values. Take this example from HubSpot Chief People Officer Katie Burke:

> One of my favourite HubSpot traditions is a peer bonus every quarter. You are essentially given $100 cash to give to another employee. We ask you to give that money out directly tied to one of HubSpot's values of HEART (humble, empathetic, adaptable, remarkable, transparent). In addition to getting a note and a nice surprise, you're getting feedback on how you actually embodied one of HubSpot's values on a day-to-day basis. It really empowers all of our employees globally not just to see that behaviour, but also reward it actively. All of our company-wide awards are focused and rooted in our overall values. If we are promoting a manager or a leader, we actually try to tie it back to something in the culture code.

Tangibly reinforcing these values gives them life. It keeps them front of mind for employees and reinforces what behaviours are encouraged and forbidden.

Lastly, for values to truly be operationalized they *must* be lived and demonstrated by your executives. The moment you allow high-profile examples that are misaligned is when you've lost. Accountability is key.

Growth by Design Talent was founded by recruiting veterans with over 35 years of experience building hypergrowth tech companies, including Airbnb, Pinterest, Facebook and Apple. Over that time, they've had a front-row seat at operationalizing core values for scale. One of their partners, Adam Ward, breaks it down.

PRACTITIONER SPOTLIGHT
Operationalizing core values

Adam Ward, Partner, Growth by Design Talent

It's not so long ago that it was rare for a company, especially one in start-up and growth-stage mode, to have defined core values. Flash forward to today and when we poll founders on their values we are almost shocked if they don't have those identified and broadly communicated. It's become a requirement in the founder's handbook.

However, most companies fail to take additional steps to operationalize their values across their people systems. This is a massive risk – particularly as you scale. From the dozens of companies we've consulted with, and in our own hands-on experience doing this foundational work at Pinterest and Airbnb, we've identified the best practices for companies that want to be intentional about assessing and positively reinforcing 'culture add' characteristics and behaviour.

Set clear definitions

Every company has its requisite value or two that is a catchy phrase but means many different things to individuals. Common ones we see are 'high horsepower', 'owner's mentality' or 'no jerks allowed'. When we press leaders of a company, let alone the employees themselves, they all come up with divergent personal meanings. Anchoring leaders, and then the company, on shared definitions of the values is critical to understanding and adoption. The most effective way to do this is to anchor it to more generally understood competencies or traits. For example, 'no jerks allowed' could translate into competencies such as collaborative, values differences and manages conflict. Ideally, there are no more than 3–4 traits per value and there are plenty of competency dictionaries out on the internet that you can reference to identify your set.

Bring it to life

Once the values are clearly defined, taking an inside-out approach is the best practice to bring the values to life for the employees. We often see the mistake of companies focusing on initially applying it to hiring new employees without first creating a shared understanding of how these values are demonstrated internally.

A great way to do this is to 'pull through' the values framework into level/role expectations language and the performance management systems (if they exist). By doing so, the values are positively reinforced through people's work. An added benefit over time is the ability to measure the correlation between candidate interview feedback on a value and demonstrated performance.

For smaller companies that may not have levels or performance management established, tying some goal/OKR language to values is recommended. You can also connect this to recognition. When employees are recognized – individually or more broadly – leaders can tie their achievement to one of the company's core values, helping employees attribute specific behaviours to values.

Apply a structured process

Like any other important aspect of hiring someone for a role, we recommend taking a structured interview approach to interviewing for values fit. Conjugating the values to competencies, and then into a standard set of questions with answer rubrics, is the gold standard. Having this framework will create a more standardized approach, thereby mitigating some of the many biases that can creep in, leading to a more consistent screen for fit.

Whether everyone is deputized to interview for fit, a curated set of 'culture carriers' or the founders themselves, a structured approach drives better interrater reliability. Some values will be easier to assess in interviews vs reference checks or work samples. It can be very tempting to try to assess all of the values within the interview process. Try to prioritize based on values that are the best indicators of success for that role or team, where possible.

We often see founders at growing companies struggle with scaling hiring for culture and they become a bottleneck to hiring by insisting on being in every interview loop even as the company grows into the low hundreds. Having a structured process will give them more confidence that the culture they are trying to build will be in good hands as they grow and scale.

It's hard to build a company. It's *really* hard to build a company with strong values and a dynamic culture where all employees feel they belong. Many companies never get there. Some never try.

What modern people teams (and leaders) get is that it doesn't happen by chance. Building these cultures takes work, effort, vigilance, intention and, at times, courage.

It also requires full buy-in from the executive team. This isn't something that can be passed over to HR to 'own'. It doesn't work that way. If your executive team believes it does, they'll probably never get there.

Case studies

Let's bring this to life with a few case studies that illustrate operationalizing your culture and values.

CASE STUDY
How Gusto embeds values assessments into interviews

Jessica Yuen, former Head of People, Gusto

With a culture rooted in values, approachability and quirkiness, one of the keys to Gusto's successful scaling has been adapting its traditions, which have evolved to match the changing needs of the company.

Gusto's founder Josh Reeves has always hired with alignment with three dimensions in mind: values, motivations and skill set. In the early days, it was up to him to determine alignment with these dimensions, and he ran an informal conversation to uncover how someone thought and approached problems – sometimes discussing prior work but other times discussing personal projects such as a home renovation. When Gusto grew to 50–60 employees, he tried to scale the aspects for determining values and motivation by having others in the company conduct similar-style conversations, but that solution lasted only so long. So Gusto adapted:

- **Original approach**: CEO interviews every candidate to evaluate candidate alignment with values, motivations and skill set.

- **Attempt 1 at scaling**: Have more employees attempt to emulate the free-form style of the CEO in assessing values and motivations.

- **Sustainable scaled approach**: Intentional programme that trains employees to run consistent and unbiased cross-functional interviews and evaluate incoming candidates for values and motivations alignment ('VMA').

Three main components helped the tradition evolve and keep it unique to Gusto:

- **Interviewers were specially selected and trained**: Employees were selected based on their interview experience, self and peer nominations, tenure at Gusto and ability to represent its community. To facilitate the training, Gusto's people team facilitated an interactive training session and prepared cross-functional VMA interviewers. Then, guided practice was next, to ensure the interviewing muscles were strengthened. Each potential interviewer shadowed two interviews and 'reverse shadowed' (where they ran the interview and were shadowed by a recruiter) three times before they conducted VMA interviews on their own. Once independently interviewing, they were also given feedback on evaluations to ensure consistency and fairness.

- **Cross-functional interviewing ensured a well-rounded experience**: Another aim of the VMA interview was for candidates to meet Gusties who work in different disciplines from their own (eg an engineer may be interviewed by a customer experience rep, a marketer by a product designer, and so on). As a result, candidates gained a new perspective on the community and interviewers got to know a potential colleague outside of their core competencies.

- **Attributes were chosen to embody the core of what to assess:** At the start of the VMA programme, a survey asked Gusties to define Gusto's culture and what traits made a successful Gustie, and then distilled this into a few attributes, some of which are still used today, such as 'service mindset' and 'intellectual curiosity'. Each attribute was evaluated in a consistent manner with specific guidance to minimize bias. An example is shown in Figure 9.1.

FIGURE 9.1   Sample attribute interview evaluation: service mindset

Positive indicators	Negative indicators
• Interested in the problems the company is trying to solve. • Anticipates the needs of others. • Shows empathy towards customers. • Takes time to help others outside of core responsibilities. • Anticipates deadlines and possible delays.	• Not interested in solving issue company is tackling. (Example: not passionate about small business) • Has only a surface-level view of customer service. • Doesn't view themselves in connection with the customer. • No actions outside of core responsibilities to serve a customer or teammate.

First Round Review (2018)

To this day, all hiring decisions at Gusto include a VMA interview.

Results

Gathering feedback is important to ensure that scaling is emphasizing the proper elements. Candidates consistently gave positive feedback on this part of the interview experience and appreciated Gusto's sincere interest in both their personal and professional journeys. About 30 per cent of Gusto employees reported wanting to serve as a future VMA interviewer, and 95 per cent of the first year's participants continued their role as a VMA interviewer. Gusto's CEO Josh Reeves believed in this approach, noting that, 'The program in place gives me confidence that we can have the same core values and philosophy at 500 people or 5,000 people as we did when we were just 5 people' (First Round Review, 2018).

Unifynd Technologies is an Indian technology company with a young workforce. They struggled with attrition, so they adopted design-thinking principles to operationalize their values throughout the recruiting and people development systems.

CASE STUDY
Reducing attrition with values-aligned people programmes

Mitasha Singh, Head of Talent, Unifynd Technologies

Company: Unifynd Technologies
Region: India
Industry: Retail Technology
Company size: 0–50
Category: Operationalizing values

What they did

We build robust, user-centric property technology products for the retail and real-estate industry, driving technological disruption in brick-and-mortar businesses. Our year of reckoning was 2019 – we tested our go-to-market strategy, aced our first deployment and tripled our team size, among many other milestones.

Based on our previous experiences, we were also focused on proactive measures to combat the biggest people challenges that would test us: high attrition owing to price sensitivity in the Indian labour market and the hidden cost of a young underutilized workforce.

Why they did it

Working with a young, diverse group of thinkers in a highly nascent start-up ecosystem, we knew that the lifetime contribution of each employee would be a huge differentiator in meeting revenue goals and customer experience.

The average voluntary attrition in the Indian tech industry, with a primary workforce of millennials and Gen Z, is ~23 per cent, with start-ups incurring heavy operational expenses at 50–80 per cent attrition (Bhattacharya, 2018).

Tying the above goal to monetary incentives would lead to a race to the bottom. We had to constantly iterate our culture and work practices to evolve into a truly agile people operations function.

How they did it

We started out by identifying the organization's core values. This would form the bedrock of talent acquisition, employee and alumni journeys, and growth. Using open-source best practices by leading start-ups of the world, we embedded flexibility and a design-thinking approach to create autonomy in every touchpoint of an employee lifecycle. In my research of employee behaviour and productivity, I discovered two academics whose work could also form very interesting benchmarks for practitioners – Dr Natasha Dow Schüll and Safi Bahcall. After studying their research and thinking about behaviour and productivity, I applied it to some of our people programmes:

- **Stake vs rank outcomes**: Creating autonomous work teams and having them centred around deliverables, cross-forming teams and de-alienating managers from work hierarchies helped create multiple 'owners' within the firm – all focused on driving their desired goals ahead.

- **Draw that line**: In an attempt not to micromanage, many new-age managers have become fearful of structures. We found that creating healthy boundaries, 'active' time for direction and clear prioritization of deliverables increased engagement and resulted in 100 per cent completion of work assigned.

- **Break those ludic loops**: We consciously alternate between 'disconnect' nudges and high-energy interactive experiences to focus on all personality types and mood cycles of our employees. Creating time-off mechanisms, peer rewards, informal meet-ups and offline engagement has led to a drastic reduction in sick days and disengaged time at work, and faster results on cross-functional teamwork.

- **To OKR or not**: It was counterintuitive to ditch OKRs after a great first quarter, but the amount of bandwidth that the leadership spent trying to make the system work was an ironical bottleneck. We've since moved to agile reviews, 30–60–90-day touchpoints, critical incident learnings and regular firm-wide brainstorming sessions. The flexibility in assessment methods has led to better founder and new manager effectiveness; with over 90 per cent of teams meeting documentation and delivery timelines.

Impact/ROI

By using key progressive people practices and approaches we were able to maintain ~5.5 per cent voluntary attrition for Q4 2019 and Q1 2020, exceed stretch goals of app-user signups, streamline technical 'release trains' and create a tech team which advocates our EVP – increasing our organic social brand following by 153 per cent.

In the spring of 2018, two of the largest companies in public relations merged. Two distinct companies with years of experience in their own unique culture were now one. This is an inside view of what it was like to create a new unified culture from that merger.

CASE STUDY
Merging culture at scale with Burson Cohn & Wolfe

Kristen Lisanti, Chief Culture Officer, Burson Cohn & Wolfe

Company: BCW
Region: North America
Industry: Public Relations
Company size: 2,500+

What they did

We developed a new culture from the largest corporate merger in PR history.

Why they did it

In the spring of 2018, the largest merger in PR history took place, combining the crisis, public affairs and the corporate communications powerhouse of Burson-Marsteller with the digital-savvy Cohn & Wolfe.

In terms of client roster and capability, it was a match made in heaven, but these two global agencies could not have been more different in terms of leadership approach, operational practices and organizational culture. As the new business came together as Burson Cohn & Wolfe, or BCW, CEO Donna Imperato decided that, for the merger to be a success, an entirely new approach to culture was needed.

Two years later, BCW is the third-largest public relations agency globally, and an unequivocal success from a merger perspective. The company is thriving, attracting the best talent in the business while retaining and growing its diverse client base. The promise of the pairing is paying off, with teams collaborating across markets, practices and disciplines (health/tech, brand/crisis, data-driven public affairs) to deliver powerful work inspired by BCW's purpose of 'Moving People'.

How they did it

Here are some of the key steps that BCW took in building its culture from the ground up.

Define and prioritize culture

In a standard merger or acquisition, most of the focus goes into ensuring that the union looks good on paper, taking for granted two major assumptions: 1) that the organizational ecosystem (aka the culture) will sort itself out; and 2) that the component companies will continue to deliver the same outcomes under new cultural conditions.

BCW made no such assumptions. Imperato hired Kristen Lisanti to serve as Chief Culture Officer and sit on the global executive team. Together, they defined culture as the ecosystem of the business, one that is inextricably linked to the work and to growth.

Begin within

Many organizational change initiatives start with business objectives and end with guidance on new policies and processes. This surface-level approach is why they fail. BCW recognized the internal experience of the team members navigating these massive changes, introduced tools and practices supporting growth mindset, mindful self-awareness and emotional intelligence practices, and committed to creating a safe and inclusive environment for everyone to take on new challenges, make mistakes and fail forward.

Design thinking

Lisanti applied a design-thinking approach to BCW's culture:

- **Step 1: Inquiry and empathy**. A three-month listening tour, including focus groups, stakeholder interviews and a global employee survey, helped Lisanti understand the potential of this new organization and the hopes, fears and needs of its people.

- **Step 2: Define and decide**. In the spring of 2019, BCW unveiled its Moving People purpose and positioning in the marketplace, along with an internal commitment to practising a growth mindset.

- **Step 3: Ideate and create**. With Moving People as the mission and growth mindset as the fuel, Lisanti engaged teams around the world to design new ways of working. From onboarding processes to finance policies, the team rallied around the opportunities to build a new kind of agency.

- **Step 4: Prototype and test**. Operational teams learned to start simple and build from the successful prototype and pilot programmes, letting go of any ways of working that proved too rigid to withstand the rapid pace of change in the industry.

- **Step 5: Iterate and evolve**. BCW's culture isn't finished, and it never will be. Like any ecosystem, it grows and evolves with every new hire, every new client, every new capability the team develops in its state of perpetual transformation.

Results/ROI

As of this printing, it has been two years since the BCW merger and the agency has grown. BCW did not lose a single client as a result of the merger, and has attracted waves of new talent from competitors to join its ranks and help build the new company.

As you've learned throughout this chapter, culture doesn't just happen. It's iterated, nurtured, refined and, in some cases – remade. It's not some static thing to be preserved. It's a dynamic manifestation of a thousand things done a thousand times.

Even if you have clearly defined values and well-aligned employees – if you're not developing and growing your talent, you're going to have a hard time holding onto them. The next chapter, 'Unlocking potential', examines progressive approaches to learning and performance that will help you grow (and retain) your employees.

References

Bhattacharya, A (2018) Most Indian Techies Quit Their Startup Jobs Within Two Years, qz.com. Available from: https://qz.com/india/1347207/indian-startups-have-an-employee-retention-problem-worse-than-bpos/ (archived at https://perma.cc/3N7L-TJNL)

Chesky, B (2020) A Message from Co-founder and CEO Brian Chesky, Airbnb Newsroom. Available from: https://news.airbnb.com/a-message-from-co-founder-and-ceo-brian-chesky/ (archived at https://perma.cc/B5HG-JPMJ)

First Round Review (2018) How Gusto Built Scalable Hiring Practices Rooted in Tradition. Available from: https://firstround.com/review/how-gusto-built-scalable-hiring-practices-rooted-in-tradition/ (archived at https://perma.cc/7QFV-SYF7)

Griffith, E (2020) Airbnb Was Like a Family, Until the Layoffs Started, *New York Times*. Available from: https://www.nytimes.com/2020/07/17/technology/airbnb-coronavirus-layoffs-.html (archived at https://perma.cc/GS2V-BU3U)

McCord, P (2014) How Netflix Reinvented HR, *Harvard Business Review*. Available from: https://hbr.org/2014/01/how-netflix-reinvented-hr (archived at https://perma.cc/Q8JG-F48Q)

Taylor, B (2008) Why Zappos Pays New Employees to Quit – And You Should Too, *Harvard Business Review*. Available from: https://hbr.org/2008/05/why-zappos-pays-new-employees (archived at https://perma.cc/R3AA-2HHR)

Umoh, R (2018) Why Amazon Pays Employees $5,000 to Quit, *CNBC*. Available from: www.cnbc.com/2018/05/21/why-amazon-pays-employees-5000-to-quit.html (archived at https://perma.cc/Z2YH-PR47)

10

Unlocking potential

Agile performance and learning

You've worked so hard to find, attract, hire, onboard and integrate your employees. How will you ensure you keep them?

'Sticky' companies are often organizations that manage to put as much thought and effort into the post-hire phase of the employee lifecycle as they do into the hire – usually more. They understand that retention is based on growth and development. If you're not providing those, you'll struggle holding onto your employees.

This chapter examines two of the key components of getting the most from your employees, which translates to helping them get the most from themselves: performance and learning. Both are core components of modern HR – and they both look very different in leading companies compared to those that still embrace legacy approaches. We'll start with performance.

Our first dance with performance

Remember your first report card? Okay, for some of us that might have been a long time ago, so let's try that again.

Remember ~~your first~~ report cards? Those school year validations/condemnations of your academic achievements/struggles? That piece of paper that summarized all of your work, as assessed by your teachers, throughout the school year and became the basis of your call placement the following year? A permanent record in your academic file.

It's easy to draw parallels between school assessments and the annual performance appraisal process that so many companies still use. Grades are replaced by ratings. Teachers are replaced by hiring managers. Gold stars are replaced by compensation adjustments. Academic records are replaced by employee files. The mechanics differ but the tenets are largely the same.

Perhaps the most striking similarity is that many companies still view the art of managing performance as an annual event. It is often a retroactive assessment of employee performance and contributions.

We have to adapt our thinking and approaches to modern times. Most of our employees were raised on real-time access from social media, internet, same-day delivery. We can create almost anything and have feedback on it that very day from our followers, connections and peer communities. We have to adapt our thinking on performance to account for this generational shift.

I'm not suggesting that instant or real-time job performance feedback is realistic (or necessary), but I think that if you wait 365 days to provide meaningful job performance feedback and discussions, you're missing the mark – and likely losing employees you might have kept.

You can't build transformative teams without effective performance development. You can't develop performance without a culture of learning. That's why I combined these disciplines in this chapter.

Unlocking performance requires both. They're separate functions in most people teams, but they're intertwined in impact. Each field has become incredibly sophisticated in today's work, from cognitive behaviour to brain science, which requires deep specialization.

This chapter doesn't explore the vastness of these fields, but is intended to broaden your thinking around performance and learning. It explores a range of approaches, considerations, technology and stories on how to approach performance and learning programmes in a more progressive way.

Performance goes agile

In 1965, three leading psychologists conducted studies on annual performance appraisal programmes published in *Harvard Business Review*, titled 'Split roles in performance appraisal' (Meyer, Kay and French, 1965). Some of the key findings included:

- Coaching should occur daily, and not be reserved for an annual event.
- Clear targets and goal setting with deadlines improves performance.
- Input by employees in goal setting improves performance.

FIGURE 10.1 What is the frequency of your employer's performance review process?

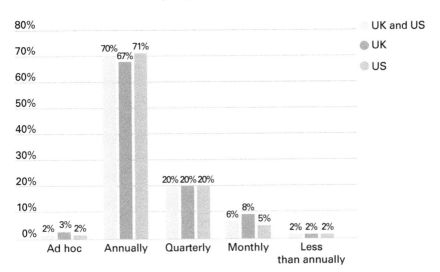

Greenhouse Workplace Intelligence Report, 2019. Reproduced with permission

Check that date again. This was 55 years ago and psychologists were already questioning the efficacy of annual performance reviews. Yet, many companies are still holding onto this relic from HR's past. According to Greenhouse's Workplace Intelligence Report from 2019, roughly 70 per cent of surveyed companies are still conducting performance reviews on an annual basis (Figure 10.1). We have work to do.

The good news is, though, that a lot of other companies have moved on. From the father of 'stack ranking' with Jack Welch at General Electric to tech titans to professional services firms, most companies viewed as having progressive and impactful people teams have abandoned annual review for more agile and ongoing performance approaches.

Karen Eber is the CEO and Chief Storyteller at Eber Leadership Group, a talent management boutique. She spent the majority of her career designing, implementing and consulting to build performance management designs across the Fortune 500, including roles as Head of Culture, Leadership Development and Chief Learning Officer in Deloitte, GE and Hewlett Packard, respectively. Having led multiple evolutions and transformations of performance approaches, she shares her unique view on considerations for building modern programmes.

PRACTITIONER SPOTLIGHT
Designing modern performance programmes

Karen Eber, CEO, Eber Leadership Group

Ask what the best shapers of organizational culture are, and performance management is often missing from that list. It is one of the strongest ways to deliver the business strategy, reinforce behaviours and develop employees. Some use performance management as a system of record, others use it for ongoing development, and others use it as a tool to enable their compensation process. Despite disruptive changes over the past 10 years, few companies claim to have figured it out.

Common mistakes

Many companies include spending significant time driving a process without enough return. Calibration meetings, completing forms and distributing small merit and compensation increase funds take time away from ongoing development and often leave employees deflated.

Performance management is shifting to support the pace and changes of work. Employees have shifting priorities and need ongoing coaching and development. Today, they also expect real-time, forward-focused feedback. This shift to ongoing development often highlights a leadership skill gap previously hidden in traditional approaches: how to have ongoing development conversations.

While it is tempting to blame the new design, this is a common growing pain and important skills for all leaders to embrace.

Technology often becomes a speedbump instead of an enabler in ongoing development. Employees focus on completing forms over the conversations out of habit. Companies should build muscle memory by starting with ongoing priority setting, touchpoints and feedback conversations before launching technology. Technology should enable conversations, not replace them.

The best app is still a conversation.

Considerations

This evolution to ongoing performance management doesn't have to require large budgets or expensive technology. Technology solutions range from PDF forms to integrated HR systems. Approaches should be designed to align with business and culture strategies. Design-thinking workshops with employees can be leveraged and help accelerate adoption.

Companies may change technology platforms more frequently – perhaps every ~5 years vs the historical 20+. Focus on necessary functionality and test potential bells and whistles with employee user testing. Technology can add great value with data analytics, helping identify skill gaps and informing how to create more of your best leaders.

Let your design inform your technology, not your technology inform your design.

Invest in equipping employees and people leaders to have development conversations and create a culture of feedback. People leaders want to understand what is expected of them and what good looks like.

Many people leaders are uncomfortable entering a conversation when they don't know where it will go. They will want prompts to know how to start difficult conversations or provide feedback. Development should include a mix of training, bite-size learning, real-time prompts, reminders and tips. Technology is a great enabler here.

Ratings continue to be messy. They aren't all good or bad, and they play an important part in some designs. Companies should examine their true role. Most make incorrect assumptions about their role and miss an opportunity for development. Some use ratings as a forcing function to ensure the process is taking place. Some use them to differentiate performance, even with a forced bell curve. Others use them as a proxy for distributing compensation. They provide a common vocabulary for performance and compensation conversations: 'You're a 1 or "exceed expectations".'

Regardless of whether ratings are used, companies should strengthen the ability for rich development conversations to help the employees understand where they stand, feel recognized and understand how to grow.

Shifting business landscapes and world events will require the agility of performance management. Many companies recognized that their designs were too rigid when Covid-19 changed priorities and prevented their normal process. Designs need to be flexible enough to support real-time shifts and deliver the intended business strategy, while reinforcing the desired culture.

The data are pretty clear at this point that more agile/ongoing methods of supporting performance drive better results. Let's look at some of the data from SHRM's 'Creating a More Human Workplace Where Employees & Business Thrive' report (Society of Human Resource Management, 2016):

- Only about half (51%) of HR leaders surveyed feel their current performance appraisal process is accurate. Yet those who conduct semi-annual or more frequent reviews are 1.5 times more likely to agree they are an accurate appraisal of employees' work, compared to organizations that conduct only annual reviews.

- Organizations that rely on more frequent performance reviews are more likely to use peer feedback, either ongoing or intermittently (38% vs 27%). Additionally, 89% of HR leaders surveyed agree that ongoing peer feedback and check-ins have a positive impact on their organizations.

- Compared to annual reviews with no peer feedback, semi-annual reviews and peer feedback are nearly twice as likely to be perceived as accurate (81% vs 42%).

- Even if an organization is not ready to forgo the traditional performance review, HR leaders can consider adopting frequent peer feedback as a supplement to improve the quality of conversations and employee development over the course of the year, the report adds.

If you're still conducting annual performance reviews, under the belief that once a year is sufficient for performance conversations, and wondering when the right time to switch is – it's now.

Shifting to agile doesn't have to be an exercise in pain. Many companies take a gradual approach rather than making the change overnight. Consider this approach from SurveyMonkey (Cantieri, 2019).

PRACTITIONER SPOTLIGHT
Shifting from annual reviews to agile reviews at Survey Monkey

Becky Cantieri, Chief People Officer, SurveyMonkey

Our performance redesign is a year-long, three-phase rollout. We refer to the overall programme as GIG, for short, which stands for growth, impact, and goals. Phase one of the rollout focuses on a quarterly GIG conversation. It avoids the high-stakes, annual discussion and increases the frequency to a quarterly discussion led by employees.

What was the impact that you've had last quarter? What can you learn from last quarter that will help you be more impactful in the quarters going forward? And then, lastly, what are your goals for the upcoming quarter? These are the questions we ask. We also tie in broad, long-term goals around professional growth. That's phase one. We've had that in place for almost a full year now.

Phase two integrates the idea of ongoing feedback. It's self-driven by employees who leverage the SurveyMonkey platform to ask for peer or manager feedback throughout the year. This could be at the conclusion of a project, a particular launch, or after a certain deliverable goes out. In those moments, it can be hard to have the courage to ask for feedback from your peers. With a structure in place, feedback can then be woven into your work for the remainder of the quarter, the year, and your upcoming GIG conversation.

The third phase will focus on formal goals as we head into the following year.

The traditional approaches to annual performance aren't cutting it any more. Like much of the evolution of HR, part of what holds us back is our tendency to evolve iteratively These gradual changes and shifts are often outpaced by societal shifts and new norms – leaving our practices outdated.

What if we took a fresh approach to our work every couple of years and asked what we'd design from the ground up in that current reality? Perhaps we'd ask if it's HR's role to even *manage* performance?

Do we really 'manage' performance?

Every journey starts with a step. The key is starting. While we're on this journey, maybe we need to question whether it's our job to 'manage' performance at all.

Does HR really 'manage' performance? Perhaps the historical framing is working against us. If the goal is to enable our employees to have the greatest impact in our organizations, we should be thinking about developing – not managing. That simple shift in framing might unlock more potential, as it orients HR in a different way.

Focusing on developing performance puts managers in a coaching position to develop their employees on an ongoing basis. Rather than largely retrospective look backs at past performance, managers can have regular check-ins centred around growth, acquisitions of new skills and removing blockers and impediments to growth.

According to a recent Gallup survey, employees cited four primary needs from their managers (Ott, 2017):

- Job clarity and priorities
- Opportunities to learn and grow
- Ongoing feedback and communication
- Accountability.

According to this same study, only one in five employees strongly agree that they've talked to their manager in the past six months about reaching their goals. If you analyse the numbers of employees who strongly agree that their managers provide meaningful feedback and support to be more effective in their jobs, you'll find similar numbers. This is a real problem with traditional approaches.

While the data show that most managers are missing the mark, the remedy is actually not that difficult. Communicate. Each of the needs referenced above can be supported with ongoing communication. Whether weekly, monthly or quarterly, ongoing check-ins increase the likelihood of alignment and engagement – two key ingredients for optimizing performance.

As we challenge our thinking and practices around measuring performance, perhaps we also need to broaden our thinking on how we apply that. M13 Talent Partner Matt Hoffman made this compelling case for measuring team performance on my podcast.

PRACTITIONER SPOTLIGHT
The case for team reviews

Matt Hoffman, Talent Partner, M13

If you think about overall team performance, it makes sense that the unit of measurement you should be looking at is the entire team (rather than the individual), because that's how and where people work now. Unless you're in one of those rare organizations where everyone is just completely siloed in a box, you should be far less interested in how employees do individually. You should be focused on how they perform within a team, and how the team performs together.

There's this continued obsession in a lot of organizations with outdated approaches like stack ranking and how to be able to measure individual performance to the nth decimal. 'You've got to focus on the top performer.' 'You've got to get rid of the under-performers.' Obviously at some level that's true. But it's not the most actionable or useful way to drive organizational performance.

Of course, there's a reasonable desire to understand how each individual performs and measure that. But then you step back; that's not how people really work – they work in teams.

We lionize individual talent, without always considering how that all-star individual fits into the broader team. Maybe we have that wrong? After all, most work is delivered by teams. As we think about reimagining performance, perhaps it's time to factor team performance into that conversation. What might that look like? Perhaps the answer lies in the next section.

OKRs: aligning individual, team and business goals

The way we think about and measure performance has evolved over the years. From management by objectives (MBOs) to key performance indicators (KPIs) to specific measurable, achievable, relevant, time-bound (SMART) goals, we regularly refine our thinking and approach. Related, we *love* acronyms.

In 1999, John Doerr adapted a goal-setting methodology he first learned at Intel to Google. Objectives and key results, otherwise known as OKRs, are one of the latest and most broadly adopted approaches. John reflected on his introduction to OKRs in the book, *Introduction to OKRs*, by Christina Wodtke (Wodtke, 2016):

I was first exposed to OKRs at Intel in the 1970s. At the time, Intel was transitioning from a memory company to a microprocessor company, and Andy Grove and the management team needed employees to focus on a set of priorities in order to make a successful transition. Creating the OKR system helped tremendously and we all bought into it. I remember being intrigued with the idea of having a beacon or North Star every quarter, which helped set my priorities. It was also incredibly powerful for me to see Andy's OKRs, my manager's OKRs, and the OKRs for my peers. I was quickly able to tie my work directly to the company's goals. I kept my OKRs pinned up in my office and wrote new OKRs every quarter, and the system has stayed with me ever since.

Following Google's embrace, OKRs quickly spread from Silicon Valley to other titans of industry, including Amazon, Adobe, Anheuser-Busch, Dell, Deloitte, Facebook, GE, Microsoft, Netflix, Salesforce, Samsung, Siemens, Viacom and many more. The OKR genie was out of the bottle and is now a core component of performance discussions.

The allure of OKRs is their ability to provide clarity and alignment from the company through the teams down to the individual. *Objectives* are often qualitative and the *key results* are often quantitative. They're often time-bound on a quarterly basis. They're also specific and measurable, so provide clarity for performance discussions.

Shifting to OKRs can create alignment, transparency and accountability within the organization. Consider this journey to OKRs from Fitbit.

PRACTITIONER SPOTLIGHT
Driving goals and accountability with OKRs

Jaison Williams, Global Head of Talent, Fitbit

Fitbit didn't start off as a health tech company. We started with one great product idea that quickly propelled us into a business, a movement, and a way of life for our users. We set lofty goals, then moved heaven and earth – sometimes scrapping or significantly shifting resources mid-stream – to achieve them. This was the part of our culture that drove our success, but also the area that leadership believed OKRs could help us improve. So our OKR journey started with a challenge to stay scrappy and agile, while becoming ruthlessly focused on delivering what's most important.

Before OKRs, we set goals at four levels as prescribed in textbooks: individual, team, department and corporate. However, this didn't translate with OKRs. In fact, it created confusion on where OKRs were really needed and whether everyone needs to 'own' an OKR. We figured out that tech teams like Engineering, Design and so on, where many people are working to deliver the same outcome, didn't need individual OKRs – and sometimes not even team OKRs.

This learning also impacted our approach to accountability. We had to change our thinking on how performance management happens to allow the business flexibility. How would our managers hold team members accountable for performance and deliverables if they didn't have individual OKRs? Could we trust that our managers could still differentiate performance, coach and provide feedback based on what each team member was responsible to deliver? Our training and communications had to reinforce what accountability in this new way of working looked like.

Equally important was making transparency a priority. Unless every employee in the company was aware of how we were performing against our most important OKRs, then we weren't enabling our own success. Transparency is something we've had to become intentional about, setting up a regular cadence and expectation with our workforce for when OKR owners update their quarterly metrics and how they are communicated out.

Six months in, employee feedback indicates a strong awareness of our priorities and associated OKRs and where everyone should be pulling together to deliver.

Whether you embrace OKRs or other performance measurement plans, the key component for modern practices is ensuring your programmes are built around regular communication and calibration.

Managing remote performance

As mentioned earlier in the book, Covid-19 dramatically accelerated the adoption of distributed and remote work. Many companies and employees who were long accustomed to working in an office shifted to remote – literally overnight for many. How does this impact performance?

The reality is that performance was often used as an excuse *not* to allow remote work. 'How do I know my employees are actually working when I can't see them?' was a common, albeit out-of-touch, response from managers.

Measuring remote performance emphasizes the real performance driver you should have been measuring all along – output. Why does it matter *where* the work gets done if the quality of the output is high? GitLab Head of Remote Darren Murph elaborates.

PRACTITIONER SPOTLIGHT
Managing performance in remote companies

Darren Murph, Head of Remote, GitLab

This is a great awakening for performance management. I've often been asked, 'How do you know if employees are working remotely?' My immediate response is, 'How did you know they were working in the office?'

What I mean by this is that it's the burden of management. The burden of leadership. It is not the direct report's burden to prove to you that they're working. There's been a lot of subjectivity and performance management in an office. You can go years building your career on likeability. In a remote setting, likeability is not the top aspect – it's results. Results are the only thing you can actually prove.

So, how do you get results? Well, it's down to management and leaders to be very articulate and prescriptive about what is expected from organizations, from departments and from individuals.

Transparency and clarity are key to tracking performance. If you look at GitLab's engineering metrics, a lot of it is based on successful merge requests that were merged into our product pipeline. If you look over in marketing and finance, the metrics are going to look different – number of media hits or the amount of money saved. It's different per department, but it's something, and it's written down and it's understood and it's transparent.

That's an action that leaders are going to have to take. If the goals are not written down, you won't have a good way to judge whether or not someone is performing.

Hopefully this chapter has sparked some ideas around how modern people teams are thinking about performance. As I'm focused in this chapter on unlocking the potential of our employees, we'll now shift to one of the other essential components – learning.

The growth mindset advantage

The average half-life of learned skill is five years, according to the 'Career and Learning: Real time, all the time' report (Pelster *et al*, 2017). Consider the average tenure from this same report, and it's clear on the importance of developing skills in our workforce while they're in our employ. Companies understand this, with the corporate training market positioned at over $200 billion according to research by Josh Bersin (2018).

Earlier in the book we explored the importance of HR leaders being life-long learners to keep up with the pace of new developments and technology impacting our field. The same thinking applies to our employees, both from the perspective of ensuring they have the skills necessary to do the (often evolving) job, and from a growth and retention standpoint.

A commitment to continual learning helps foster a growth mindset, a highly sought-after trait that demonstrates a mix of humility and desire to learn and grow. 'I've never done that before, but I'd love to learn.' And then going out and learning. Growth mindset allows employees to be agile in their impact, deliver on stretch assignments and ultimately maximize their value to the team and company. HubSpot Chief People Officer Katie Burke weighs in on the importance of growth mindset:

> One of the things I hope excites people who join our team is that we really want to build a 21st-century HR team. That requires all of us to have a growth mindset and to be flexible and willing to learn. Unfortunately, there isn't a school yet that churns out 21st-century HR leaders, so we're creating a bit of a playbook as we grow. We're learning from people we admire as we grow, but none of us, including me, has it all figured out. The number one thing I look for when interviewing someone for our team is a comfort level with transparency, but also a comfort and humility with saying they don't know everything and are willing to learn and adapt to the organization as we scale.

As Katie mentions, growth mindset is one of the most important traits for modern HR operators. The complexity of today's problem-set that people teams most account for is massive – and increasing. The year 2020 is a great illustration of why it's so important for HR practitioners to adapt and learn – quickly.

The same goes for our employees. If we're not developing our employees, we're not likely to retain them. Fortunately, we have a tremendous array of tools are our disposal in 2020 – online, offline, peer-based, crowdsourced, and the biggest educational library the world has ever known – Google.

University of Google

How many times have you used Google today? This week? This month?

There are 70,000 searches on Google every second (Prater, 2019). That's over 5.8 billion searches per day. Almost all of the world's information is at our fingertips. It's an unlimited buffet for curious minds.

When it comes to learning, Google and other digital platforms allow the initiated to quickly find answers to (almost) all of life's questions. Need to change a filter in your fridge? Google has you covered. Finally getting around to learning how to play that guitar that's been collecting dust in your basement? YouTube has hundreds of recorded instructors waiting to teach you. Trying to determine how to craft global pandemic return-to-work plans? As the chapter on open source showed, the internet has you covered.

The key to learning and development (L&D) is leveraging the right resources at the right times that cater to the right formats for the right employees. There's art in that alignment.

PRACTITIONER SPOTLIGHT
Learning is the currency of today's economy

Michael Fraccaro, Chief People Officer, Mastercard

Learning is the true currency of today's economy. There's so much disruption from so many sources. If you stand still, you won't progress.

As an organization, we're continually evolving. To keep pace and advance our strategy, continuous learning is the key. That applies at all levels – from the organization to leadership to the individual employee. The best way to thrive in a constantly shifting landscape is to ensure you have that discipline built into the organization and that you're wired for continual learning.

Quite often we think of learning as only happening in a classroom setting or in the confines of a self-paced training module. In reality, almost every interaction you have – even reading a newspaper – is potentially part of your learning.

You've got to break it down and start thinking in terms of how the different experiences and exposures that make up everyone's job can be part of their learning journey. Within organizations, we have the opportunity to reframe how people think about learning and help them realize that learning is a habit that they can build into their day-to-day routine.

As Michael mentions, building *habits* of learning is key. Gone are the days when HR viewed learning as purely a classroom-based activity. Sure, that format is still appropriate at times, but the vehicles for learning have broadened exponentially since those classes were the only way to learn. We now have tools like on-demand micro-learning, virtual and augmented reality, aspirational learning to develop skills for the jobs you *want* – not just that job you *have*, and much more.

The current state of learning in 2020 is dynamic, driven by technology and often fluid in order to adapt to the changing needs of the business, teams and individuals. Let's explore where L&D leaders are spending their time today from LinkedIn's 2020 Workplace Learning Report (LinkedIn, 2020):

- 29% Building or sourcing learning programmes and content
- 17% Building and delivering compliance training
- 16% Promoting learning programmes to employees
- 15% Identifying skills gaps
- 15% Spending time with managers to identify learning needs
- 10% Championing learning programmes to executives.

That last bullet is key. To foster a culture of learning, these efforts must be embraced and championed by the executive team. If they're perceived simply as owned and facilitated by HR, with no overarching leadership champions, they're likely to fall flat.

So how do you get that buy-in? Put them in charge of some of the curriculum. A leadership course facilitated by an external trainer no one knows might be a hard sell. A leadership course taught by a member of your executive team will often draw more attention. The power of the C-suite in championing learning programmes is real. Harness it.

Learning in the flow of work

Work has become… complicated. Our employees are constantly pulled and pushed from one thing to the next, and that was before Covid turned everyone's lives upside down. The average US worker spends 25 per cent of their day reading or answering email. Between email notifications, Slack pings, calls, texts and WhatsApp messages interrupting them throughout the day, it's amazing they still have time for work.

This is the environment that essentially killed traditional approaches to classroom-based training and learning. An environment that gave rise to new methods of micro-learning, on-demand training and what Josh Bersin calls 'learning in the flow of work'.

According to Bersin's research, the average employee has 24 minutes a week to learn (Bersin, 2018). That reality has led to a shift in thinking from the learning community about how to deliver training in a consumable format, given the limited employee learning bandwidth. Bersin breaks down this shift as 'micro' and 'macro' learning:

- Micro-learning (I need help now)
  - 2 minutes or less
  - Topics or problem based
  - Search by asking a question (bots are great tools for this)
  - Video or text
  - Indexed and searchable
  - Content rated for quality and utility
  - Delivery vehicles: videos, articles, code samples, tools
- Macro-learning (I want to learn something new)
  - Several hours or days
  - Definitions, concepts, principles, practices
  - Exercises graded by others
  - People to talk with, learn from
  - Coaching and support needed
  - Delivery vehicles: courses, MOOCs, programmes.

As we continue down the evolutionary track from on-demand learning to 'learning in the flow of work', we'll begin leveraging technology that will send automated prompts to employees with learning materials based on predetermined milestones: promotions, new teams, relocations, new projects and so on.

This 'push' training coupled with robust libraries of on-demand learning content will enable and empower our employees to take the initiative in their own learning and development. This is a perfect illustration of one of the fundamental shifts from legacy to modern thinking in HR from Chapter 4 – *from command and control to decentralize and empower*. By empowering our employees to take control of their own education and development, we're truly unlocking their potential.

Let's take a look at a few case studies to see some of these approaches in practice.

Additional practitioner spotlights

These practitioner spotlights provide examples of developing your management layer of the organization.

PRACTITIONER SPOTLIGHT
Building management development programmes to retain middle management

Joy Sybesma, former Chief People & Culture Officer, Kargo

As Kargo scaled, we faced a common issue of needing to communicate and decide things more quickly. This became increasingly difficult, as our management team had grown to 40+ people. We tried many iterations of who was part of the group, what the group would work on and so on, but the executive team continued to have a range of issues brought to us to solve.

While our executive team was functioning well, we realized our management layer needed more guidance and support to meet our expectations. This management cohort was highly sought-after and had a lot of institutional knowledge and cultural clout – so we knew their retention was crucial. We decided to invest in a 'management development programme' to ensure we kept our emerging leaders engaged and growing.

The charter given to the managers

Our objective was to: Build individual leadership skills and team camaraderie to equip the management team to translate the needs of the organization down and expectations of employees up for better synergy, efficiency and results. Act as translators between employees and company. Become a trusting team to operate the company autonomously.

We developed the following plan to bring that to life.

360 feedback + individual development plan

We will do a 360-degree feedback review to give you a picture of how managers are perceived today, by yourself, your team, your colleagues and your manager. Each management team member will have this as a starting point to build an individual development plan (IDP). That plan will be 6–12 months in duration and will focus on key areas of strength to maximize and key areas of focus to demonstrate improvement in. People Operations will partner with you and your manager to create your IDP and roadmap of projects to work towards honing your skills.

The ways you will work towards your IDP will be threefold:

1 delegation of tasks/R&Rs (rules and regulations) (both down and up);

2 monthly group work and peer mentorship from the management team;

3 individual coaching through Pilot (explained below) and people operations.

Pilot coaching

Kargo is partnering with a software-based coaching platform called Pilot to support each management team member in their IDP and overall journey. The entire group will be on a one-year curriculum path that they will pursue simultaneously yet autonomously. The sessions and outcomes will be confidential to the management team member and their Pilot coach. The intention is to give an outside perspective from a confidential and neutral third party to better support and develop this team.

In addition to working on yourself, the management group coming together as a team is mission-critical.

Communication cadence: to build a team you need to build relationships and trust. To accomplish this, we will meet formally as a team monthly offsite for our Management Team Monthly (MTM). These meetings will provide a framework and carve out space to establish trust and become a team.

Additionally, you will meet with the executive team quarterly for the review and planning meeting to present:

- Feedback on the progress from the past quarter

- Ideas for groups for the quarter ahead.

These conversations will be a key way you translate up to the exec team on behalf of the organization. Finally, the expectation is that the management team and subsets of the team will also meet organically to build relationships and solve problems.

So why are we doing all this? Our desired outcomes are outlined below.

Desired end result(s)

- Each member makes progress and realizes accomplishments towards their IDP.

- Stronger internal relationships fostered.

- Improved 360 performance reviews.

- Improved overall business performance.

Accountability

As a member of the management team, your performance metrics will be based on self (values and accountabilities), as well as your management effectiveness (radical candour).

I left Kargo a few months into the programme but saw incredible motivation and engagement and retention of this key layer of talent as a result. I'm now the Chief People Officer at Dataiku where I am currently building a global version of this programme.

PRACTITIONER SPOTLIGHT
Increasing manager Net Promoter Score (NPS) through performance training

Mai Ton, Founder, EMP HR Consulting

In a lot of companies where I've worked, programmes to train new managers are sparse or non-existent. As an HR leader, I felt compelled to craft my own training programmes to get new managers up to speed quickly. It was my goal to train managers and give them a space to learn and feel safe expressing that they were out of their comfort zones. I also knew that if I could activate all the managers in the company, it would increase engagement scores company-wide, decrease turnover and lead to better business results.

Over the course of five months, I had the chance to show that my own in-house L&D programme had a direct effect on the business. Here's how I did it.

First, I solved the need to train my managers by creating my own content and teaching it each week during lunch-and-learn sessions. I tackled bite-size learning segments covering things like 'how to have difficult conversations', 'how to place an employee on a performance improvement plan (PIP)', 'how to give feedback', 'how to motivate your team' and 'how to have effective 1:1 conversations'. My coursework was created based on what I thought my own managers were struggling with day-to-day.

Second, I collected feedback from these weekly sessions so that I could measure the efficacy of these sessions and also how managers actually performed leading their teams. I inserted one specific NPS question in our quarterly engagement survey: 'I would recommend my manager as a great manager to others', to measure how successful our managers were in real life.

When I started the teaching sessions, manager NPS scored in the 60s (out of 100). As the sessions continued, I saw a direct correlation between offering these weekly sessions and the score of the manager NPS question. By the time I hit week 20 of these sessions, the scores on this one question increased to 80+, so it was clear that attendees were getting value. When I saw the increased scores on that manager NPS question, I believed that the managers who attended my sessions actually applied the content to managing their teams. Manager NPS scores remained in the 80s for the next three quarters.

Having strong and engaged managers led to stronger engagement scores from employees. We moved about five points on our company-wide engagement scores and we decreased turnover to less than 5 per cent per quarter (which is pretty good for a fast-growing start-up company). This increased manager and engagement scores, and we started winning various accolades that come from having a great place to work, which gave us more publicity and more customers.

The great thing for me was that I had a chance to show how one of my people programmes, in this case, weekly L&D sessions, directly impacted our scores and our business outcomes. After all, we all know that when you take care of employees, they will take care of your business.

To be effective as a people leader, both to your teams and to your executives, this example shows the importance of understanding how learning affects your performance and how that is measured and tracked. Resources, budgets and bandwidth are finite. Modern people leaders don't do things for the sake of doing them – they measure, scrutinize and monitor their programmes regularly to ensure they're delivering value to the business – which frames one of the more important questions for modern people practitioners.

Do you know you're making an impact on the business? I mean, really *know*. In the last chapter, 'The house that data built', we'll explore the evolution of data and people analytics to help you measure the impact of all this work.

References

Bersin, J (2018) A New Paradigm for Corporate Training: Learning in the Flow of Work. Available from: https://joshbersin.com/2018/06/a-new-paradigm-for-corporate-training-learning-in-the-flow-of-work/#_ftn6 (archived at https://perma.cc/2UHT-8R3S)

Cantieri, B (2019) Our Journey to Reimagine Performance Reviews at SurveyMonkey. Available from: www.surveymonkey.com/curiosity/our-journey-to-reimagine-performance-reviews-at-surveymonkey/ (archived at https://perma.cc/8BAK-GBRQ)

LinkedIn Learning (2020) 2020 Workplace Learning Report. Available from: https://learning.linkedin.com/resources/workplace-learning-report (archived at https://perma.cc/8M2Z-S8YC)

Meyer, H, Kay, E and French, J (1965) Split Roles in Performance Appraisal, *Harvard Business Review*. Available from: https://hbr.org/1965/01/split-roles-in-performance-appraisal (archived at https://perma.cc/Z75H-DRZK)

Ott, B (2017) 3 Reasons Why Performance Development Wins in the Workplace, *Gallup*. Available from: www.gallup.com/workplace/231620/why-performance-development-wins-workplace.aspx (archived at https://perma.cc/7DNR-ASRM)

Pelster, B *et al* (2017) Career and Learning: Real Time, All the Time, *Deloitte Insights*. Available from: www2.deloitte.com/us/en/insights/focus/human-capital-trends/2017/learning-in-the-digital-age.html (archived at https://perma.cc/36VY-XUQE)

Prater, M (2019) 25 Google Search Statistics to Bookmark ASAP, HubSpot. Available from: https://blog.hubspot.com/marketing/google-search-statistics (archived at https://perma.cc/7332-Z56K)

Society of Human Resource Management (2016) Creating a More Human Workplace Where Employees and Business Thrive. Available from: www.shrm.org/hr-today/trends-and-forecasting/special-reports-and-expert-views/Documents/Human-Workplace.pdf (archived at https://perma.cc/F477-CW5H)

Wodtke, C (2016) *Introduction to OKRs*, O'Reilly Media Inc, Sebastapol, California

11

The house that data built

A great home can't be built without a solid foundation. The same thinking applies to people analytics, yet instead of concrete we're talking about data integrity, uniformity and integrations.

Data themselves itself isn't to HR. We've been collecting data on spreadsheets and HR systems for years. We've always been big on data and reporting, and yet we've only just recently embraced analytics and insights. This chapter will examine that journey and explore insights from some of the leading thinkers in people analytics.

If you've been in this space long enough, you have an Excel story. It's really a badge of honour for us old-timers in the space. Mine sticks with me.

Back in the mid-2000s I was running global recruiting for Ticketmaster. We had businesses around the world and many had their own applicant tracking systems (or none). Needless to say, there was no integration or common real-time reporting dashboards.

There was a point in time when we were preparing to spin out from our parent company, InterActiveCorp (IAC), and become public as a stand-alone business. Our headcount was under close scrutiny and we had several machinations of hiring freezes, pauses, holds, prioritizations and so on. What this meant in practice was that I had to build a common Excel spreadsheet that every regional HR Directory used to compile all of their open positions, offers, and stages of every open role in their region.

Every Friday, I had to collect, collate and reconcile every regional spreadsheet with ours for the United States and compile a master global document for our executive team. Every. Friday. For months.

My fingers are still unsteady from that experience as I recount and type that memory. That was my first deep, and somewhat traumatic, dive into reporting at scale.

Fortunately for all of us, the tools and practices have evolved dramatically since then. The level of sophistication in best-in-class teams is like comparing ping-pong to VR gaming. It's a totally different class.

The history of analytics

Before we explore the modern state of people analytics, we should understand how we got here. There are few humans on the planet better positioned for that discussion than the founder and CEO of People Analytics and Future of Work community and event series, Al Adamson.

He views the evolution of people analytics in stages, and sees us as currently in the 3.0 stage. He breaks down the evolution as follows (Adamson, 2017):

- People Analytics 1.0: Research & Analysis (1924–present)
    - Description: Academically inspired individual, team, & organizational studies that analyse the past with the hope of improving the future
    - Data: Specific, solicited, observational
    - For whom? Executives
- People Analytics 2.0: Data Aggregation & Visualization (2001–present)
    - Description: Dashboards, scorecards, drill-down, self-service, data-mining, exception reporting & alerts, democratizing data & insights
    - Data: Transactional, descriptive
    - For whom? Executives, HR business partners, HR analysts
- People Analytics 3.0 Productization/'Solutionize' (2015–present)
    - Description: Apps, chatbots, AI, machine learning, wearables, digitized processes, networked intelligence, well-being, personal development
    - Data: Behavioural, passive, intention-based
    - For whom? Executives, HR business partners, team leaders, employees.

It's important to note from the timeline that the dates run concurrently. Just because our capabilities are at the people analytics 3.0 stage, it doesn't mean we're all there. In fact, much like the capabilities and approach gap in HR and people operations that this book examines, the field and capabilities for people analytics is also a spectrum.

On one side, companies are harnessing predictive analytics to forecast talent needs of the business a year out or more. On the other side, practitioners are still grappling with pivot tables and macros on Excel.

These phases are a good way to think about the evolutionary shift in people analytics, not just in terms of how they are processed, but in who is involved. Adamson argues that previously, leaders would commission people analytics projects with an 'organization-first mindset' to understand how to optimize sales, employee productivity and other business outcomes.

Al Adamson breaks down the history and evolution:

> Historically people analytics has been commissioned by leaders to better understand how they can best optimize employee productivity, innovation, customer satisfaction, sales, profitability, or some other business outcome. It's been about efficiency and effectiveness: 'Am I, as an executive, using my budget (payroll, bonuses, benefits, training, employee perks, etc) wisely to achieve desired outcomes?'
>
> All fine and good, yet this has been done with an organization-first mindset, with little regard to people's humanity apart from their role in achieving those outcomes. The human benefit has often emerged as a fortunate externality at best, an unwelcome accident at worst (because it might have to be maintained or even invested in over time).
>
> Now, however, this is fundamentally shifting, and it's shifting for good. People Analytics 3.0 is helping humanize the corporate experience. As it does so, it provides incentive (both conscious and unconscious) for workers to provide better data (more accurate, frequent, specific, etc). Better data mean better insights. Better insights means better decisions: risk is reduced and the likelihood that desired outcomes are achieved elevates beyond where it would have been otherwise. All great things.

For many HR and people practitioners, analytics can be scary and over-whelming with its (potential) complexity. Just the idea of people analytics is enough to get your heart rate going a few beats faster. I see this a lot in companies with firmly established practices and programmes that lack embedded analytics capabilities.

Last year I sat down with Insight222 Executive Director David Green to get his thoughts on the evolution of people analytics from fringe to foundational:

> People analytics has become transformative. It was something on the periphery of HR which only some companies were doing. Now I see it being very central to HR strategy moving forward. There's a number of reasons for that. People see the good work that the pioneers have been doing in this space.
>
> We're producing much more data; as consumers, as employees and as organizations. We're living in an interesting time. Politically, economically,

socially. A lot of disruption is going on within organizations and if an organization is to grow and survive, then they really need to understand their people who are going to help them and ultimately it's then understanding the data around the people that can help them make better decisions.

David is right. To really harness the transformative potential of people analytics, we have to know what to measure, why we're measuring it and how to interpret those results. To do so, we need frameworks to gauge where we are on the pendulum of capability.

My first introduction to modern people analytics was Josh Bersin's Talent Analytics Maturity Model in 2014. It was the early days of HR Open Source and I was working with a start-up, OPOWER, to build a case study on their journey to build people analytics capability. They modelled their multiyear roadmap using Josh Bersin's model with an aspirational goal of reaching Level 4 in three years.

Bersin's Talent Analytics Maturity Model was a framework that many companies used to benchmark their people analytics capabilities (Bersin, 2014). For readers who aren't familiar with this model, I'm adding below:

- Level 1: Reactive – Operational Reporting
  - Ad hoc operational reporting
  - Reactive to business demands, data in isolation and difficult to analyse
- Level 2: Proactive – Advanced Reporting
  - Operational reporting for benchmarking and decision making
  - Multidimensional analysis and dashboards
- Level 3: Strategic Analytics
  - Segmentation, statistical analysis, development of 'people models'
  - Analysis of dimensions to understand cause and delivery of actionable solutions
- Level 4: Predictive Analytics
  - Development of predictive models, scenario planning
  - Risk analysis and mitigation, integration with strategic planning.

All companies are somewhere on this spectrum. In 2014 when this was released, only 4 per cent of companies had reaches the pinnacle of predictive analytics, but a lot has happened in this space since then and Josh Bersin has iterated the model over time, as well as reporting on company adoption.

In 2018, 84 per cent of companies were still in operational mode and had not yet advanced to the more impactful and less administrative phases of people analytics. To better align with current thinking, technology and approaches, Bersin updated the model, and it will be useful to us to understand each aspect in more detail (Bersin, 2020).

LEVEL 1: TRUSTED REPORTING AND ALERTS

This level is defined by reactive reporting of operational and compliance measures, plus a focus on data accuracy, consistency and timeliness. The focus is on making HR and talent better, including ERP, talent, recruiting, learning, diversity, compensation and rewards.

Key milestones include:

- Data management, integration, and shared data dictionary;
- Governance of data definitions;
- Reporting and integration tools;
- Strong IT partnership;
- Sound tool set for dashboards;
- User access to data.

The majority of HR/people teams are still at this level. If we're honest, many still struggle with reporting accuracy because they work across manual systems – or toggle between multiple systems that aren't integrated, so true and accurate reporting requires a manual mashup of data.

LEVEL 2: MANAGEMENT INSIGHTS AND ACTION

At this level, organizations engage in proactive reporting for decision making, analysis of trends and benchmarks, and produce customizable, self-service dashboards. The focus is on identifying performance engagement, retention and culture issues through feedback, conversations and surveys; well-being, location, psychometric data assessments and 360 data; reskilling of HR business partners.

Key milestones include:

- Integration of analytics team with performance, talent, engagement and other assessment offerings;
- Ethics and trust standards for data privacy;
- Clear communication to users.

This is the optimal level for most teams and the entry point to modern people capabilities. If you can achieve and reside at this stage, you'll be designing and refining impactful people programmes for your business.

LEVEL 3: PRODUCTIVITY AND WORK REDESIGN

At this level, organizations produce statistical analysis, identify issues and actionable solutions, centralize staff and integrate data. Organizations should take a consultative approach to individual business units, show expertise in network analysis, have an analytics team embedded in the business, and leverage tools for organizational network analysis (ONA).

Key milestones include:

- Understanding of how the organization works;
- ONA and/or email metadata;
- Map of database relationships that includes understanding of organizational design, management practices, high-performer behaviours and misbehaviours.

At this level you'll have a dedicated people analytics team that has a holistic view of all of your people data, including their interdependencies. Level 3 allows people teams to *begin* developing predictive analytics to identify risks to the business and strategic opportunities before they present themselves.

LEVEL 4: AI-ENABLED ACTION PLATFORMS

At this level, organizations are developing predictive models and data governance models, carrying out scenario planning, and analytics are integrated with business and workforce planning. Organizations at this top level should provide tools to help managers improve behaviours, leverage employee segmentation and journeys, and integrate AI-driven chatbots and other systems of employee engagement.

The key milestone is:

- Established process for delivering action and insights to managers and bringing data together into employee experience solutions, journeys and problem-solving projects.

This is *The Jetsons*-level analytics (a reference my fellow GenXers will no doubt recognize, but admittedly will require a quick google search for most readers). This is near self-actualized levels of analytics. Very few companies have the budget, resources and tools to operate at this level in 2020.

As the above framings from Al, David and Josh reinforce, it's important to recognize that we're all at different stages of the people analytics journey. I imagine many readers will self-identify at each of these stages, but the majority of you will likely be in levels two and three.

For the purposes of this chapter, I'll be focusing more on the advanced stages to provide context on that journey and on how companies and practitioners are using data and analytics to drive their businesses forward.

This is a complex and sizable field, so I won't claim to provide (remotely) all the context you need. My aim is to cover some of the history and considerations – including ethical implications, diversity, recruiting, workforce planning – as a starting point in your journey towards those top levels of people analytics mastery. Let's dig in.

RO(Why)

The business case for investing in people analytics is pretty clear. According to research by Insight222, companies with advanced people analytics capabilities have a 30 per cent higher stock price, 79 per cent higher return on equity and 56 per cent higher profit margins (Green, 2019).

It's no surprise that this directly correlates with an increase in people analytics professionals, as well as a deeper prioritization for the field. Some of the recent results from LinkedIn's 2020 Global Talent Trends report include (LinkedIn, 2020):

- There has been a 242% increase in HR professionals with data analysis skills over the past 5 years.
- Fifty-five per cent of talent professionals still need help putting basic people analytics into practice.
- Seventy-five per cent say that people analytics will be a major priority for their company over the next five years.

We're already using analytics to solve a range of business and people issues, as Figure 11.1 shows, from performance to workforce planning to identifying skill gaps and a range of other HR/people problems. However, with many talent professionals still requiring training or support to use them, it's vital we think about how to embed them into our HR practices. The sophistication of best-in-class programmes, approaches and tools allows the field to move firmly from transacting to strategic.

FIGURE 11.1 Most popular people analytics practices today and in 2025

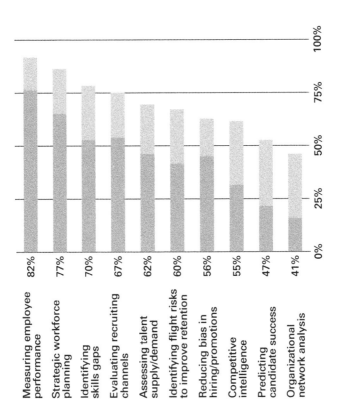

Most popular people analytics practices today and in 2025

Percentage of talent professionals who say their companies currently use these practices or plan to within the next 5 years.

■ Currently in use ■ Planned future use

Measuring employee performance	82%
Strategic workforce planning	77%
Identifying skills gaps	70%
Evaluating recruiting channels	67%
Assessing talent supply/demand	62%
Identifying flight risks to improve retention	60%
Reducing bias in hiring/promotions	56%
Competitive intelligence	55%
Predicting candidate success	47%
Organizational network analysis	41%

0%   25%   50%   75%   100%

LinkedIn Global Talent Trends, p 31. Reproduced with permission

For large and enterprise companies especially, identifying and fixing a small issue may feel incremental – but when applied at scale it might result in millions of dollars in cost savings.

Nielsen recognized they were having an issue with attrition (Steiner, 2017). They tasked their head of a newly formed people analytics team, Piyush Mathur, to find out why. After building a model to confirm and identify the root cause of their attrition problems, they identified and addressed the issue – which slashed regrettable voluntary turnover by nearly half and saved the company millions of dollars.

Nielsen has since built a robust people analytics capability (Louie, 2018). Their mantra of 'business outcomes first' guides their analytics vision and prioritizes having impacting business outcomes lead their priorities. These means their capabilities include:

- instant answers to talent-related questions;
- a constant read on the pulse of the organization;
- a sixth sense of when action needs to be taken;
- deep insights on major talent issues and areas; and
- a view into future talent needs and trends.

Realizing that vision depends on their ability to manage their workforce, create opportunities for their employees and improve their talent to a fundamentally higher level. They're building the capabilities they need to achieve this on a few different dimensions:

> **Data:** Data is the lifeblood of any analytic effort. People data is notoriously messy and disconnected. We have a significant effort underway to improve the quality and completeness of our people data and integrate it with other critical data sets (e.g., financial, operational).

In an automobile analogy, data is the petrol. Without it, you go nowhere:

> **Technology:** Data only becomes valuable when it is accessible and usable. We are launching an analytics platform that brings our people data to bear in the form of use-case-driven reporting (eg understanding workforce trends, major drivers of attrition, the efficiency of our hiring process), with the ability to see aggregated insights and drill down to individual information to take action.

As my painful Excel headcount tracking memory that opened the chapter shows, you can do analytics in low-tech ways. The good news? You don't have to. Most of our core HR technology systems have at least a base level of analytics capabilities. With a bigger budget, the sky is the limit as there are hundred (thousands?) of analytics tools on the market at this point in people analytics' maturity:

> **People:** We are increasing the analytic capabilities of our HR associates through a People Analytics Community of Practice, which provides training and access to resources (eg current tools, past studies) and promotes the sharing of best practices across the organization.

All of the companies at Level 4 of the various maturity models will have dedicated people analytics teams. You just can't reach that level of sophistication without that dedicated focus. The great news for practitioners who aspire to get there is the global community of leaders in this space who've embraced open-source approaches and are happy to share their learnings with you:

> **Approach:** We are putting the policies and processes in place to ensure we protect the privacy of our associates around the world, utilizing data in ways that are transparent and beyond reproach.

Nielsen's last point on transparency and privacy is really important – particularly for global companies operating across countries with different data privacy laws and regulations. We'll explore that more deeply later in this chapter when we get into the ethical implications of people analytics.

For Nielsen, having this clarity in their people analytics foundation is smart. It provides clarity and alignment, sets expectations and presents a clear foundation for their efforts.

In most companies there are near infinite numbers of business challenges that people analytics can help unlock. You need to have a clear sense of how you prioritize and tackle these challenges so you can focus your (often finite) resources on solving the right problems at the right time.

2020 vision: analytics in workforce planning

One of the biggest use cases for people analytics is workforce planning. The ability to predict and understand what talent resources you'll need, and when, is a significant advantage to a business.

This can only be realized in some of the advanced levels of the models shown earlier in this chapter from Al Adamson and Josh Bersin. If you don't have that technology, integration and infrastructure in place, this will be an exercise in Excel wizardry that would make Harry Potter proud.

One of the hallmarks of legacy HR is that they're often reacting to the business needs. That transactional, and often behind, view is one of the biggest frustrations executives have about our field.

Modern people teams are operating from the front. Because workforce planning is future-oriented, it's a key aspect of modern HR teams' success. By embracing and embedding people analytics capabilities, modern people teams are able to predict and proactively address challenges and opportunities much earlier than their legacy-oriented contemporaries. That allows them to make a significant impact to the business, and avoid one of the labels often placed on old-school HR teams – *'invisible or in trouble'*.

Those new to the field are probably wondering where to start. In LinkedIn's 2020 Global Talent Trends Report, Ross Sparkman, author of *Strategic Workforce Planning: Developing optimized talent strategies for future growth* (2019), broke down a fundamental way of approaching analytics in workforce planning (LinkedIn, 2020):

- **Estimate future company demand**: First you need to gauge how many new and replacement hires will be required in the months or years ahead. Gather as much data as possible about current turnover and work with business strategists to understand where and how growth will occur.

  – Sample inputs: Attrition rates, retirement rates, historical correlations between labour force and production, cost constraints, and feedback from on-the-ground managers.

- **Assess the external talent market**: Once you've assessed future needs, it's time to study the external landscape to find the best places to look for the required skills, diversity, level of seniority, and other factors.

  – Potential data sources: HR industry tools (such as LinkedIn), government reports and macro trends, such as population, education and migration.

- **Make recommendations**: How will the company find the talent it needs? Your advice may be as simple as targeting a specific geography for recruiting. But if analysis shows that your company's needs are incompatible with the talent landscape, it's time to get creative.

  – Possible solutions: Open an office in a different location.

  – Use succession planning and compensation to address attrition. Set up an internal training programme to build a workforce with the needed skills.

The framework above is a great illustration of the sequencing and stages of a workforce planning exercise. Imagine the strategic value to the business

FIGURE 11.2 Tackling any problem with the IMPACT framework

	Question	Action to take	Stakeholder responsible
Identify	What's the business issue we're trying to solve?	Create a problem statement, propose a hypothesis, ensure legal compliance.	Business
Measure	What's the strategic priority of the issue?	Benchmark the severity of the issue and define what success looks like.	People analytics team and business
Plan	What's our plan for insight and action?	Check against past analyses, plan type of testing and data gathering.	People analytics team and business
Analyze	What are the findings from our analytics?	Find actionable insights, confirm statistical confidence.	People analytics team
Communicate	What do we recommend and how?	Decide on the right medium to convey results and recommendations, develop plan to track impact.	People analytics team and business
Track	What's the impact of actions taken?	Monitor results after intervention and socialize any important findings.	People analytics team and business

LinkedIn Global Talent Trends, p 39. Reproduced with permission

when your HR and people department can do a full talent-market assessment and make accurate recommendations on where to open that new office based on clear potential workforce data. Talk about moving from reactive to proactive.

Best-in-class people teams not only have this capability, but it's clearly understood and called upon from the C-suite. Having a decision support matrix helps them identify, prioritize and involve the right stakeholders in their projects. The example in Figure 11.2 reflects the IMPACT matrix used by LinkedIn's own people analytics team when evaluating projects.

The importance of having this rigour ensures you're focusing your limited resources on the right problems. As mentioned earlier in the chapter, there are always going to be problems to solve – they just might not be the right problems to solve. Insight222 Executive Director David Green shares an example.

PRACTITIONER SPOTLIGHT
The importance of measuring the right things

David Green, Executive Director, Insight222

If you give data to a bunch of analysts, they'll find something, but they might not find something particularly interesting or important to the business.

I was in India a couple of years ago, meeting with the chief analytics officer of a very large company. He had a supportive CEO and he and the team had done some great work in other areas of analytics – not in HR. He thought it was about time they did something in HR and looked externally to see what other companies had done.

There were a lot of analytics projects around attrition, so they decided to develop a flight risk model. They spent six months developing it. They tested it. They told me it was over 90 per cent accurate.

Then they went to HR and no one cared because their attrition rate, as a business, was so low. It wasn't a problem.

Great work. Wrong problem.

Great work. Wrong problem. Those are words you don't want to hear when allocating your limited people analytics resources on business issues. Make sure you're asking the right questions to ensure the business need and business impact are aligned before you undertake new people analytics projects.

Using data to drive diversity

As mentioned in Chapter 3, 'Building a company for everyone', data and analytics are often key components of a successful DEI strategy. To really be insightful, the data must be granular in the different classifications of gender, race and other employee classes. To extract actionable insights, it's not enough to know your turnover numbers for men vs women; you have to drill down further to be able to gauge turnover for Latinx vs Black vs White women. Only with this ability to segment and understand specific employee populations can you truly identify trends and insights.

The general rule of analysing data is that larger data sets yield better insights. While true, this may push some organizations to group categories (ie white vs PoC) in order to build larger data sets. This is a mistake, as this *Harvard Business Review* article, 'The mistake companies make when they use data to plan diversity efforts' (Wullert, Gilmartin and Simard, 2019), explains:

> As companies collect more and more data on their workforce, there are going to be groups for whom the available data are more limited than others. Small numbers cannot be a rationale to stall progress. Concluding that little can be said with limited data renders underrepresented groups more invisible and creates a roadblock to meaningful change. To create lasting and impactful change, organizations should be willing to analyse small numbers, gather detailed interview data on employee experiences, engage managers as allies for change, and hold themselves accountable to making small numbers grow.

Don't be afraid of small numbers. While larger data sets are optimal, it's more important to work with what you have if you want to effect change. If you truly make the effort to understand those small numbers, that knowledge may give you the keys to unlock that path to making those small numbers enable big impact.

Ethics in the age of analytics

'With great power comes great responsibility.' Spiderman's Uncle Ben may have used those words to guide a young Spidey, but they ring true when considering the ethical implications of analytics. When we have the power to build predictive analytics models that identify risks, like turnover, before they happen – how and where we use them matters.

Consider the following real examples of ethics in people analytics from IBM's 'The Grey Area: Ethical dilemmas in HR analytics' (Green, Guenole and Feinzig, 2018):

- New technology permits identification of employees who are making negative comments about their employer on public websites. What should we consider before proceeding?
- We would like to integrate data sets from different systems such as employee opinion surveys and performance management for strategic insight that will help with workforce planning. Is it okay to do so?

- We would like to survey our employees about a sensitive topic, and were told we should not because it will make the workers think about things they wouldn't have thought about otherwise. Is this a valid reason not to proceed?

- We can detect potential employee health risks through wearables and sleep monitors. Should we use this information to make decisions about employees? What if that employee is an airline pilot, for example, and their potential health risk could be dangerous for customers?

Maybe you've grappled with one of the questions above. How did you approach it? Was the decision yours? Should it have been?

With great power comes great responsibility. We have the tools and technology at our fingertips to make data-based assumptions where we had only anecdotal ideas in the past. However, just because we *can* doesn't mean we *should*. We have to consider the ethical, and at times moral, basis for these projects.

An article from CapGemini, 'Walking the tightrope of people analytics – balancing value and trus*t*' (CapGemini, 2020), explored some of the practical considerations HR faces when launching people analytics projects:

> Consider this example of how a People Analytics project can go wrong: let's assume your organization has an attrition problem. So, you set up a People Analytics project and tackle the topic. After a couple of data-crunching rounds, you discover that employees with characteristic 'X' are more likely to leave the organization. Perfect! You can and probably want to engage with employees with the characteristic 'X' to see what is happening with them, what can be done, what can be changed etc. Great project, great result.
>
> But do you then also tell Recruitment to hire fewer people with characteristic 'X'? Or do you keep this result a secret? Can you even keep this insight secret, and can you unlearn it? What if team members move to a different role? Is there a difference – in your national regulations, or in the public perception – if characteristic 'X' means 'daily commute' or 'gender of employee' or race, or religion? You can see how you're suddenly walking a tightrope and any misstep may drastically hurt your organization's reputation and employee trust.

The ethical quandaries aren't anecdotal. We now have the ability to leverage data to make predictive inferences about our workforce that could easily lead to unethical decisions if we're not careful. So how do we ensure we're asking the right questions to guide our work ethically? These are questions HR leaders should be asking, as referenced in the 'Walking the tightrope of people analytics' article:

- How do I balance the interests of the employer and the employee when conducting people analytics projects at scale?
- How do I structure my people analytics projects and build in the right checks and balances to deliver proportionate value to both management and employees?
- How do I ensure fairness and transparency in every project?
- How do I prevent illegal/immoral application of results?

As you build out your analytics capabilities and determine what projects to undertake, it's vital to ensure there is an ethical review component as you determine what problems to solve. Asking the questions above won't give you absolute clarity on the ethical implications, but they will help guide your thinking and understanding of the right approach. The challenge HR leaders face is that the resolution of the ethical questions is often neither clear or simple. It can lie in a grey area open to subjective human interpretation, and may have multiple and complex effects.

One of the challenges organizations face is that views towards ethical behaviour aren't universal. In 2018, IBM released a white paper by David Green, Sheri Feinzig and Nigel Guenole, titled 'The Grey Area: Ethical dilemmas in HR analytics' (Green *et al*, 2018). The study surveyed over 20,000 workers in 44 countries for their perspectives on data use in HR analytics. The feedback and perspectives resulted in four classifications of ethical outlooks:

- **Absolutists:** Assume the best possible outcomes occur when universal moral rules are followed. *'I believe the rules are the rules.'*
- **Situationalists:** Reject moral rules and advocate individualistic analysis of each situation. *'The rules are made for the guidance of the wise. If a new policy means better results and benefits for everyone involved, it should be enforced.'*
- **Subjectivists:** Want evaluations based on personal values rather than universal moral principles. *'It's my way or the highway. I personally can't get behind a policy that ignores potential risks, so I can't see why anybody else would be comfortable with that.'*
- **Exceptionalists:** Want moral rules to guide judgements but recognize the need for exceptions. *'The exception that proves the rule. I don't personally love this idea, but I can see how others might benefit from it.'*

The fact is that the very definition of ethical interpretation adds another layer of complexity to an already ambiguous situation. The potential for abuse and misuse of data is high if we don't account for ethics in our process. It's vital that HR teams understand and mitigate these risks, and at times requests, to use people data in this way.

With great power comes great responsibility. We must use it wisely.

Building your own house

I realize that this chapter contains a lot to take in. The reality is that this is a massively complex space where only specialists can truly go deep. Most practitioners won't need this level of depth, but they should all have a grasp of the potential, impact and considerations surrounding people analytics.

As someone new to people analytics, you might be reading this chapter and wondering how you can possibly move from Level 1 of Bersin's model to Level 4. Don't worry – you're far from alone. As David Green reinforces, the key is to just get started:

> It's never too late to get started in people analytics. There's still many organizations that are already in the early stages of getting started. Grasp the nettle by the horns and get on with it. I think the most important thing is to really think about what are the business challenges that your organization faces. Then think about the people elements of those business challenges and how data analysis could potentially help you get insights that could allow you to solve that challenge.
>
> Think cross-functionally. This is not something that you can do in isolation in HR. If you're going to solve business challenges, you need to bring HR data and combine it with business data, perhaps some external data as well. There will be some people, perhaps, in HR who have some of the skills that can get you started. Maybe find some HR business partners that are analytically minded and curious enough that will help you get the right attention of the right people in the business. Then you can start talking to them about things that you could potentially do to impact the business.

I highly recommend following the contributors in this chapter for ideas and learning. Most of them offer free newsletter, resources and so on. That's how I've learned about this space – and they've forgotten more than I know. You've got this.

Let's take a look at how some companies are leveraging people analytics below.

Case study

One of the most common uses of people analytics and reporting is to better understand employee turnover. This is a massive cost to business – both in terms of brain drain and the practical investment of recruiting. In the following case study, Luno demonstrates how they addressed turnover by looking more closely at the data.

CASE STUDY
How Luno used data to turn around turnover

Kelly Jackson, Chief People Officer, Luno

Company: Luno
Region: Europe
Industry: Banking and Financial Services
Company size: 201–500

What they did

We reviewed the candidate scorecards of all Lunauts who left within their first 90 days, looking for any predictive indicators that correlated with the short tenure.

Why they did it

To improve our quality of hire and use the data as a basis for creating an exceptional interview culture and candidate experience

How they did it

We had two sample groups; group one had left Luno within their first 90 days in 2019 and group two contained a random sample of current employees who had rated highly in their previous performance check-in.

For both groups we re-read their candidate scorecards from each stage of the hiring process, and were looking specifically at the commentary in the scorecards for common patterns which could be used in future interviews as warning flags that either an offer should not be made, or that an area should be more deeply probed in the next assessment stage. The data were also used to inform the skills we needed to develop in our hiring community and the elements of the candidate experience we needed to focus on to make it an exceptional experience.

We found that in group one, 100 per cent were recorded as a 'yes' or 'strong yes' but all had commentary indicators that their skills and/or experience would be misaligned to the role they were interviewing for. For example, interviewers projected skills onto the candidate based on their background or type of companies worked at, without probing for the evidence to support this. Alternatively, they assumed that the candidate could be taught the required skills if they passed the culture and values interview – again a misalignment between experience and need from the business.

The patterns seen in the commentary led us to one conclusion: that the overall rating was being inconsistently applied and carried more weight than it should have done, without being verified.

The analysis also showed a lack of consistency in our Moontality (our values) assessment. This has led to the introduction of independent Moontality interview panels – cultural champion interviewers agnostic to the hiring team, and skilled in behavioural competency interviewing.

Finally, there was no evidence in the commentary of group one candidates of any of our high-performance behavioural indicators. However, in comparison, group two had commentary referencing those behaviours within their scorecards – although a wider sample group is needed to validate whether the scorecards of those identified as high performing also contained any red flags.

Impact/ROI

Reduce last quarter's mis-hires (those who leave within the first 90 days) by 3 per cent – currently 8 per cent. Decrease the percentage of candidates who strongly agree that process is not challenging: 20 per cent against benchmark of 7 per cent. Decrease the number of candidates who felt that interviewers were not well prepared or performing skilfully: 12 per cent against benchmark of 4 per cent.

All journeys begin with a step. Don't compare yourself to best-in-class organizations, as they have years of experience, and in many cases millions of dollars, invested into the journey that got them there. Start small. Scale. Learn. Scale some more. You can do this. To build a modern people team and capability, you must.

Hopefully your head is full of ideas after reading these 11 chapters. In the conclusion, we'll bring it all together, with tips and ideas on how to build a career as a modern HR practitioner. I'll also share some resources where you can continue to find tools, information and community for practising modern HR.

References

Adamson, A (2017) People Analytics 3.0, LinkedIn. Available from: www.linkedin.
com/pulse/people-analytics-30-al-adamsen/ (archived at https://perma.cc/
BSH2-WB8V)

Bersin, J (2014) The Datafication of HR, *Deloitte*. Available from: www2.deloitte.
com/us/en/insights/deloitte-review/issue-14/dr14-datafication-of-hr.html
(archived at https://perma.cc/83C8-3EQ3)

Bersin, J (2020) Resource Spotlight: A New Maturity Model for Analytics.
Available from: https://bersinacademy.com/blog/2020/04/resource-spotlight-a-
new-maturity-model-for-analytics (archived at https://perma.cc/BWQ6-DBRW)

CapGemini (2020) Walking the Tightrope of People Analytics – Balancing Value
and Trust. Available from: www.capgemini.com/2020/05/walking-the-tightrope-
of-people-analytics-balancing-value-and-trust/ (archived at https://perma.cc/
QF9N-PTJY)

Green, D (2019) How to Create More Impact with People Analytics, Insight222.
Available from: www.slideshare.net/DavidGreen21/how-to-create-more-impact-
with-people-analytics (archived at https://perma.cc/3C4Z-VYD5)

Green, D, Guenole, N and Feinzig, S (2018) The Grey Area: Ethical dilemmas in
HR analytics, IBM. Available from: www.ibm.com/watson/talent/
talent-management-institute/ethical-dilemmas-hr-analytics/desktop/index.html
(archived at https://perma.cc/6PFE-LEE4)

LinkedIn (2020) Global Talent Trends 2020. Available from: https://business.
linkedin.com/talent-solutions/recruiting-tips/global-talent-trends-2020#two
(archived at https://perma.cc/AY5F-XP8Z)

Louie, C (2018) An Analytics-Powered Approach to Talent, *Nielsen*. Available
from: www.nielsen.com/us/en/news-center/2018/analytics-powered-approach-
talent/ (archived at https://perma.cc/9ZL5-9AVN)

Sparkman, R (2018) *Strategic Workforce Planning: Developing optimized talent
strategies for future growth*, Kogan Page, London

Steiner, K (2017) People Analytics Isn't as Hard as You Think – Nielsen Proves
Why. Available from: https://business.linkedin.com/talent-solutions/
blog/employee-retention/2017/how-nielsen-used-people-analytics-to-increase-
retention-and-saved-millions-of-dollars (archived at https://perma.cc/
R6FA-4LS5)

Wullert, K, Gilmartin, S and Simard, C (2019) The Mistake Companies Make
When They Use Data to Plan Diversity Efforts, *Harvard Business Review*.
Available from: https://hbr.org/2019/04/the-mistake-companies-make-when-
they-use-data-to-plan-diversity-efforts (archived at https://perma.cc/
V97H-Z3Z8)

Conclusion

Trying to capture the breadth, depth and nuance of the field of HR is quite an undertaking. No single book can do it justice, but I hope I have covered enough here to lay the groundwork for how modern HR and people practitioners should be thinking about the field.

As you ponder what you've read, know that very few practitioners go deep in all these areas. I certainly don't. The field of HR has become too specialized and sophisticated to know everything about every function.

Considering the learning resources at your fingertips, the truth is you don't need to. Your ability to build a dynamic network and plug into the data/experts/resources you need is often the skill that distinguishes the very best practitioners.

Some of the most important attributes for success in this field right now include a growth mindset, learning agility and network equity. How do you build those?

Building a career as a modern HR operator

I've interviewed hundreds of modern HR practitioners over the years. They all have unique approaches and perspectives, but also share some common views and thinking on what's led them to success. I wanted to distil those traits and couple them with my own career learnings to leave you with some tangible advice on building a great career in HR, people operations, talent, recruiting or whatever discipline you choose to pursue:

1 **Build your network thoughtfully:** When a company hires you, they're actually hiring the skills and knowledge you possess in your head – as well as the networked knowledge you have the ability to tap into to solve their problems. Be deliberate with your network. Cultivate it like

you would tend a garden. Make it a point to add value and help your connections whenever you can. Build where you know you have gaps. That collective intellect will pay dividends throughout your career.

2 **Prioritize (and schedule) learning:** The field of HR and people operations is only going to increase in complexity. Internal factors, external factors, generational factors, economic and global factors, technology and so on – the variables are endless. Most HR roles are under-resourced and overburdened. That's just the reality of the job. You have to find ways to push against that gravity pulling your head down into the work and look around to see what's changing. Make time for learning. Protect it. Block your calendar. Whatever you need to do, do it. This investment in yourself is vital if you hope to stay on top of this dynamic field.

3 **Create a personal board of directors:** Most of us have mentors. That concept of mentors goes back to Homer's *Odyssey* (Schmidt, 2018). I feel that's too narrow a view for today's world. What we really need are personal boards of directors. A group of advisors, reflecting different disciplines, roles, backgrounds and experience levels. A personal advisory board will keep you honest and focused. They'll push you to pursue things you didn't think you could do – and help you avoid the things you shouldn't be doing.

4 **Check your blind spots:** We all have blind spots – gaps in our expertise, understanding or thinking that can cause us to make bad decisions. Check them. Be open and humble about what you don't know, and curious enough to find those answers. We're all a work in progress. Don't be afraid to seek out perspectives you know differ from your own and see what you can learn from them.

5 **Give it away:** One of my favourite authors in Austin Kleon, an Austin-based artist who writes about creativity and the creative process. His second book, *Show Your Work* (2014), was a blueprint for working out loud and infusing open-source approaches in your work. Give freely. Found a great hack? Share it. Built a new forecasting tool? Give it away. The continued evolution of the field is dependent on our ability to break down silos and accelerate others through our own intentional sharing efforts.

6 **Be kind to yourself:** The field of modern HR can be rough. Disappointing. And let's be honest, at times depressing. We're on the front lines of the highest of highs and lowest of lows of all our employees. Burnout is common. I often heard the analogy of 'putting your oxygen mask on before others' during the Covid-19 crisis of 2020. You must be able to prioritize your own self-care and well-being in order to stay in this field.

7   **Practise resiliency**: If you stay in this field long enough, you will have the scars to prove it. Projects will fail. You'll be blamed for things you were not involved in. That's just the nature of the work. You'll need thick skin and an ability to bounce back from setbacks to build a career in this field.

8   **Be brave**: To be a modern people operator requires bravery. Don't compromise your ethics and lose your voice when it counts. The business and employees are counting on you – even when it's hard. Even when they don't know it. You are the expert in this field. Stand up for what you know to be right.

9   **Feed curiosity**: The one common trait in every modern people leader I know is insatiable curiosity. The world of modern HR is so complex you'll struggle without it. Whether your hack is building a 'things to learn' list, devouring books or blogs, building things, or whatever else lights you up – make sure you're finding outlets to learn and try new things. Bonus points if they're outside the field of HR and people operations.

10   **Build a good name**: I wish I could remember who gave me this advice early in my career, but it still resonates deeply. Employers and roles will come and go. Accolades, awards and recognition will fade. Your name is the one thing you really own. How do you want to be remembered? How do you want to honour the mentors who've invested in you? Where do you want to leave the field? If we want to make this industry better, we have to give more to it than we take from it. We have to pay it forward and be helpful.

Learning beyond this book

It's impossible to write a timeless business book if the aim is highlighting progressive practices. I knew if that was my goal, I'd have to find a way to build a digital platform to accompany the book that would include ongoing updates with new resources, tools, articles, developments and so on – so I built that!

Read

You can visit redefininghr.com, a dynamic website including links for the tools, articles and resources listed in this book. I'll also be building out a resource and content library with fresh articles, links and tools supporting modern HR practices.

Listen

If you liked learning how some of the HR executives featured in this book think and operate, I recommend subscribing to the 'Redefining HR' podcast (link on the above website). Each episode features conversations from leading HR and business executives across companies including Spotify, HubSpot, Mastercard, Vayner Media, Basecamp and more.

Engage

Be sure to connect with me on LinkedIn (linkedin.com/in/larsschmidt), Twitter (@Lars) and Instagram (@ThisIsLars) to stay in touch beyond this book.

Final thoughts

I want to thank you for taking the time to read this book. I feel fortunate to be in this field, and to share what I've learned over my career with you.

There's never been a better time to work in the field of HR. I genuinely believe that. There's so much opportunity to pursue whatever outlet and discipline lights you up. There are countless resources out there to support your learning and growth. Social media have given us all the opportunity to share what we're learning and discovering, and make connections with peers around the world that was never possible before.

The world is getting smaller. Our experience and expertise are expanding. Our businesses and employees need us more than ever. This is our time to rise to this moment and break those legacy perceptions of what it means to practise HR.

HR is indeed being redefined – by you, and countless peers around the world who believe in making work better for employees: building businesses with a foundation of ethics, inclusivity and empathy.

I know someone reading this is going to write the next book on modern HR. I can't wait to read it.

References

Kleon, A (2014) *Show Your Work!: 10 ways to share your creativity and get discovered*, Workman Publishing, New York

Schmidt, L (2018) The 5 People You Must Have in Your Network, *Fast Company*. Available from: www.fastcompany.com/90246816/the-5-people-you-must-have-in-your-network (archived at https://perma.cc/6PVR-VMQ8)

INDEX

CPSIA information can be obtained
at www.ICGtesting.com
Printed in the USA
LVHW010216171220
674185LV00003B/5